The Vietnam War
from the Other Side

The Vietnam War from the Other Side

The Vietnamese Communists' Perspective

ANG CHENG GUAN

RoutledgeCurzon
Taylor & Francis Group

First Published in 2002
by RoutledgeCurzon
11 New Fetter Lane, London EC4P 4EE

Simultaneously published in the USA and Canada
by RoutledgeCurzon
29 West 35th Street, New York, NY 10001

RoutledgeCurzon is an imprint of the Taylor & Francis Group

© 2002 Ang Cheng Guan

Typeset in Goudy by LaserScript Ltd, Mitcham, Surrey

Printed and bound in Great Britain by
MPG Books Ltd, Bodmin

British Library Cataloguing in Publication Data
A catalogue record for this book is available from the British Library

Library of Congress Cataloging in Publication Data
A catalog record for this book has been requested

ISBN 0–7007–1615–7

In memory of Ralph Smith

Contents

Maps

Indo-China: South Vietnam's main towns, railways and roads xi
North and South Vietnam's provinces   xii
South Vietnam's major war zones and battles   xiii

Introduction   1

1 Prelude to the Armed Struggle   13
The 6th Plenary Session of the Lao Dong Party   13
Le Duan's 14-point plan   15
Le Duan's thesis: 'The road to the South'   18
2nd Conference of the Nam Bo Regional Committee   20
The 12th Plenary Session and the modernisation of the
    VPA   21
A re-think of the 'North-first' strategy   24
Activities leading to the 15th Plenary Session of the Lao
    Dong Party   26
The 15th Plenary Session of the Lao Dong Party and
    ensuing developments   29
Developments following the passing of Law 10/59   33
Le Duan   37
Chinese and Russian attitudes towards the resumption of
    armed struggle   37

2 The Armed Struggle Begins — 41

The armed struggle resumes — 41
Hanoi and the growing Sino-Soviet rivalry — 44
Developments in Laos — 48
The 3rd Party Congress of the Lao Dong Party — 52
Communist activities in the South — 54
Directive of 31 January 1961 — 56
Developments in the VPA — 58
Further developments in Laos — 59
The proposed International Conference on Vietnam — 62
Le Duan's July 1962 letter to the South — 64
The military situation in the South — 65
The Battle of Ap Bac — 67
Modernisation of the VPA reviewed — 68
Ngo Dinh Diem's death — 69

3 The Armed Struggle Intensifies — 73

The 9th Plenary Session of the Lao Dong Party — 73
Military preparations — 75
Developments in Laos and Cambodia — 76
Hanoi and the Sino-Soviet rift — 78
Special Political Conference (27–28 March 1964) — 79
The Tonkin Gulf incident and its aftermath — 80
Preparations for the winter–spring 1965 offensive — 83
Military offensive (I): The Binh Gia Campaign — 84
Kosygin's visit to Hanoi — 86
Hanoi's 4-point plan — 86
Military offensive (II): (a) The Dong Xoai Campaign — 90
Military offensive (II): (b) The Ba Gia Campaign — 92
Developments in the VPA — 94
Military preparations in the South — 99
Military offensive (III) — 101
Developments in 1965 reviewed — 103
Responding to the US counter-offensive — 104
Fighting and negotiating — 107
Ho Chi Minh — 109
Stalemate — 110

4 Breaking the Stalemate   **113**
  Military situation in early 1967 reviewed   113
  Nguyen Chi Thanh and the Tet Offensive proposal   116
  Ho Chi Minh's health   119
  Preparations for the Tet Offensive   120
  The Tet Offensive (or 'General Offensive General
    Uprising') – Phase I   126
  The decision to negotiate   131
  The Tet Offensive – Phase II   132
  The Tet Offensive – Phase III   133
  The military situation in 1969   135
  Differences within the Hanoi leadership   138
  Hanoi and Sino-Soviet relations   139
  Ho Chi Minh's final months   140

Notes   **145**
Selected Bibliography   **175**
Index   **191**

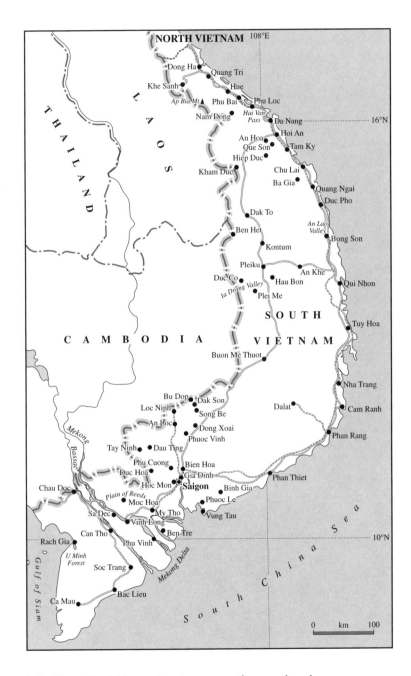

Indo-China: South Vietnam's main towns, railways and roads

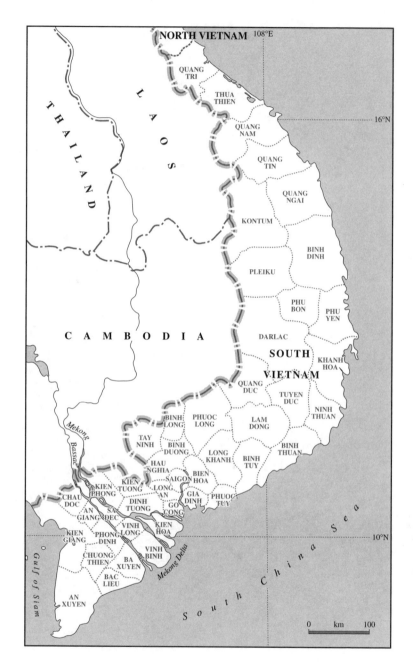

North and South Vietnam's provinces

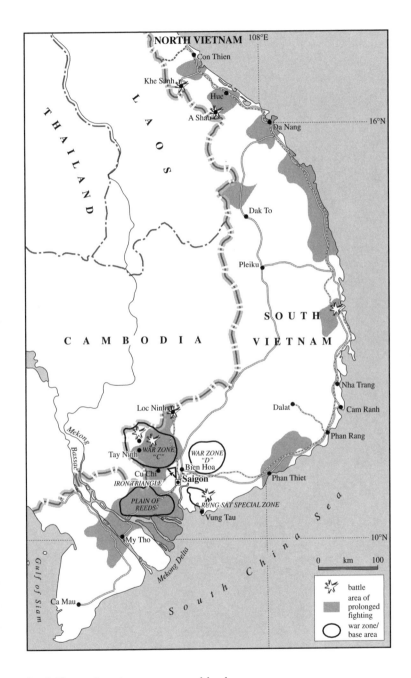

South Vietnam's major war zones and battles

Introduction

The literature on the Vietnam War in the English Language is voluminous and continues to grow. The writings have however focused predominantly on the decisions of the United States (US) and its role in the war. Scholarly writings that present the communist perspective(s) of the war are meagre by comparison. There are two explanations for this disproportion. The first is the prevalent assumption in the 1950s and 1960s that the Vietnam War was but a part of the machination of Beijing and/or Moscow to control the non-communist world. As such, except for a few scholars, most do not view Hanoi as an independent entity and do not consider the North Vietnamese communist perspective worthy of serious study on its own terms. The realisation that this assumption was too simplistic, if not altogether mistaken, only came about gradually in the 1970s. The second explanation is the relative difficulty of access to the archives of the communist governments. Despite the end of the Cold War, it is unlikely that scholars were able to fully exploit the complete archives of the former communist governments. Indeed, it is highly improbable that they would ever be able to tap the archives of the few remaining communist ones, and in this case Vietnam, for some time to come. Furthermore, because of the years of deprivation during and after the war, the Vietnamese communists had not preserved their documents as well as they could have. Given that non-communist official documents and materials are much more easily obtainable, it is only to be expected that researchers will continue to write about the war from the perspective(s) of the 'non-communist West' and in particular, the US. What this means for the historiography of the Vietnam War is that the gap between what one knows about American decision-making with regard to the war on the one hand, and that of the Vietnamese communists on the other, can only widen.

It is important that this problem of lack of access, real as it is and frustrating as it may be, should not discourage the historian from trying to come to grips with the communist side of the Vietnam War. Indeed, to gain a more balanced and impartial understanding of the Vietnam War, it is imperative that the communist side of the war be documented and described as carefully and as objectively as possible. Only when this task has been satisfactorily accomplished can one proceed to the next step, which is to appraise and evaluate the actions, successes and failures of one side or the other. In the view of this author, too many premature judgements have been passed on American decision-making and the conduct of the war without having given adequate consideration to understanding how the war was actually perceived and conducted on the communist side.

R.B. Smith identified three broad phases in the evolution of Western scholarship on the communist side of the Vietnam War. The first generation of writings relied mainly on official media materials. The works of the second generation were largely based on documents seized or collected during the war. One of the more valuable 'second generation' contributions is Carlyle A. Thayer's two-volume Political Science doctoral thesis, 'The Origins of the National Liberation Front for the Liberation of South Vietnam' (September 1977), published in 1989 as War by Other Means: National Liberation and Revolution in Vietnam 1956–1960. In his writing, Thayer thoroughly documented the 13 plenary sessions of the Lao Dong Party Central Committee, the three Politburo meetings, the seventh and eighth sessions of the National Assembly and the three conferences of the Nam Bo Regional Committee, all of which took place between 1954 and 1959. Another contemporary work is R.B. Smith's three-volume (to date) An International History of the Vietnam War, published between 1983 and 1991. Smith started his account from 1955 and his Volume III recounts the events up to 1966. *An International History of the Vietnam War* is a seminal work and Smith was one of the first historians to recognise the need to examine the communist side of the war. He was of the view that as the history of a game of chess cannot be documented by only recording the moves of the black player, similarly, the history of the Vietnam War would not be completely understood without examining the moves of all players in the field. In any study of the history of the Vietnamese communists' struggle, it will be remiss not to mention the contributions of William J. Duiker and William S. Turley. In 1981, Duiker published *The Communist Road to Power in Vietnam*, a pioneering study of the Vietnamese communists' rise to power from its origins to the end of the Vietnam War in 1975. His most recent book on the Vietnam War is *Sacred War: Nationalism and Revolution in a Divided Vietnam* (published in 1995). It covers in a concise manner all the wars which the Vietnamese had fought in the past, including the Vietnam War. William Turley's *The Second IndoChina War: A Short Political and Military History, 1954–1975* is still recommended as one of the most readable and balanced accounts of the war which gives equal weight to the goals and strategies of both sides. It was, however, published more than ten years ago in 1986 and hence could benefit from an update.

Since the end of the Cold War, a number of books and journal articles on various aspects of the communist side of the war have been published. These form the third generation of writings on the communist side of the Vietnam War. What differentiates these writings from those published earlier is the greater use of communist materials that have become available only in the last decade. Besides seized documents, we now have an invaluable collection of North Vietnamese, Chinese and Russian primary and secondary sources in both their original languages and in translation. Those who have made use of these more recent materials in their writings include Chen Jian, Qiang Zhai, Ronnie Ford, Ilya Gaiduk, Robert K. Brigham and this author. The first two authors are the leading scholars on China's involvement in the Vietnam War; their research was based primarily on Chinese sources. Ilya Gaiduk's publication on

Russia's role made use of limited documents from the Russian archives. Ronnie Ford has written on the 1968 Tet Offensive using North Vietnamese communist sources. In his work about the foreign relations of the National Liberation Front (NLF), Robert Brigham consulted Vietnamese communist sources, particularly oral interviews. These historical studies have both broadened and deepened our knowledge of '*the other side*' of the war. Thus far, this small pool of 'third generation' writings has in the main focused on Chinese and Soviet relations with Vietnam, and episodes of the war which have captured international attention, namely the Khe Sanh siege and the 1968 Tet Offensive. Most of the presentations at a recent conference entitled '*New Evidence on China, Southeast Asia, and the Vietnam War*', organised by the Cold War International History Project and Hong Kong University in January 2000, were based on newly available Western, Chinese and Russian sources.

This study is the first of a projected two-volume history of the Vietnam War based principally, although not solely, on Vietnamese communist sources. It attempts to re-construct the evolution of decision-making on the communist side of the Vietnam War, particularly between the years 1954 to 1969, and to show the progression of the Vietnamese communists' struggle from one that was essentially political in nature to a full-scale war. It attempts to integrate the activities and perspectives of all three allies on the communist side, namely, North Vietnam, China and the Soviet Union, but with the Vietnamese communists' holding centre-stage. The author is mindful of the fact that the North Vietnamese historical accounts (as well as western accounts of the war) have not given sufficient attention and credit to the role of the South Vietnamese communists in the struggle against the US. Hence, in this study, the author will also be addressing the significance of the role of the southern revolutionaries, a concern shared by Ngo Vinh Long and David Hunt.[1] In writing the history of this period, this author owes much to the contributions of the first, second and third generations of Vietnam War scholars. This author's research, which is based largely on official communist histories of the war (then not available to Carlyle Thayer, Ralph Smith,

William Duiker and William Turley), builds on their ground-breaking scholarship.

The most 'heavily mined' North Vietnam communist sources for this study are the various official histories of the Vietnamese People's Army (VPA). The first volume of the *Lich Su Quan Doi Nhan Dan Viet Nam* (The Official History of the Vietnamese People's Army) covering the period 1930 to1954 was published in 1974 to commemorate 30 years of the formation of the VPA. The second volume, which covered the years 1954 to 1968, was published 14 years later in 1988 to mark the forty-fifth year of the VPA and the hundredth year of Ho Chi Minh's birth. A sequel to Volume Two was planned with the intention of bringing the account up to 1975. It was not until 1993 that another major step was taken to document the history of the war. In November of that year, the General Staff and the Political Department of the VPA organised a conference to discuss the teaching of military history in Vietnam. After taking into account the proposals of the Director of Schools and the Rector of the Institute of Military History, amongst others, in December 1993, the Chief of Staff issued a directive to draw up both the syllabus and materials for the teaching of military history in the schools, universities and military establishments. In March 1994, a committee and editorial board was formed for this purpose. Its work stretched from March 1994 to July 1996. The writings and materials on various aspects of the Vietnam War were finally submitted to the Ministry of National Defence in August 1996 and were endorsed by the then Minister of Defence, Doan Khue, in October that year. The exercise also spawned many other related research initiatives on the Vietnam War. Some of these communist sources consulted by this author for the writing of this book are listed in the bibliography. In 1994, there was a change of mind about producing a sequel to Volume Two of the *Lich Su Quan Doi Nhan Dan Viet Nam* The new plan was to publish a revised and updated version of *Lich Su Quan Doi Nhan Dan Viet Nam* (Volume Two). This took another five years. On the fifty-fifth anniversary of the VPA in 1999, Hanoi issued a fifth reprint of Volume One and the third reprint of Volume Two, which contained the content of the original Volume Two with three additional chapters, bringing the history of the Vietnam War to its conclusion in 1975.

There are those who are dismissive of 'official histories' (particularly those from the North Vietnamese side), as mere communist propaganda and therefore unreliable as source materials for historical research. In this respect, the author is fully aware of 'the natural tendency (of the communist accounts) to concentrate more on achievements than on setbacks, and to interpret the ambiguous outcome of some engagements as victories for the communist side'.² While it is true that 'official accounts' are not as impartial as archival sources, they are by no means worthless. As R.B. Smith further observed, 'the communist accounts are more likely to indicate the way in which specific operations fitted into Hanoi's developing assessment of the strategic situation'.³ The Hanoi leadership naturally has its own interpretation of the events but the historian has a responsibility to take an even-handed approach by presenting both sides of the story. Despite the limitation of the official histories, one should not dismiss them outright. Rather, they should be perused carefully and judiciously, and then, by juxtaposing and relating them with the non-communist and other independent accounts, there is the chance that one can reconstruct a more complete and authentic picture, or at least something akin to what actually took place.

This study spans the period from July 1954 until 1969. Whereas most US-centric accounts of the Vietnam War begin in 1965, from the perspective of the Vietnamese communists, July 1954 marked the beginning of a new phase in the Vietnamese struggle for the reunification of the country. Even as the negotiations were going on at Geneva, the Vietnamese communist leadership had decided that North and South Vietnam could not be peacefully reunified and that they must immediately prepare for an eventual military confrontation with the US.

By 1956 when it was obvious (though not unexpected) that there would not be an election to reunify the country as specified in the 1954 Geneva Agreement, a 'debate' started amongst the Vietnamese communist leadership on the best strategy to achieve the goal of reunification. This 'debate' continued right into the late 1960s. The goal of reunification was never in doubt but the differences regarding the pace to achieve that goal was a recurrent issue of contention throughout. In the beginning and for a brief period until 1957, there was a consensus at the highest level that the top priority ought to be the rebuilding of North Vietnam's shattered economy and modernising the VPA. Towards the end of 1957, however, the communists in South Vietnam were beginning to feel the heat of Ngo Dinh Diem's actions against them. Although, the first indication of a change of mind by the Hanoi leadership could be detected in December 1957, up till March 1958, a military campaign to achieve reunification was still considered neither feasible nor achievable.

By mid-1958, Diem's renewed efforts to exterminate the Southern communists, culminating in the passing of Law 10/59 (6 May 1959), were fatally damaging the revolutionary struggle in the South. According to a Vietnamese communist source, at the end of 1958 and in early 1959, Diem's policy of terror in the South had reached its height.[4] Wilfred Burchett described the period 1958–1959 as the 'blackest, most hopeless years for the people in South Vietnam.[5] Hanoi realised that it could no longer continue to advocate restraint without both losing the allegiance of the Southern communists and the reunification struggle to Diem. The difficult decision to renew the military struggle in the South, taken at the landmark 15th Plenary Session of the Lao Dong Party held in January 1959 and which was not publicised till a week after the promulgation of Law 10/59 in May, must be seen in this context. All these events are covered in detail in Chapter One.

But as Chapter Two will show, even then, when put into action, the political struggle still pre-dominated. This was so because the North, specifically the military, was still far from ready to handle an expansion of the war. This was evident from the 13 January 1961 directive issued by the Lao Dong Party. Also, developments in Laos, which were not necessarily within the control of Hanoi but which had an impact on Vietnam, consumed much of the Vietnamese communists' energy and engaged their full attention in 1960 and 1961.

Chapter Three takes the story from the unexpected death of Ngo Dinh Diem in November 1963 which led to the next landmark decision taken at the 9th Plenary Session in November/December 1963. The decision of the 9th Plenary Session can be viewed as a shift of gears in line with the policy adopted at the 15th Plenary Session in 1959. The decision to further escalate the military struggle was to preempt the Americans and to gain as much strategic advantage as possible before the anticipated direct American intervention in the fighting. Those who favoured the escalation of the military struggle had a stronger case in 1963 than in 1959. According to most of the American intelligence reports, from about August 1963, the combat capability of the southern communists had been improving and they had scored not a few successes. In a 13 December 1963 memorandum, it was reported that the South Vietnamese government had been unable to materially reduce the strength of the communists in spite of the increased number of non-communist offensive operations.[6] Those amongst the leadership who continued to advocate caution argued that the targets set in the 2nd Five-Year Military Plan (1961–1965) had yet to be fully achieved. Compounding that, the North was also experiencing the worst drought since 1954.[7] The Gulf of Tonkin incident in August 1964 (like the promulgation of Law 10/59 in May 1959) inadvertently strengthened the pro-escalation camp.

The decision of the 9th Plenary Session did not mean that the Vietnamese communists had thrown all caution to the wind. Indeed, if one were to scrutinise the events following both the 1959 and 1963 decisions, one would find that the Hanoi leadership were extremely hesitant and cautious about the military struggle. In 1963, while the objective of the Vietnamese communists was to try to win the reunification struggle before the Americans intervene directly in the war, Hanoi also did not wish to give the US a pretext to attack North Vietnam. The escalation of the military struggle therefore needed to be handled very adroitly. This came across most clearly in a conversation of both Pham Van Dong and Hoang Van Hoan with Mao Zedong on 5 October 1964. According to Dong, Hanoi would try to confine the war within the sphere of a special war, and would try to defeat the enemy within that sphere. It would try not to let the Americans turn the war into a limited war or expand it into North Vietnam. The various secret negotiations should also be understood in the context of the military struggle. The Vietnamese communists realised very early on that it was not possible to achieve on the diplomatic table that which they could not obtain on the battlefield. Regarding negotiations, Mao commented that the North Vietnamese had 'earned the qualification to negotiate'. However, it is another matter whether or not the negotiation would succeed. Zhou reminded his audience that Beijing had been talking to the US for nine years and there had been more than 120 meetings and the Sino-American ambassadorial talks were still continuing in Warsaw.[8]

In early 1965, the Vietnamese communists were still not confident of being able to confront the Americans in a 'limited war'. They knew all along that they would never be able to defeat 'the strongest in the world' in a straight fight. The strategy was therefore to force the Americans to withdraw through negotiations. In the view of the Hanoi leadership, this was only achievable when they could defeat the US air war, exhaust the US troops in the South and weaken the will of the American politicians and soldiers.[9] American troops eventually landed on Danang in March 1965. On hindsight, that event perhaps marked the beginning of American direct military intervention in the reunification struggle, which the Vietnamese communists had predicted in 1954 and had hitherto been trying to delay from happening. As Chapter Four will show, for the next two years, the war was fought to a stalemate. Hence, to break that stalemate, which could only lead to a communist defeat if left to drag on, in the spring of 1967, the Vietnamese communists endorsed the plan for the 'General Offensive General Uprising' (or the *Tet Offensive*).[10]

The failure of all three phases of the 'General Offensive General Uprising' to achieve the objectives as spelt out by Le Duan in his letter of 18 January 1968 led to the resumption of the 'debate' between the 'escalation camp' and the 'protracted war camp' within the Vietnamese communist leadership. An added dimension that had to be considered in 1968 was the question of whether it was then the appropriate time to negotiate with the enemy.

Intertwined into the above was the broader debate within the communist bloc between the Soviet strategy of peaceful coexistence (read: no fighting, negotiation) and the Chinese strategy of supporting national liberation struggles in the colonial countries (read: protracted struggle, no negotiation). Although the Vietnamese communists refrained from talking about the Sino-Soviet rift in public, they were acutely concerned about its negative effect on their struggle. The significance of both Russian and Chinese moral and material support to the Vietnamese communist national liberation struggle is well-known. It was impossible for Hanoi to stand apart, much as they wanted to, from the Sino-Soviet rivalry that had been brewing since 1956 and which worsened as the years went by. Those such as Vo Nguyen Giap, Hoang Minh Chinh and Nguyen Kien Giang who advocated a more cautious pace were crudely labeled as 'pro-Soviet' while Le Duan and others who shared his view on speeding up the struggle became known as 'pro-China'.[11] (It is perhaps worth noting that Le Duan was later re-labeled as 'pro-Soviet'.) Le Duan, in fact had played a moderating role in debate over the pace of the re-unification struggle from 1956 until November 1963 before becoming more 'hawkish' (than the Chinese would have liked) after the death of Diem and particularly after the Gulf of Tonkin incident. Ho Chi Minh was the only Vietnamese leader who had the stature and the willingness to mediate between the two communist giants. But Ho's health was declining from 1964 and he no longer oversaw the day-to-day decisions, which were gradually being made by Le Duan and his associates. This study attempts to trace on the one hand, the physical weakening of Ho Chi Minh, and on the other, the gradual rise of Le Duan from the 1950s through the 1960s.

Although the Vietnam War was not over until April 1975, 1969 is an appropriate juncture to conclude this volume for two reasons. On the communist side, their heavy casualties during the 1968 Tet Offensive compelled the Hanoi leadership to reexamine its strategy. The communists were finally agreeable to negotiations which began in Paris in 1968. (The four-party talks only began in January 1969.) Ho Chi Minh who had been the unifying force in the Vietnamese communist leadership passed away in September of the same year. On the American side, on 8 June 1969, Richard Nixon, the newly elected President of the United States, announced the new policy of '*Vietnamisation*' and from September 1969, the US began withdrawing significant number of its troops from Vietnam. Meanwhile, the schism within the communist bloc, which Nixon was subsequently able to exploit, reached the point of a military clash between China and the Soviet Union. 1969 thus marked the end of one phase and the beginning of a new phase in the war. A more practical reason for ending this volume in 1969 is the need to await a larger body of both communist and non-communist primary materials pertaining to the post-1969 period to become available, since both Vietnamese communist and Chinese sources pertaining to the Vietnam War from 1967 are scanty and patchy compared to the earlier period. It is the author's intention to write a sequel to this volume covering the period 1969 to the end of the Vietnam War in 1975.

Chapter One
Prelude to the Armed Struggle

The 6th Plenary Session of the Lao Dong Party

The 6th Plenary Session of the Lao Dong Party Central Committee (15–18 July 1954) is the appropriate point to begin the reconstruction of the history of the Vietnam War from the perspective of the Vietnamese communists. According to the *Lich Su Quan Doi Nhan Dan Viet Nam*, the 6th Plenary Session was the beginning of a new phase in the history of the Vietnamese people 'the period of resisting the Americans to save the country'. Significantly, the session was held when the Geneva Conference was meeting on the other side of the globe. At the plenary session the Hanoi leadership acknowledged that the country could not be reunified by peaceful means and Ho Chi Minh already identified the US as the new enemy.[1] The Vietnamese communists were cognisant of the fact that the US was an opponent not to be treated flippantly. They were fighting a new aggressor that had the greatest economic potential and the most powerful armed forces amongst the imperialist powers.[2] In the *Lich Su Quan Doi Nhan Dan Viet Nam*, the Americans were depicted as being the most influential and dangerous counter-revolutionaries they had ever confronted.

The meeting decided on two courses of action. The first was to rebuild the economy and lay the foundation for socialism in the North, badly damaged by the many years of struggle against the French, so that it could be a strong base for the reunification of the country. They hoped to achieve this goal within a period of three years from 1955 to 1957. The second course of action was to transform the VPA into a modern and regular revolutionary army that would not only be responsible for the security of the country but also would partake in the reconstruction of the economy. No deadline was set for this as it was expected to be a long and complex process.[3]

The Chinese shared the view that it would be impossible for Vietnam to be reunited peacefully. Based on their own experience in fighting the Guomintang, they were of the opinion that the Vietnamese communists should prepare for a protracted struggle which meant that they should lie low for a period of time, muster strength, keep in touch with the people and wait for an opportunity to strike.[4] Chinese assistance had been a critical factor in the success of the Vietnamese communists against the French. Thus, despite their disagreements with the Chinese during the Geneva Conference,[5] the Hanoi leadership continued to consult Beijing about the reunification strategy.[6] In July/August 1955, Beijing had decided to withdraw their military advisers (who had been sent to North Vietnam in July/August 1950) in three phases – September/October 1955, end of 1955 and spring 1956. The North Vietnamese leaders, however, requested for continued Russian assistance in the form of military specialists to help in the modernisation of the VPA.[7]

Although Moscow was the co-chairman of the 1954 Geneva Conference, it did not play an active role in ensuring that the general election stipulated in the Geneva agreements was held.[8] Moscow did not pay much attention to Southeast Asia and left Southeast Asian affairs to the discretion of China. Some time between 1955 and 1956, a gentleman's agreement was apparently reached between the two countries whereby Burma, Thailand, Laos Cambodia, Malaya and Vietnam would fall within the Chinese sphere of operation. India, Afghanistan, and all of Asia to the west of those countries would come under the Russian sphere. The exception was Indonesia where both the interests of Moscow and Beijing overlapped.[9]

In February 1956, Khrushchev declared at the 20th Congress of the Communist Party of the Soviet Union (CPSU) that war was not inevitable between the socialist and capitalist camps, and both camps could peacefully coexist with each other.[10] Under this new policy (which Hanoi did not agree with),[11] both North and South Vietnam should coexist peacefully and engage in friendly economic competition. Moscow was confident that as the socialist mode of production in the North was far superior to that of the capitalist South, over time the latter would naturally yearn to be unified with the North.[12] Although Moscow supported the Chinese suggestion that a new and enlarged Geneva Conference be convened to discuss the enforcement of the 1954 Geneva Accord, in 1956, Khrushchev, through the Soviet ambassador in Washington, also floated the idea of admitting both North and South Vietnam to the United Nations.[13] In November 1956, when Zhou Enlai visited Hanoi, he described Khrushchev's action as a 'selling out' and assured Ho Chi Minh that China would not be 'a party to this betrayal.'[14]

Le Duan's 14-point plan

Meanwhile, in December 1955, Ngo Dinh Diem announced that he would conduct unilateral election in South Vietnam the following year. According to the evaluation of the United States Country Team, the Vietnamese communists' subversive capability in the South had declined since mid-1955. Diem's policies and actions in the South had caused the Vietnamese communists to lose much of their earlier bases of support. The consolidation of the Saigon government's position and new security arrangements, particularly in the central provinces, had also severely curtailed the strength of the communist resistance.[15] Thus, although there were some attempts by the Vietnamese communists to sabotage the unilateral election in the South on 4 March 1956, they were unable to disrupt it.[16]

The setbacks suffered by the communist cadres in the South and their attendant low morale prompted Le Duan to put forward a 14-point action plan that called for a more aggressive and militant approach to complement the political struggle in the South.[17] The plan called for military action to support the political activities in the South, the creation of support bases and more battalions and the consolidation of the military organisations in the inter-zones. As Cambodia was considered to be of strategic importance, it also recommended an increase in the budget for activities in Cambodia and for senior cadres to be posted there. It also called for the consolidation of the leading organisations and the creation of a support base to aid activities there.

In late March 1956, the Hanoi leadership met to consider the 14-point plan that had been endorsed by the Nam Bo Regional Committee.[18] The leadership surmised that the Vietnamese communists were not ready to step up the military struggle in the South. Furthermore, their two allies, China and the Soviet Union, whose support they would need, were also not in favour of any move that could lead to a new military confrontation. It thus rejected the 14-point plan and directed Le Duan and his associates in the South to continue to exploit the agrarian issues in the South.[19]

In the light of Hanoi's rejection of the 14-point plan, in early April, senior party officials in Nam Bo convened a special conference to re-evaluate the situation in the South. The meeting concluded that the tactical use of violence had not only failed to yield the desired result, but had also undermined Hanoi's diplomatic efforts to resolve the issue. As such, any further use of violence at that point of time would be inappropriate. It then decided on a new approach focussing on the economic struggle.[20] However, not everyone was pleased with the decision. Some were unhappy that Hanoi had imposed the new strategy upon them.

Despite the decision taken at the meeting, the Hanoi leadership was not totally dismissive of the use of violence to achieve reunification. This was discernible in the closing speech made by Ho Chi Minh at the 9th Plenary Session (enlarged) of the Lao Dong Central Committee on 27 April 1956 when he said, 'Although it is possible that certain countries may achieve socialism by peaceful means, we must understand that in those countries where the administrative machinery, the military powers and the secret police of the bourgeois class are still powerful, the proletariat must prepare for an armed struggle. While noting the possibility of achieving the territorial unification of Vietnam through peaceful means, we must not forget the American imperialists and their lackeys still occupy one half of our national territory and are preparing for war. That is why, while holding high the flag of peace, we must be prudent and vigilant.'[21]

An official North Vietnamese historical record noted that during this period, 'the struggle of the people in the South to achieve the unification of Vietnam became increasingly fierce ... The revolutionary movement demanded guidance that was appropriate to a situation that was undergoing new develop-ment.'[22] There were certain quarters amongst the Vietnamese communists who felt that the 'North Vietnam first' policy needed to be balanced by more consideration for the situation in the South. While they did not necessarily object to the strategy adopted by the Hanoi leadership, they felt that more attention needed to be paid to the problems faced by those in the South.[23]

The Politburo convened a meeting on 8–9 June 1956 and subsequently issued a directive on 19 June that clarified the roles and responsibilities of the southern cadres in the revolutionary struggle. According to the directive, the struggle at that point of time was necessarily a political and not a military one. Therefore, they should resort to arms only in circumstances that called for self-defence. The establishment of a popular front and the consolidation of the Party in the South were to be the key tasks. In this regard, the strategy was to focus on the development of the armed forces and to consolidate those forces that they already control. They were instructed to organise self-defence forces, develop more base areas and arouse the political consciousness of the masses and, when possible, attempt to free those who had been arrested.[24] On the same day, in a letter written to the Southern cadres who had regrouped in the North, Ho Chi Minh affirmed that North Vietnam was the foundation of the struggle to achieve the liberation and reunification of the country. Whatever was being done for North Vietnam was not only to increase the strength of the North but that of the South as well.[25]

Due to difficulties in communication, a number of regions in the South did not receive the 19 June directive. After the failed attempt to reunite the country in July, some comrades in the Plain of Reeds (region in Kien Phong and Kien Tuong provinces and parts of Dinh Tuong, Long An and Hau Nghia provinces) were already making preparations to restart armed struggle. On 18 August, the Politburo had to send another letter to the Nam Bo Regional Committee reiterating the main points of the June directive.[26]

The general election, which was supposed to be conducted not later than July 1956 under the supervision of the International Supervisory and Control Commission (ISCC) as stipulated in the Final Declaration of the 1954 Geneva Conference regarding Vietnam, failed to take place. Thus the prediction of the Hanoi leadership at the 6th Plenary Session in 1954 that Vietnam could not be unified by peaceful means had proven correct. Surprisingly, all three parties involved – Hanoi, Beijing and Moscow – each allowed the deadline to pass somewhat uneventfully. Nevertheless, up to the end of July 1956 and for some time after, Hanoi continued to press for a meeting to discuss the general election. The political and diplomatic charade had to be maintained. Le Duan explained that Hanoi had to continually call for the general election to be held (as stipulated in the Geneva Accord) because of its propaganda value in presenting the North Vietnamese as the aggrieved party.[27] The Hanoi leadership also had to show the communist cadres, expecially those in the South, who had been told to expect reunification in 1956 that efforts were being made towards that end. It was also a convenient camouflage for Hanoi's preparation for the anticipated confrontation with the US-Diem regime.

Le Duan's thesis: 'The road to the South'

Readers would recall that at the 6th Plenary Session in July 1954, it was decided that the first target was to restore the war-shattered economy, pave the way for North Vietnam's economic recovery and advance to socialism within three years (1955–1957).[28] Since the consolidation of the North was seen as a prerequisite for the reunification of Vietnam, any delay in the timetable would automatically prolong the reunification process. From August 1956 onwards, the agrarian reform debacle in the North and the increasing disaffection of the intellectuals with the policies of the Lao Dong Party consumed much of the attention of the Hanoi leadership and threatened to derail the schedule. Hanoi had to convince the Southern cadres that had gathered in the North and those in the South that the leadership was working hard on the reunification agenda and to persuade them to be patient.[29] This responsibility was delegated to Le Duan and he was directed by the Politburo in August 1956 to remain in the South to guide the revolutionary struggle. Le Duan had by then completed the thesis, '*Duong Loi Cach Mang Mien Nam*' (*The Road to the South*), which elucidated the path in which the struggle in the South would gradually develop into a violent revolution.[30] In August, he travelled from U Minh (the area extending along the coast of the Gulf of Siam in An Xuyen Province) across the Plain of Reeds up to Ben Tre. He instructed the Southern comrades not to conduct any further struggle in the name of the religious sects. He also entrusted Comrade Sau Duong to write a thesis on the proper conduct of armed propaganda.[31]

The Lao Dong Party Central Committee held its 11th Plenary Session in December 1956, which affirmed that revolution was the correct way to liberate South Vietnam.[32] At that session, it was agreed in principle that Le Duan's blueprint, '*Duong Loi Cach Mang Mien Nam*', would serve as the basis of a three-pronged strategy: (1) The consolidation of the North, (2) Sustaining the struggle in the South, and (3) Winning international support for their cause.[33] Although the available official Vietnamese sources acknowledged that the Lao Dong Party's strategy for the South was based on the '*Duong Loi Cach Mang Mien Nam*', Tran Van Tra noted that it was neither formalised nor fully implemented till three years later.[34] For the meanwhile, the strategy for the reunification of the country as enunciated at the 6th Plenary Session remained essentially unchanged.[35]

The 6th session of the DRV National Assembly (29 December 1956–25 January 1957) reiterated the decisions of the 11th Plenary Session. The immediate task was to quickly complete the rectification of the mistakes of the agrarian reform. In the area of defence, the National Assembly approved the demobilisation of 80,000 volunteers and the introduction of compulsory military service. In his address to the National Assembly, Pham Van Dong stated that peaceful coexistence would remain the cornerstone of the North Vietnam's foreign policy. In particular, Hanoi would improve relations with Cambodia and Laos. As for the reunification of the country, Dong repeated the call for consultations between the North and the South on the general election.[36]

2nd Conference of the Nam Bo Regional Committee

Soon after the 11th Plenary Session, the second Conference of the Nam Bo Regional Committee was held in Phnom Penh in December under the chairmanship of Le Duan and Nguyen Van Linh, the Committee's General-Secretary. The meeting approved the paper drafted by Nguyen Minh Duong on the organisation and activities of the self-defence forces. It passed a resolution which stated that since South Vietnam was then engaged in a political struggle, it was not appropriate to conduct guerrilla warfare. However, it was necessary to create self-defence and armed propaganda forces in support of the political struggle and for the eventual violent revolution. The meeting agreed to build up the propaganda forces and secret armed units; establish base areas in the forested mountains in eastern Nam Bo, the Plain of Reeds and the U Minh area; win the hearts and minds of the disaffected; and eliminate traitors.[37] Nguyen Huu Xuyen was appointed to oversee the establishment of the armed forces in the South.[38]

One of the most important decisions that emerged from the Conference was the lifting of the restriction on the use of force in the South. According to the *Lich Su Quan Doi Nhan Dan Viet Nam*, the meeting concurred that armed propaganda would be permitted with the caveat that the military struggle in the South would not be intensified until the North was ready. In other words, although the Southern cadres would be given more freedom of action, at the same time, they were cautioned against embarking on premature adventures.

Soon after the Conference, Le Duan left for North Vietnam to assume the position of acting secretary-general and to assist Ho Chi Minh in the running of the Party.[39] Hoang Van Hoan recalled that Le Duan was considered to be the most appropriate person to assist Ho manage the party in the immediate period after the agrarian reform debacle in the North[40] as he had had some experience implementing agrarian reforms in the South. Bui Tin disclosed that although Ho's preferred choice for the post was Vo Nguyen Giap, Le Duan had the support of the very influential head of the Party Organisation Department, Le Duc Tho.[41] According to Hoan, Le Duc Tho was Le Duan's most trusted follower.[42] Moreover, the consensual impression was that Le Duan, who had previously done time in Poulo Condore during the French period and who authored the '*Duong Loi Cach Mang Mien Nam*', could be trusted to carry out the struggle for the reunification of the country. Bui Tin remembered Le Duan being adamant in his belief that, to achieve reunification, war with the US was inevitable.

The 12th Plenary Session and the modernisation of the VPA

Readers would recall that at the 6th Plenary Session a decision was taken to modernise the VPA. The subject was revived at the 12th Plenary Session of the Lao Dong Party Central Committee in March 1957. Vo Nguyen Giap described the 12th Plenary Session as marking 'a new step of development in the party's military theory in general and in its theory on building the armed forces in particular.'[43] He reiterated that it was imperative that the VPA be modernised and regularised if it were to be effective in pursuing its dual mission of protecting the North and unifying the country.[44] The leadership concurred but cautioned against hasty and impractical changes. The view was that military modernisation should proceed in tandem with the pace of the economic reconstruction of the North, although it was envisaged to be a Herculean task considering the existing shape of the VPA and the economic condition of the North. Nevertheless, the leadership set the goal of completing the military transformation by 1959. All aspects of the military, for example, staffing, training and weaponry, would be gradually reconfigured according to modern doctrines of warfare with the help of North Vietnam's communist allies.[45] The first step was to replace the prevailing voluntary enlistment with obligatory military service, as approved by the National Assembly at its recent 6th Session.[46] It was evident from the meeting that Hanoi was not planning to reunify the country by military means before 1959.

Judging from a number of remarks and observations made by Ho Chi Minh during that period, it seemed that the modernisation process had some unintended negative consequences. On 16 May 1957, while addressing a group of middle and senior ranking officers from the Ministry of Defence attending a re-education class to study the decisions of the 12th Plenary Session, Ho warned against individualism, meritocracy, arrogance, envy, jealousy and the danger of dividing the people, party and army. He stressed the need for unity in the military hierarchy as well as amongst the cadres and fighters from the North and South, within and outside the Party. He reminded the class of the responsibility of the military and of the need to raise the level of its socialist consciousness.[47] In another talk to the military units of the Military Region Department (Military Region IV), on 15 June 1957, Ho again warned against 'falling into the hole of individualism', jealousy and envy. He emphasised the importance of manual labour and cautioned against belittling such work. According to Ho, while mental labour was important, manual labour was paramount. He observed that party consciousness was not yet sufficiently developed in the VPA. He exhorted the army to raise their alertness, put more effort into their military training and political education, and to economise. Ho again spoke of the need for unity in every part of the army and warned against divisions between the North and South fighters.[48]

The lack of 'party consciousness' in VPA was an issue that continued to occupy the minds of the Hanoi leadership in the subsequent two years. For example, in November 1958, the General Political Directorate, under Nguyen Chi Thanh, completed the study of the politico-military role of the VPA during the period of struggle against the French. According to the study, which confirmed the primacy of Party leadership, the highest principle of party leadership was collective leadership. The history of the army was first and foremost the history of the Party leading the army both in times of war and peace. It stressed that this principle must always be respected even with the modernisation and regularisation of the army. The study recommended the strengthening of party committees in the military. In the same month, the Central Military Committee held a conference for political commissars in the VPA to disseminate the guidelines regarding the role of politics in the military. The aim of the conference was to clarify the responsibility of the political organisation in the VPA and to affirm the leadership of the Party over the military.[49]

In a speech made on 2 September 1957 to commemorate the 12th anniversary of the independence of North Vietnam, Ho reiterated the basic task of the North, which was to restore the economy and to incrementally improve the livelihood of the people. He argued for the necessity to lay a strong foundation before moving on to the next stage. Meanwhile, the South must persevere in its economic struggle. Ho highlighted the experiences of North Korea and the German Democratic Republic which, like North Vietnam, were also concerned about the reunification of their countries.[50] He repeated the call for Hanoi and Saigon to establish contact as a first step towards convening a consultative conference on the general election. He had recently returned from a near two-month visit to 'fraternal countries in the socialist bloc' to strengthen ties and garner support for the Vietnamese communists' cause, firmly convinced that it was premature to step up the struggle in the South.

A re-think of the 'North-first' strategy

However, two months later, there was a re-think of the 'North-first' approach, which had been the operative strategy since July 1954. The change in stance was prompted by two factors, namely the precarious situation in the South and the Moscow Conference.

In South Vietnam, from the latter part of 1957 onwards, many communist cadres in the Mekong Delta region (from Go Cong province down to the Ca Mau Peninsula), My Tho province, the Plain of Reeds (region in Kien Phong and Kien Tuong provinces and parts of Dinh Tuong, Long An and Hau Nghia provinces), U Minh jungle (the area extending along the coast of the Gulf of Siam in An Xuyen Province) and Resistance Zone D (the region 20 miles northwest of Saigon) were either arrested or killed. The self-defence organisations in the countryside were destroyed, the armed forces in the resistance bases were being decimated and the resistance army of the religious sects had also dwindled into a token force.[51]

In November, Ho, together with Le Duan and Pham Hung (who would later be appointed Vice-Premier at the 8th Session of the National Assembly in April 1958), travelled to Moscow for the Moscow Conference that was held in conjunction with the 40th anniversary celebration of the October Revolution.(It is worth noting that both Le Duan and Pham Hung were closely associated with the communist revolutionary movement in South Vietnam.)[52] The Moscow Conference was divided into two main sessions with the first session (14–16 November) being attended only by the representatives of the 12 communists' and workers' parties of the socialist countries, including China and North Vietnam.[53] The Conference was especially significant for the Vietnamese communists because, for the first time since the 20th CPSU Congress in February 1956, Moscow conceded that under certain circumstances, a non-peaceful transition to socialism was possible and might even be unavoidable. Implicit in the Moscow Declaration was acquiescence to the use of non-peaceful means to achieve the reunification of Vietnam.

Soon after the Moscow gathering, at the 13th Plenary Session in late December 1957, Ho elucidated the intrinsic relationship between the two revolutionary strategies and the two revolutionary responsibilities. According to him, the Vietnamese were concurrently engaged in carrying out two equally important revolutionary strategies: a people's democratic revolution and a socialist revolution. It would be a mistake to underestimate either. The consolidation of the North and its advancement towards socialism was a decisive factor for the victory of the revolution. The North must become a socialist society so that it would serve as a solid base for the reunification of the country. At the same time, the revolutionary strength of the South must be nurtured, as it constituted the direct and decisive factor for the victory of the struggle in the South. In short, Ho was saying that the struggle in the South was to be considered of equal importance to the revolution in the North. According to the *Lich Su Quan Doi Nhan Dan Viet Nam*, Ho's speech at the 13th Plenary Session was especially significant as it clarified the path along which to carry out the socialist revolution in the North and the people's democratic revolution in the South.[54]

At the beginning of 1958, Le Duan met with the cadres responsible for Inter-zone V (the southern half of Trung Bo). The communist activities in Inter-zone V had drastically deteriorated as a consequence of Diem's renewed efforts to exterminate the communists. Le Duan observed that Inter-zone V comprised three regions: the towns, the delta and the central highlands. In his analysis, if the highlands were strong and stable, then the delta would be secure. Therefore, it would be logical for the communists to swiftly establish small squads or, even better, platoon-sized armed forces to operate independently in the highlands to protect their activities there. At the opportune time, this guerrilla movement could effectively support the main offensive. The cadres in charge of Inter-zone V were directed to urgently build many safe base areas to assist the guerrilla activities and to steer the economic struggle in the delta areas and in the towns.[55]

Meanwhile, from 27 December 1957 to 14 January 1958, the Lao Dong Party Central Committee organised a conference for more than 200 high and middle level cadres from Hanoi and the provinces to study the Moscow Declaration. Le Duan and

Truong Chinh also briefed them on the situation of the country. The cadres were told that the target of restoring the war-shattered economy within three years (1955–1957) had been achieved, that the foundation for a socialist economy had been laid and the socialist revolution had begun.[56] The new three-year economic plan (1958–1960) was subsequently spelt out in detail during the 8th Session of the National Assembly (16–29 April 1958).

In mid-March 1958, the Central Military Committee drew up a new military plan to increase the security and defence of the North, particularly of the north-western and western part of Inter-zone IV.[57] (It is noteworthy that the north-west and west Inter-zone IV adjoined the Pathet Lao-controlled provinces of Sam Neua and PhongSaly which had extremely close ties with the Vietnamese communists). It also decided to delay the completion of modernisation programme of the VPA from 1959 to 1960 to bring it in tandem with the new three-year economic plan (1958–1960). This would be consistent with the earlier decision that military modernisation must be kept up to speed with the country's economic development. In the same period, the Council of Ministers also met to discuss, amongst other matters, military service and reward, military rank and salaries, the establishment of the army reserve and the participation of the military in production work. A decision was taken to channel more troops to economic reconstruction. To this end, part of the armed forces was transferred to farm production units.[58] All these activities indicated that up until March 1958 a military campaign for reunification was still not in the cards and was not imminent till at least after 1960.

Activities leading to the 15th Plenary Session of the Lao Dong Party

By mid-1958, Ngo Dinh Diem's campaign to exterminate the communists began to seriously hurt the revolutionary movement in South Vietnam[59] to an extent and degree that Hanoi had to respond in a more substantive way. It was within this context that the Lao Dong Party resurrected the idea of an armed struggle in the South. In the summer of that year, the Lao Dong Central Committee sent two documents to their Chinese counterpart for their views. They were entitled '*Regarding the basic tasks of the Vietnamese communists in the new phase*' and '*Views on uniting the line of struggle with the revolutionary struggle in the South*'. In a written reply[60] the Chinese expressed the view that the time was still not favourable and queried whether Hanoi was in fact ready to expose their armed forces in South Vietnam.[61] Also, in the summer of 1958, Ho Chi Minh apparently made a trip to Beidaihe and Beijing to meet Zhou Enlai and Deng Xiaoping to discuss the matter. According to one Chinese account, at that meeting, Ho sought the views of the Chinese on a document outlining the strategy of the Vietnamese communists' struggle against the Americans in the South. Beijing opined that the socialist revolution in the North should be the fundamental and most urgent task. Their advice on the revolutionary struggle in the South was the same as that given in 1954, which was that the Vietnamese communists should continue to lie low, build up and consolidate their military strength, win over the masses and wait for the right moment to strike. The Chinese, however, presented the Vietnamese with 50,000 AK-47 assault rifles.[62]

Meanwhile, in August 1958, the Nam Bo Regional Committee held its third conference under the chairmanship of Nguyen Van Linh. The meeting resolved that, given the current revolutionary situation in South Vietnam, it was necessary to apply some degree of military force to assist the political struggle and gradually use the armed forces to defeat the enemy. The Nam Bo Regional Committee decided to establish two revolutionary base areas: Zone A situated in the north-east of Saigon (extending from Ma Da to Bu Champ in Thu Dau Mot Province) and Zone B situated to the north-west of Saigon in Duong Minh Chau District, Tay Ninh Province. It was also decided to create the Eastern Nam Bo Command as the command centre of the armed struggle in the South. Some of the forces in the eastern Nam Bo provinces were grouped into four companies under this Command. Its formation would help the

Nam Bo Regional Committee to unify its control of the armed forces and their activities in the South.[63] These decisions were conveyed to the Lao Dong Party Central Committee in Hanoi.[64]

In the summer/fall of 1958, the Inter-zone V Party Committee held a meeting chaired by Vo Chi Cong to discuss their strategy. Taking into account the analysis given by Le Duan, the meeting decided that they would accelerate the development of the western parts of the lowland provinces in Inter-zone V and the Central Highlands. The objective was to recover and expand their base of support. The plan was to build up storage bases for rice, salt, etc., and to mobilise the people in preparation for the revolution. They would organise a number of platoons and arm them with whatever weapons they could muster. These armed troops would be used for self-defence, to support their political struggle, as well as to protect their economic activities and the villages. They would also attempt to free their comrades who had been arrested by the government and to exterminate those that were traitors to their cause. The committee decided that they could no longer rely solely on political struggle but 'must use limited armed struggle co-ordinated with political struggle' in order to annihilate the enemy.[65]

In November 1958, the Lao Dong Party held its 14th Plenary Session to discuss three reports: the report by Le Duan on the world situation, the report on the three-year economic plan (1958–1960) by Nguyen Duy Trinh, and that by Truong Chinh on land reform. The meeting decided on the immediate need to accelerate the socialist transformation of the North and to develop the state-run economy as the leading force of the national economy.[66] Surprisingly, although it was unlikely that the meeting did not broach the subject of the situation in South Vietnam, reports on the meeting were silent on the issue. Probably the leadership had not at hand sufficient information to make a decision. Soon after the 14th Plenary Session, Le Duan travelled to the South on an extended inspection tour to assess the situation there.[67] Meanwhile, the Southern revolutionaries were told that political struggle remained the main thrust of the revolution in the South. This was confirmed by a document issued by the Nam Bo Regional Committee entitled '*Situation and Tasks for 1959*', stating that political struggle should remain the basis of the revolution in the South despite its acknowledgement that the Diem regime was gaining the upper hand in the struggle.[68]

The 15th Plenary Session of the Lao Dong Party and ensuing developments

Less than two months after the 14th Plenary Session was held in November 1958, the Hanoi leadership met again for the 15th Plenary Session in January 1959. There is no information on the precise date of the entire session except that it began with a closed-door meeting followed by an enlarged one. If one had to venture a guess, it must have taken place after Le Duan returned from his visit to the South in early January. The closed-door session could have ended before 11 January 1959 because Le Thanh Nghi, a member of the Politburo, arrived on that day in Beijing to meet up with the North Vietnamese economic delegation that had been in China since December 1958.[69] Nghi, who was Minister of Industry and Director of the Industrial section in the Prime Minister's office, was the leader of the economic delegation. It was most likely that he had remained behind for the closed-door segment of the 15th Plenary Session. Those who attended the enlarged meeting, which was chaired by Ho Chi Minh, included representatives from the Nam Bo Regional Committee, the inter-provincial committee of Inter-zone V and representatives from all the party committees from the provinces in Central Vietnam.[70] The full 15th Plenary Session ended on 13 January 1959.[71]

No details were forthcoming on the proceedings of the closed-door segment except that a resolution was passed which called for the liberation of South Vietnam from imperialism and feudalism, and for the completion of the people's democratic revolution. The meeting agreed that in order to establish the foundation for the revolution in the South, it was essential to use mass uprisings to first seize power. Subsequently, the course of the revolution would have to be contingent on the situation on the ground as it unfolded. The critical factor was the strength of the masses and the armed forces should only play a complementary and supportive role. Because of the American presence, it was anticipated that the struggle would be a protracted one.[72] Tran Van Tra pointed out that Le Duan's '*Duong Loi Cach Mang Mien Nam*', written almost three years ago, was finally adopted in full.[73]

The *CRIMP Document* disclosed that at the 15th Plenary Session, the meeting had regarded the struggle to reunite the country as part of the world revolution and believed that a Vietnamese victory would encourage struggles for liberation in Asia, Africa and Latin America. The meeting agreed on the need to establish a popular front in the South and also to support the communist struggle in Laos and Cambodia. Although the 15th Plenary Session specified the responsibilities and strategic aims of the revolution in the South, questions such as how the aims and responsibilities of the revolution were to be implemented, and what forms and procedures should the struggle take, were left unanswered. There was probably insufficient information then on the revolutionary situation in the South for the formulation of a precise strategy. The limited knowledge they had of the experiences of 'friendly nations' also provided little guidance. It took another two years before a clearer programme was eventually mapped out.[74]

In his closing address at the session, Ho said, 'The task of saving our country is a responsibility of the whole party ... (We) must consider the southern region of Vietnam as part of our country's revolution and to see our country's revolution as part of the world's revolution ... We must spread out and fly high the flag of peace because that has great benefit for us. But peace does not mean that we do not prepare our military forces ... If we organise our political strength well, when the need comes to resort to arms, it will not be difficult.'[75] At the end of the session, all the participants from the South were entrusted with the urgent responsibility to return home to prepare for and guide the revolution.[76] Significantly, the decision of the 15th Plenary Session was not made public till five months later on 13 May 1959.

The VPA stepped up their training programme soon after the 15th Plenary Session had ended. All military units were rallied to be involved in studying the situation in the South and the duties of the revolution. The 324th Division and the 305th Brigade stepped up their military exercises to include mobile vehicles in the mountainous and delta terrains, combined assaults with the infantry, and combined infantry-artillery attacks on enemy key positions. A number of detachments from the 305th Brigade also began to train their troops in parachuting. The 330th Division conducted offensive and defensive exercises in delta-like terrain. The 335th Battalion experimented with offensive and defensive manoeuvres in mountainous terrain under varied conditions in preparation to fight in Laos. In Military Region IV, the troops were studying and practising the procedures of organising and protecting the cadres in the South.[77] The 338th Division, comprising the regrouped Southern cadres and a number of infantry regiments, was responsible for the training of cadres and fighters for their mission in the South. Tens of thousands of cadres and fighters, who either had lived in the South or were familiar with the terrain in South Vietnam, started training in preparation to be sent there.[78] In short, during this period, the VPA were gearing up for the order to launch the offensive in the South. However, at the same time DRV troops were reported to have encroached into the demilitarised zone between North and South Vietnam. The Saigon government protested to the ISCC that North Vietnamese troops had entered A Choc, situated in the demilitarised zone south of the demarcation line, on 10 January 1959.[79]

In February 1959, the Central Military Committee met Le Duan to consider how the development of base areas and the revolutionary armed forces in the South could be accelerated. The Committee also discussed the role of the North in the revolution and the readiness of the VPA to respond to any contingency. Le Duan told the senior officers that while the leadership prefer not to take the route of war, they must be ready to fight if the US were to declare war on them. He opined that a war provoked by the enemy would be an excellent opportunity for the communists to reunite the country. It was not known if the senior military officers had any reservations on intensifying the struggle in the South before the completion of the modernisation of the VPA in 1960. The Central Military Committee concurred that the modernisation of the VPA had to be accelerated.[80]

In March 1959, the Politburo issued a directive on the mission of creating a revolutionary base in the Central Highlands, which included the mountainous areas of Inter-zone V and the jungle and mountain areas of north-east Nam Bo. They had analysed the situation and was convinced that the Central Highlands was a very strategic region that had to be secured before the US-Diem regime could construct a military complex there. The directive instructed that the base area should be developed principally through political means, which included proselytising amongst the people; promoting ethnic solidarity and self-sufficiency; the construction of a political administration base; building up of revolutionary armed forces; and campaigning among enemy soldiers. The Politburo further directed the armed forces in the South to be developed, as there was the need for a strong military force to protect the bases. For the meantime, the armed forces should aim to be able to carry out guerrilla warfare on a limited scale to help the political struggle. The long-range goal was for it to become the main force in the overthrow of the US-Diem regime and to defend the future revolutionary administration.[81]

The attitude of the Vietnamese communists to the armed struggle was clearly reflected in the discussions that took place during the visit of the Hungarian party and government delegation to Hanoi (19–26 April 1959). Janos Radvanyi recalled that during one of the discussions, the subject of the situation in South Vietnam was raised. Ho Chi Minh yielded the floor to Le Duan whom he introduced as the Politburo member in charge of South Vietnamese affairs and that he had recently returned from an extended tour of the South. Le Duan explained that the situation in the South was gradually turning to the advantage of the North. Political workers and party cadres had been instructed to mingle with the peasants in the countryside and the intellectuals in the cities and, when possible, to infiltrate the army and government. In the sphere of political agitation and propaganda, party cadres were told to exploit every opportunity to expose the corruption of the Diem regime and to support popular grievances. Although he admitted that there were difficulties, Le Duan appeared confident that the Diem regime would eventually collapse.

During the discussion, Pham Van Dong disclosed that the South Vietnamese guerrilla leaders residing in Hanoi were pressing the Politburo to endorse unrestrained military action in the South. While he understood their feelings, Dong thought that it was folly to do so before the North was strong enough and before the situation was ripe in the South. However, according to Radvanyi, 'in a half-finished sentence he hinted that the Southern comrades should not be asked to wait too long.'[82]

While in Hanoi, Radvanyi also had a brief opportunity to meet with Nguyen Huu Tho(?) who was adamant that the South was ready for revolutionary guerrilla activity and lamented that the guerrillas must stay their hand because Hanoi insisted that the time was not right for action. This would concur with the *CRIMP Document* which revealed that, since the end of 1958, many felt that the situation was ripe for an armed movement against the Diem regime but the leadership of the Nam Bo Regional Committee hesitated principally because it was against the Party line.[83] Tho had further asked Radvanyi whether Ho, Pham Van Dong or Le Duan had divulged to the Hungarians any new plans regarding the liberation of the South.[84] Radvanyi reported that the Hanoi leadership regarded the South Vietnamese living in Hanoi, 'like poor relations – to be tolerated but virtually ignored.'

Developments following the passing of Law 10/59

Ngo Dinh Diem's policy of terror in the South[85] reached its height on 6 May 1959 with his promulgation of the notorious Law 10/59 that provided for the establishment of special military tribunals to try anyone suspected to be involved in communist activities.[86] Le Duan recalled that, 'before the law was passed, there were only hundreds who were wholeheartedly prepared to fight the enemy. Since the passing of that law, masses regardless of their political inclinations rose against Diem.'[87] On 7 May, Le Duan instructed the Nam Bo Regional Committee to focus all efforts on the establishment of base areas in Nam Bo, particularly in the eastern part, through political work. At the same time, the armed forces and self-defence forces should also be developed.[88]

On 13 May 1959, a week after the passing of Law 10/59, the Hanoi leadership finally issued a communiqué on the decision to reunify the country made at the 15th Plenary Session in January 1959. According to the communiqué, North Vietnam had completed the people's democratic revolution and was in the process of a socialist revolution. This was significant as it determined the direction and the next stage of the development of the Vietnamese revolution. In the North, the most urgent task was building socialism as it was directly related to the struggle for national reunification. While North Vietnam had always respected the 1954 Geneva Agreements, the Diem regime and the US had been undermining the Agreements. The communiqué paid tribute to the struggle of the southern compatriots and stated in very broad terms that the entire people would unite and strive to achieve reunification.[89] The *Nhan Dan* editorial on the communiqué was somewhat more precise but equally circumspect. It stated that 'the people were determined to struggle resolutely and gallantly and use every means and methods – if necessary – to attain their objectives.'[90]

Soon after, the Central Military Committee established a unit under its direct supervision to look into the possibility of opening a land-route that would link the North and the South. The aim of the envisaged road, which later became the famed 'Ho Chi Minh Trail', was to facilitate the movement of cadres, weapons and other necessary supplies from the North into South Vietnam. On 19 May, Vo Bam, Deputy-Director of the Office Agricultural Collectivisation was appointed to head the unit.[91] Military Transportation Group 559 was formed to construct the first North-South road and to organise the transfer of weapons and supplies to the South, specifically to Inter-zone V. Group 559 consisted of two battalions. The 301st Battalion comprised 500 cadres and soldiers specially selected from the 305th Division who had previous experience fighting the French in Inter-zone V. The other battalion was the 603rd Battalion, code-name 'Gianh River Fishing Team', formed in June and comprising 107 cadres and soldiers. The 603rd Battalion was in charge of the sea-route to the South. Besides these two battalions, there was a separate Group 759, formed in July and based at the coastal region of Do Son-Haiphong. It began as a small group of cadres, directly under the General Staff of the VPA, who were assigned to look into the logistics of organising a maritime route to transport weapons, ammunition and equipment to the South.[92] Amongst its members were Vo Nguyen Giap, Hoang Tung and Tran Quang Huy.[93] US intelligence sources also identified the formation in May 1959 of the 70th Battalion, which operated at the Laotian panhandle. It was tasked with the responsibilities of transporting weapons, ammunition, mail and supplies to South Vietnam through the Laotian trails; serving as guides to the infiltration groups; and helping the sick and injured cadres return to the North.[94]

The initial plan was to build a road to reach the northern bank of the Ben Hai River. But after a meeting in May 1959 with Hanh (member of the Party Committee of Quang Tri Province) and Quyet (member of the Party Central Committee of Inter-zone V), it was decided that, for the road to be useful, it had to be extended to join Highway 9. By the first week of June, a new route, punctuated with nine relay stations (two in the region above the Ben Hai River and seven in Inter-zone V) and which cut through the central region south of the 17th parallel, had been drawn up. The most difficult and dangerous part of the route was where it crossed Highway 9, between Khe Sanh and Lower Laos. It was called the 'neuralgic point' because it was 'bristled with enemy positions and was controlled day and night by armoured patrols'.[95] By 20 August 1959, the 301st Battalion had completed relay station Number 9 in Pa Lin (west of Thua Thien), which for the first time made it possible to transport up to 500 kilograms of material to Inter-zone V.

To avoid detection or engagement with the enemy, the weapons and other equipment were camouflaged as products meant for sale and the cadres were advised to minimise contacts with the population. By the end of 1959, the 301st Battalion had transferred to Pa Lin 1,667 rifles, 788 bayonets, and 188 kilograms of explosives as well as binoculars, compasses and topographic maps. In addition, the units carried another 1,174 rifles of all types, bullets and ammunition when they man-oeuvred into the South through the newly built roads. All these weapons and equipment were for the troops in Inter-zone V and the newly formed self-defence forces in the Central Highlands and the plains, as well as the provinces in central Vietnam.[96]

Apparently, during this period there was also much military action along the Laotian border adjacent to North Vietnam. There was then no concrete proof but only circumstantial evidence pointing to any North Vietnamese involvement .[97] At that time, Hanoi in fact denied all charges that its military units were involved in the fighting in Laos. However, in 1970, Langer and Zasloff were able to establish that the North Vietnamese were involved in the fighting during the summer of 1959. Their principal source of information was an intelligence officer of the rank of captain in the G-2 section of the Royal Laotian Armed Forces whom they interviewed over an eight-month period.[98] A North Vietnamese economic cadre's notebook also revealed that in May 1959, Hanoi began to pay greater attention to the revolutionary movement in Laos.[99] In 1980, the North Vietnamese finally disclosed that in 1959 they had reached an agreement with the Pathet Lao on the creation of a team of Vietnamese military specialists to work alongside the Pathet Lao forces. Group 959 was created in September 1959 to serve as specialists to the Pathet Lao forces, organise the logistics and the supply of Vietnamese material as well as to supervise the Vietnamese communist units operating in Sam Neua, Xieng Khouang and Vientiane. Group 959 remained active till 1973.[100] According to a 1994 Vietnamese source, from the moment the decision was taken to open the Ho Chi Minh Trail for the purpose of infiltration, it was understood that Laos and Cambodia would have to be involved in the Vietnamese struggle.[101]

Le Duan

One episode, which illustrates Le Duan's consultative style of leadership (which changed in later years), is perhaps worth re-telling here. Tran Van Tra recounted a meeting in the summer of 1959 between himself, Nguyen Van Vinh and Le Duan which gives us an idea of the extent of Le Duan's authority in 1959. Tra had heard a BBC news bulletin of a skirmish between a platoon of Diem's troops and a Vietnamese communist platoon in the Plain of Reeds. It was reported that both sides had withdrawn after two hours of fighting, without suffering any casualties. Tra was amazed by the news and concluded that either the BBC reporting had been inaccurate or the training of the Southern communist cadres had left much to be desired. The next day, he visited his long-time friend, Nguyen Van Vinh, and they both concurred that there was an urgent need to step up the training of the communist cadres in the South and that it would be conducted by the regrouped Southern cadres in the North. Both men then met with Le Duan, who, according to Tra, was the de facto First Secretary of the Lao Dong Party Central Committee. They presented Le Duan with the proposal to send 100 young cadres from the North to the South. After much deliberation, Le Duan said that it would be difficult to proceed with the proposal as the Politburo had not decided on the matter. When Tran and Vinh persisted, Le Duan asked whether the number could be reduced. A new figure of 50 was proposed. Le Duan again hesitated but finally agreed to bear the responsibility if the number was smaller. They finally agreed on 25. The team was selected by June 1959 and was ready to be dispatched to the South by Christmas 1959. By then, the Party Central Committee had given its blessings.[102]

Chinese and Russian attitudes towards the resumption of armed struggle

It was not known if Ho Chi Minh informed the Soviet leaders of the decision of the 15th Plenary Session when he was in Moscow for the 21st CPSU Congress on 27 January 1959. Even if he had done so, it was unlikely that he was able to get much Russian support. Immediately after the 15th Plenary Session, Hanoi had tried unsuccessfully to exploit the 'Phu Loi incident' to rally support from Moscow and China to support the military struggle.[103] At the Congress, Khrushchev reiterated his belief that war between the two camps was not inevitable. In his analysis, economic progress in the Soviet Union and the socialist countries could only lead to more countries outside the socialist bloc aspiring to identify with the socialist bloc. The international situation would change radically when the Soviet Union become the world's leading industrial power and China become a mighty industrial power, and when all the socialist countries together produce half the world's industrial output. The new correlation of power would be so obvious that even the most obdurate imperialists would realise the hopelessness of any attempt to launch a war against the socialist camp.[104]

According to Radvanyi, when the Hungarian party and government delegation met Khrushchev in Moscow during their visit from 16–17 May 1959, Khrushchev showed no interest at all in Vietnam. The conversation ranged from the Berlin question to the current Conference of Foreign Ministers in Geneva to his low opinion of the Chinese Great Leap Forward. But when the Hungarian Prime Minister, Munnich, tried to engage him on some of the highlights of their Hanoi visit, Khrushchev 'all but yawned in his face', an attitude which puzzled Radvanyi. He opined, 'in as much as the 15th Plenum of the Central Committee of the Lao Dong Party in May(?) had for the first time called for an armed struggle against the Diem clique and Americans ... Khrushchev, for reasons unknown to me, seemed totally unconcerned.'[105]

Ho visited the Soviet Union again in July, ostensibly on vacation.[106] At about the same time, Khrushchev was visiting Poland from 14 to 23 July; and US Vice-President, Richard Nixon, was in Moscow from 23 July till 2 August. While in the Soviet Union, Ho would have seen all the favourable publicity in the Russian media regarding Khrushchev's forthcoming visit to the US in September at the invitation of President Eisenhower.

The Chinese position can be gleaned from an interview that Mao gave to Anna Louise Strong on 13 March 1959. Mao believed there would always be wars but one should not fear the imperialists because that would only induce them to action. In his own words, 'one should oppose them, but with care.'[107] A month later, in his speech at the 16th enlarged session of the Supreme State Conference on 14 April 1959, Mao explained why China did not simply attack Taiwan. He compared the Quemoy (Jinmen) Crisis of August 1958 with the Tibet problem, and explained that it was easier for the PLA (People's Liberation Army) to move into Tibet than into Taiwan as the latter had a treaty with the US whereas the former did not.[108]

The Hungarian party and government delegation was in Beijing from 29 April 1959 to 7 May 1959 after visiting Hanoi from 19–26 April. Radvanyi reported that in contrast with the Russians, the Chinese were keen to hear about their visit to Vietnam. Chinese Foreign Minister Chen Yi and Wang Youtien, Director of the Soviet and East European Department in the Chinese Foreign Ministry, were particularly interested in what they knew of the South Vietnamese situation. Also, Chen Yi expected the Vietnamese communists to start the reunification process soon. The subject of Vietnam was raised again at a meeting with Mao Zedong. Mao spoke of Ho as an old friend with whom he had enjoyed harmonious relations and blamed Stalin for Ho's difficulties. It was Mao's hope that the communists would come to power in France, thus making possible the resolution of the Vietnam problem within the framework of a French Union under Maurice Thorez and Jacques Duclos. Mao also stated that the Chinese would continue to back the Vietnamese in their efforts to liberate the country.[109]

Ho Chi Minh spent the month of August 1959 in China where he met Zhou Enlai. In Han Suyin's account, Ho, during his meeting with Zhou in August 1959, expressed concern about the forthcoming Khrushchev-Eisenhower summit and its implications for Vietnam. Ho also informed Zhou of his intention to create a liberation front in South Vietnam and to use military means to achieve the reunification of the country. Zhou assured Ho that China would give approximately $500 million worth of weaponry, equipment and funds to support the liberation struggle at the end of 1959.[110] This account corresponds with that of Hoang Van Hoan who recalled that when the North Vietnamese eventually made public the decision to renew the struggle to unify the country on 13 May 1959,[111] the Chinese considered it 'a reasonable idea and agreed to provide military aid.'[112] A Chinese source similarly noted that when the North Vietnamese proposed an armed defence struggle in the South after the promulgation of Law 10/59, China supported the idea.[113] However, for reasons still unclear, Beijing failed to deliver the promised military aid at the end of 1959.

Chapter Two
The Armed Struggle Begins

The armed struggle resumes

The Southern representatives who attended the 15th Plenary Session returned to their respective bases in the South between August and December 1959. The Tra Bong uprising (in the mountain-region district in the western part of Quang Ngai province) was one of the first local uprisings in the transition phase of the revolution in the South in 1959. It involved the Inter-zone Party Committee, Provincial Party Committee, the surrounding districts in Quang Ngai and Quang Nam provinces and the provincial and inter-zone armed forces.[1] It started on 28 August 1959, when 16,000 ethnic minority people in Tra Bong, with the support of the 339th platoon, started an uprising under the leadership of the District Party Committee and the Provincial Party Committee. They eliminated Diem administrations in 16 villages, forced the abandonment of seven posts, killed 161 traitors and set up revolutionary administrations in the hamlets and villages. The uprisings quickly spread to the neighbouring villages in the districts of Son Tra, Ba To and Minh Long. On 26 September 1959, the communists ambushed two companies of the 23rd Division, resulting in the death of 12 soldiers and the loss of all the weapons.[2]

By September 1959, more reached home after the long and arduous journey from Hanoi. It took another month or thereabouts to make the necessary military preparations.[3] So in some parts of South Vietnam, the armed struggle was launched in October.[4] It took another two months for the 15th Plenary Session resolution to be disseminated to all the provinces in the Nam Bo and Inter-zone V.[5] According to historian Tran Huu Dinh, it was towards the end of 1959 that the leadership of the Nam Bo Regional Committee finally reached home (via Cambodia) to organise the resistance movement there.[6]

Hence from 1960, there were mass revolts all over South Vietnam. In a January 1960 special report on the internal security situation in South Vietnam, the US Embassy in Saigon noted that for the first time there were attacks by the communists on large South Vietnamese Army units. Le Duan recalled that 'the simultaneous uprisings that broke out during this period marked an important leap forward. They moved the South Vietnamese revolution to the offensive and the revolutionary high tide developed in all areas with the co-ordination of both forms of political and armed struggles ... Armed struggle and political struggle together are the fundamental form of violence of the South Vietnamese revolution, and co-ordinating armed struggle with political struggle is the fundamental law of the method of the South Vietnamese.'[7]

In Ben Tre, from 17–24 January, there were uprisings in 47 villages in the districts of Mo Cay, Giong Trom, Chau Thanh, Ba Tri and Thanh Phu. Although they began as unarmed mass uprisings, the communists very quickly captured guns and other weapons. With the weapons captured at Binh Khanh, the communists were able to arm three squads to support uprisings in Minh Tan, Thanh Phu and Mo Cay. They also managed to create a number of platoons and the 264th company, their first. On 21 January, the Saigon government dispatched an amphibious battalion into Phuoc Hiep village to recapture Dinh Thuy and Binh Khanh but were surrounded by the 264th company and armed squads from the three villages. A number of the marines were killed and more weapons were captured. In February, the Ben Tre provincial committee created a second company, the 269th, at Bao Island (comprising Giong Trom, Ba Tri and Chau Thanh). On 4 February, the Ben Tre provincial committee and the Mo Cay district committees organised 200 women from Phuoc Hiep village and 5,000 women from the adjoining villages into resistance groups.[8] According to the *Lich Su Quan Doi Nhan Dan Viet Nam*, the practice of attacking the enemy by combining the political struggle with the armed struggle was first employed during the Ben Tre uprisings.[9] From the uprisings in Ben Tre onwards, concerted uprisings swept across the provinces of Nam Bo. Terrorism and guerrilla action, once regarded by the US Country Team as a long-term threat to the Diem regime, was now South Vietnam's 'number one problem'.[10]

Despite the uprisings, the communist leadership exercised extreme caution. To pre-empt the uprisings from spiralling out of control, on 28 March 1960, the Nam Bo Regional Committee sent an urgent letter to all the branches in the South warning against any premature intensification of the military struggle. The letter reiterated that the Party's policy remained one of 'strongly pushing the political struggle ahead and combining it to the right degree with armed activities'. The letter explained that the time was not yet ripe for a direct revolution to overthrow the Diem regime because while the enemy had been weakened and demoralised, they still had the capability to retaliate in a massive way. The balance of forces was not yet to their advantage and any premature resort to violence would only put the communist forces in a dangerous and vulnerable position.[11] The letter also revealed that the 3rd Party Congress would be held in September 1960 and one of the agenda items was the discussion of the line and task of both the Party and people at the current stage of the revolution.[12]

In a speech on 20 April to commemorate Lenin's 90th birthday anniversary, Le Duan reiterated that it was not the appropriate time to fight a full-scale war in the South. In his view, although the South was governed by the laws of a colonial and feudal regime and should theoretically follow the path to liberation as prescribed by Lenin, the people's democratic revolution of the South was occurring when the world had changed fundamentally. In various parts of the world, the forces of socialism were gaining supremacy while capitalism was weakening. This meant that there were growing possibilities to frustrate imperialism and achieve lasting peace. In addition, North Vietnam, the firm base for the revolution in the South, had been completely liberated and was advancing towards socialism. From this he concluded that, 'We can and must *guide and restrict* within the South the solving of the contradiction between imperialism and the colonies in our country' (emphasis added).[13]

Le Duan's caution could also be prompted by developments in the VPA in the first nine months of 1960. It is notable that there is a conspicuous lack of information in the *Lich Su Quan Doi Nhan Dan Viet Nam* about the activities of the VPA during those months. The Czech ambassador reported that there was 'quite a serious malaise' in the army and many units were dispersed to different parts of the country. Vo Nguyen Giap was kept busy visiting the units to track down the problem.[14] The problem could be related to the implementation of the Military Obligation Law approved at the 12th Plenary Session and promulgated in April 1960 as part of the effort of the Hanoi leadership to transform the VPA into a professional army. With the passing of the new law, the VPA would no longer be a volunteer army. Troops could henceforth be mobilised swiftly for any contingency and also be channelled into economic construction.[15]

Hanoi and the growing Sino-Soviet rivalry

At this juncture it is appropriate to highlight two issues that had a significant and direct bearing on the Vietnamese communist side of the Vietnam War. The first issue concerns Hanoi's relations with Beijing and Moscow.

Any decision to intensify the armed struggle in the South must necessarily take into consideration the views of Beijing and Moscow, Hanoi's principal supporters. As noted before, Beijing was sympathetic to the Vietnamese communists' cause, more so than Moscow. But the Chinese leaders were not supportive of any intensification of the military struggle. Readers would recall that in August 1959, at a meeting with Ho Chi Minh in Beijing, Zhou had agreed to provide military aid in support of the Southern struggle by the end of 1959. Beijing apparently reneged on its promise for fear of exacerbating the military struggle. This evidently displeased the Hanoi leadership. The French Delegate-General, Monsieur Chambon recalled that, in a speech at a New Year gathering with the diplomatic corp on 1 January 1960, Ho Chi Minh went out of his way to lavish praise on the Soviet Union[16] but made no mention of China at all. British officials in Hanoi also noted that until March 1960, North Vietnamese reports on China were perfunctory and scarce whereas much publicity was given to the activities of Khrushchev.[17] Sino-Vietnamese relations however appeared to have recovered by May. On 1 May, it was announced that the Chinese delegation led by Zhou Enlai would visit North Vietnam from 9–12 May 1960.[18] The relationship between them was once again portrayed to be as 'close as the teeth and the lips'.

The Sino-Vietnamese talks that took place on 11, 12 and 13 May 1960 are significant. Contemporary reports on the talks revealed little except for the fact that both sides arrived at completely identical views of all questions discussed.[19] According to the 1980 North Vietnamese account, during the Sino-Vietnamese meeting(s) in May 1960, the Chinese said that although they believed that political and military struggle were both equally important, it was not possible to win political power immediately because, even if they succeeded in overthrowing Diem, there was still the US to contend with. It would, therefore, have to be a protracted struggle. The North could support the South politically and help in formulating policies, but it must principally nurture in them the spirit of self-reliance. When the chances of success were certain, the North could then aid the South militarily by secretly supplying arms but should not provide direct assistance.[20] A Chinese source recorded that in mid-May 1960, the North Vietnamese and Chinese leaders met first in Hanoi and then in Beijing to discuss the question of revolutionary struggle in the South. During their discussions, Zhou Enlai agreed with Pham Van Dong that the South must be liberated. Both Zhou and Deng Xiaoping were of the opinion that a combination of political and military struggle should be applied. Political struggle should be employed predominantly in the cities, with military struggle playing a supporting role. In the countryside, though military struggle could take precedence, there was also the need to win political support. Dong concurred with their views.[21] Hoang Van Hoan recalled that, after being fully apprised of the situation in South Vietnam in May, the Chinese had a better understanding of the Vietnamese communists' position regarding armed struggle in the South and fully supported it.[22]

However, nothing substantial developed out of the above meetings for another year. In early 1962, the North Vietnamese and Chinese leaders met again to discuss Chinese military assistance for the struggle in the South.[23] Another meeting followed this up, this time with Ho Chi Minh and Nguyen Chi Thanh, in Beijing in the summer. The Chinese eventually supplied 90,000 guns of all assortments for equipping the 230 infantry battalions, thus marking the beginning of Chinese aid in promoting the development, strengthening and expansion of the communist military arsenal in the South.[24] (Thereafter, whenever Zhou Enlai made reference to Chinese assistance to the Vietnamese struggle in South Vietnam, he cited 1962 as the starting point.) Chinese assistance increased thereon as the war gradually expanded.[25]

Meanwhile, Sino-Soviet relations, which had been uneasy since the 20th CPSU Congress in February 1956, deteriorated further. Their disagreements had so far been kept fairly muted until the Bucharest conference in June 1960 when the Russians decided to involve the other senior party members in the communist bloc in their ideological dispute. As the Bucharest conference was unable to resolve their differences, it was decided that an all-party conference would be convened in November in Moscow to settle the matter. In July 1960, Moscow suddenly recalled 1,390 experts working in China as well as terminated 343 contracts for the service of Soviet experts and 257 projects of scientific and technical co-operation. It also ordered their experts to take back with them all blueprints and technical data.[26]

Hanoi was able to avoid taking sides in the Sino-Soviet dispute. On 28 June, the *Nhan Dan* published the full text of the Bucharest communiqué with an editorial entitled 'To strengthen solidarity and unity of mind among the brother-parties is constantly our foremost task'. In his report to the 2nd National Assembly (7–15 July 1960), Pham Van Dong told the assembly not to expect an easy and quick victory in the struggle for reunification. However, under the leadership of the Soviet Union and China, the collapse of imperialism was inevitable. He emphasised the significance of the 1957 Moscow Declaration recently reaffirmed in the Bucharest communiqué. On 9 July, the *Nhan Dan* again published the full text of the Bucharest communiqué together with the complete 29 June 1960 editorials of *Pravda* and *Rennin Ribao* concerning the Bucharest communiqué.[27] In a communiqué dated 14 August 1960, the Hanoi leadership emphasised the need for solidarity and unity in the socialist camp and stated that they would do their utmost to strengthen the unity of the socialist camp. In August 1960, Ho Chi Minh travelled to Yalta to meet Khrushchev with the intention of helping to reconcile Hanoi's two communist allies. During that meeting, Ho was constantly interrupted by Khrushchev who stuck to his anti-Chinese position.[28]

The Moscow Conference met from 10 November to 1 December 1960 to settle the unresolved issues at Bucharest. The Chinese objected to a point in the official statement and refused to be a signatory. Ho Chi Minh appealed to Khrushchev to accede to the Chinese because 'China was a big country with a big party and they could not allow a schism in the communist movement'. Khrushchev retorted that the Soviet Union was by no means a small country, to which Ho replied, 'For us, it is doubly difficult. Don't forget, China is our neighbour.'[29] Ho also coaxed Liu Shaoqi to meet privately with Khrushchev on the conference statement.[30] The parties eventually compromised on a statement that reiterated the correctness of the Five Principles of peaceful coexistence. But it also considered national liberation wars as progressive and having revolutionary significance. How these two policies were to be reconciled in practice was not clarified. The Statement also mentioned that, depending on the specific conditions of the particular country, colonial countries could achieve their independence through armed struggle or through non-military means. In countries where the imperialists had established war bases, it was necessary to step up the struggle for their annihilation. There could only be true independence when all the patriotic forces of the nations unite in a single national-democratic front to wage a determined struggle against imperialism and the remnants of feudalism. There was, however, no mention of the specific ways to achieve that.[31] At the end of the conference, Sino-Soviet differences were not resolved. For the Vietnamese communists, the Moscow Statement at the very least provided an endorsement of Hanoi's current reunification strategy.

Developments in Laos

The second issue that had an impact on the Vietnamese communists' side of the Vietnam War was the prevailing political situation in Laos. Vo Bam recalled that in early 1960, troops operating on the Ho Chi Minh Trail started to take a short cut near Khe Sanh by crossing a privately owned coffee plantation. On one occasion, a batch of rifles was negligently left at relay station 5 that subsequently led to a regiment-sized sweep of the area by Diem's troops. When Vo Bam reported the incident to Le Duan, the latter suggested that they try to find an alternative route that would attract less enemy attention. The alternative route that Vo Bam proposed was to travel southwards on the western side of the Truong Son Range, which was in Laotian territory.[32] Given the importance of the Ho Chi Minh Trail to the struggle in the South, it was to be expected that Hanoi could not be disinterested in the developments there.

According to the *Lich Su Quan Doi Nhan Dan Viet Nam*, the united struggle of Laos and Vietnam against the common enemy – the American imperialists – was a special relationship based on the traditional closeness of the two countries and the spirit of proletarian internationalism between the two parties and armies. And it was this unity which created the condition for the success of both the revolutions in Vietnam and Laos.[33] The irony is that in 1960 and early 1961, it was Laos rather than South Vietnam that captured international attention. In the view of President

Eisenhower, if Laos should fall to the communists, then it would just be a matter of time before South Vietnam, Cambodia, Thailand and Burma would follow. Laos was key to the entire area of Southeast Asia. Vietnam then was considered less critical.[34]

The crisis in Laos was essentially a struggle for power between the Pathet Lao (supported by Hanoi) and the RLG (Royal Laotian Government, backed by the US). On 25 December 1959, the US-backed Committee for the Defence of National Interests (CDNI) and the Royal Laotian Army carried out a coup that forced the Phoui Sananikone government to resign. On 5 January 1960, Hanoi accused CDNI of colluding with the US imperialists to turn South Vietnam and Laos into US military bases. A provisional government, headed ostensibly by the elder statesman Kou Abhay, was formed on 7 January 1960. However, the real power behind the provisional government was General Nosavan and the CDNI. On 30 January 1960, the Laotian Council of Ministers announced that general election would take place on 24 April 1960. By introducing electoral laws weighted against the left-wing parties, the RLG hoped to prevent the NLHX (Neo Lao Hak Xat/Lao Patriotic Front) Party from gaining any political power. Nevertheless, the NLHX fielded nine candidates. On 21 April, General Phoumi Nosavan told the British ambassador that the results of the election were a foregone conclusion.[35] The Royal Laotian Army carried out mopping-up operations during the campaign period. The election itself was also blatantly rigged, apparently with assistance from CIA agents. For example, in Sam Neua, the Pathet Lao stronghold, the NLHX candidate unbelievably received only 13 votes compared to the 6,508 votes of the RLG candidate.[36] Needless to say, the RLG won a landslide victory on 24 April 1960.

The participation of the NLHX in the elections despite the odds provided the cover for the Pathet Lao forces to prepare for an eventual military offensive. According to British Embassy sources in Vientiane, in the past months, the 2nd Battalion as well as other elements that had received training in North Vietnam had been returning to Laos and positioning themselves strategically all over the country. It was estimated that between

200 and 400 regular units had infiltrated into Southern Laos as well as Central and Northern Laos[37] and on the night of 23 May 1960, after being detained for ten months, Souphanouvong and 15 other NHLX prisoners escaped from Phone Kheng police camp outside Vientiane. According to British assessments then, even before the escape of the NLHX leaders, the Pathet Lao were already in a position to launch a very effective and successful military campaign if they chose to do so.[38]

Like a bolt from the blue, on 9 August 1960, the 'revolutionary forces' led by Captain Kong Lae, Commander of the 2nd Paratroops Battalion, carried out a coup in Vientiane.[39] Kong Lae, who did not have any political affiliation, explained that he had organised the coup in order to stop the civil war, eliminate corruption amongst public servants (including military commanders and officials), and rid the country of foreign armed forces, specifically those of the US. The Revolutionary Committee, he declared, would maintain the neutrality of Laos and establish friendly and neighbourly relations with all countries.[40] On 11 August, Kong Lae proclaimed Souvanna Phouma as the chosen Premier of the Revolutionary Government. Souvanna Phouma presented his new government to the National Assembly on 16 August. In his policy statement, Souvanna Phouma stated that he planned to implement the agreements he had reached with the Pathet Lao as spelt out in the 1957 Vientiane Agreement that had been jettisoned by the previous administration. Meanwhile, the US-backed Phoumi Nosavan was rallying his forces for an offensive to retake Vientiane. It was rumoured that Bangkok might intervene militarily to forestall a communist take-over of Laos. If Phoumi Nosavan was to launch a counter-offensive, a civil war in Laos would be inevitable and the involvement of either US and/or SEATO forces in support of Phoumi Nosavan could not be discounted. The North Vietnamese communists would also find it difficult not to be embroiled in such a war. British officials in Vientiane noted that the Pathet Lao had shown astonishing forbearance when they could have easily taken advantage of the crisis in Laos to seize power.[41] Neither Hanoi nor the Pathet Lao was, however, ready for such a war.

Phoumi Nosavan's first (but unsuccessful) counter-offensive to retake Vientiane began with the move on Paksane on 19 September. Kong Lae's paratroopers, with the assistance of the Pathet Lao, forced his troops to retreat down the Mekong Valley to the south bank of the Ca Dinh River. On 26 September, the Pathet Lao armed forces, with the support of the Vietnamese communist troops, captured the city of Sam Neua and gained control of most of the province. This gave the Pathet Lao a large base area, which bordered North Vietnam, and which could be expanded northwards, southwards and westwards. British officials based at Vientiane noted that the Pathet Lao's strength had increased throughout the country and Souvanna Phouma had lost whatever control he had over Kong Lae who in turn was completely dependent on the Pathet Lao.[42] Also, with the capture of Sam Neua, Hanoi was able to organise and co-ordinate the revolution in Laos without serious hindrance until their complete victory in 1975.[43] Although the Pathet Lao had the upper hand, the NLHX Central Committee continued to pursue peaceful negotiations with Souvanna Phouma on the basis of the 1957 Vientiane Agreement.

In the ongoing civil war, Hanoi and Moscow supported the Kong Lae-Pathet Lao forces[44] while the US supported the Phoumi Nosavan faction.[45] The Laotian crisis presented an opportunity for Moscow to gain the foothold in Laos that it had been trying to secure since June 1956. In October 1960, Laos finally established diplomatic relations with the Soviet Union. In the context of the growing Sino-Soviet rivalry, the liaison could not have come at a better time for Moscow. President Eisenhower saw some indications that Moscow was concerned over communist pressures in Laos and in Southeast Asia emanating from China and North Vietnam.[46] The Soviet ambassador to Thailand confirmed this observation when he told Marshal Sarit that Soviet activities in Laos were in part meant to keep China from intervening in that country.[47] Beijing closely monitored the developments in Laos but, up till the end of 1960, they were unwilling to take any initiative of their own which might involve them in the civil war and were contented to let the Russians and North Vietnamese run the show. Beijing, however, was vigilant of any attempts to turn Laos into a base against China.[48]

On 8 December, Colonel Kouprasith Abbay who supported the Phoumi Nosavan-faction carried out a coup against Souvanna Phouma.[49] This led to the fight for Vientiane between Kong Lae's paratroopers and the forces of Phoumi Nosavan (with the direct support of the Thais).[50] Neither the Pathet Lao nor the North Vietnamese took part in the Vientiane battle[51] although they gave indirect support. From Hanoi and Haiphong, the Russians airlifted fuel, ammunition and combat rations to Kong Lae. North Vietnamese military personnel were also parachuted in to augment Kong Lae's forces outside Vientiane.[52] On 14 December, in a message to the co-chairmen of the Geneva Conference, Nehru proposed that the International Commission in Laos be reactivated.[53] Hanoi, Beijing and Phnom Penh supported the proposal. Kong Lae eventually withdrew from Vientiane on 15 December. On 22 December, Moscow delivered a note to its counterpart at Whitehall proposing that a new conference involving all the participants of the 1954 Geneva Conference be convened to resolve the situation in Laos and that the ISCC should resume its activity as suggested by Nehru.[54]

The 3rd Party Congress of the Lao Dong Party

Meanwhile in North Vietnam, the 3rd Party Congress of the Lao Dong Party convened on 5 September 1960.[55] A congress of the ruling party was an event of great significance as it gave a picture of the existing situation in the country, revealed the difficulties they were facing, the progress made, as well as its future goals and direction. In this case, it attracted even more attention because the 2nd Congress was held nine years ago. In his political report, Le Duan stated that Vietnam's revolution at that stage shared a common objective, which was the reunification of the country. It also had two strategic tasks that were mutually reinforcing. The first was to carry out a socialist revolution in the North, and the second was to complete the national people's democratic revolution through the removal of the colonial and semi-feudal regime in South Vietnam. The immediate task of the revolution in the South was to create a broad national united front against the US-Diem regime, with the worker-peasant alliance as the core. The struggle for national reunification would have to be gradual and it might take different forms depending on the changing circumstances. For the North, the task was to carry out the socialist transformation of agriculture and light industries while giving priority to the development of heavy industries.[56]

In his report at the congress, Vo Nguyen Giap highlighted the need for the defence budget and other resources to be curtailed so that manpower and material resources could be channelled to economic construction in the North, which had become the central task of the Party. This statement was the strongest indication that the modernisation of the VPA had hitherto been slowed down.[57] The 3rd Party Congress decided that the modernisation of the VPA would have to be intensified. The dual revolutionary strategy spelt out during the Congress would serve as the basis for the VPA to chart its direction in the new era.[58]

Pham Van Dong, in his report on Hanoi's foreign policy, stated that North Vietnam would further strengthen the solidarity and unity within the socialist bloc. He praised the Soviet Union and China alike for their unflinching struggle against US imperialism. He reiterated the desire of Hanoi to establish friendly relations with Cambodia on the basis of the Five Principles of peaceful coexistence and the establishment of friendly relations with Laos if it respected the Geneva and Vientiane Agreements.[59]

According to the *Lich Su Quan Doi Nhan Dan Viet Nam*, the 3rd Party Congress was a milestone in the country's revolutionary struggle. After five years, the North had completed the restoration of its economy and was on the road towards socialism while the uprisings in the South were developing satisfactorily. The dual revolutionary strategy as envisaged by the Central Committee was emerging clearer by the day. In Laos, after the escape of the 2nd Battalion, a politico-military struggle was developing. In the world, the socialist system was in the ascendant. The VPA was also intensifying its preparation for the eventuality that it was called upon to move into South Vietnam and Laos.[60]

With regards to the issue of peaceful co-existence, Bui Tin recalled that the Russian and Chinese attitude towards the issue of peaceful co-existence was a bone of contention within the Hanoi leadership. Truong Chinh was amongst those who supported the Russian position regarding peaceful coexistence first propounded at the 20th CPSU Congress whereas Le Duan supported the Chinese opposition to it. The latter was able to carry the majority of the Politburo and the Central Committee with him. The confirmation of Le Duan as the First-Secretary of the Lao Dong Party at the congress further strengthened his hand. Those who held contrary views from his were branded as 'revisionists' and 'opponents of the Party'.[61]

Communist activities in the South

According to a Special National Intelligence Estimate (of 23 August 1960), the US Country Team reported that in the first five months of 1960, Vietnamese communist terrorism had continued to intensify, and support from the North appeared to have increased. Senior cadres and military supplies such as communication equipment were believed to be entering the South via the land routes through Laos and Cambodia or by sea on junks along the eastern coastline.[62]

In July 1960, the Nam Bo Regional committee held its 5th Plenary Session in War Zone D. Encouraged by their recent victories, they agreed to press harder on the Diem regime. The meeting decided to launch simultaneous uprisings throughout the country starting on 23 September 1960, which was also the 15th anniversary of the resistance in the South. The provincial committees of south Central Vietnam and Inter-zone V also decided to initiate a new wave of armed activities from September 1960. From the middle of September onwards, mass uprisings instigated and led by the communists, and supported by armed units, swept the South.[63] The uprisings, along the lines of the earlier ones in Ben Tre, started on 14 September in the provinces of Ca Mau, Rach Gia, Soc Trang, Vinh Long, Chau Doc, Long Xuyen, and Can Tho (in western Nam Bo). On 23 and 24 September, uprisings were launched in the provinces of Long An, Ben Tre, Kien Phong and Kien Tuong (in central Nam Bo). There were also uprisings in eastern Nam Bo in the areas surrounding Saigon-Gia Dinh-Tay Ninh, Ben Cat, Dau Tieng, Cu Chi, Hoc Mon to Lai Thieu, Thu Duc, Tan Binh, Di An, Nha Be, Binh Chanh as well as in Trung Bo and Inter-zone V.[64]

On 20 December 1960, the National Liberation Front for South Vietnam (NLFSV) was established in Tan Lap village, Chau Thanh district (presently, Tan Bien district, Tay Ninh province).[65] The idea of a united front strategy was first suggested at the June 1956 Politburo meeting and was made a policy at the 15th Plenary Session in January 1959. It was also discussed between Ho Chi Minh and Zhou Enlai in Beijing in August 1959. (Beijing was the first to recognise the NLFSV.) In autumn of that year, Nguyen Van Hieu met with Ho Chi Minh in Hanoi to discuss its platform. By the end of 1959, the manifesto and political programme were finalised and the date for the inaugural meeting was fixed.[66] The intention to establish a united front was officially announced by Le Duan in his political report during the recent 3rd Party Congress in September. The NLFSV Provisional Committee subsequently decided to strengthen its presence in the Saigon-Cholon area where it was weakest by forming the Saigon/Cholon/GiaDinh Committee on 31 January 1961.[67]

The Hanoi leadership wanted to ensure that the military activities in the South were centrally co-ordinated. To this end, a military committee for all the zones, provinces, hamlets and villages was thus created to serve as the command centre. The military committee would also be responsible for recruitment and logistics. It was also decided that the armed forces in the South should be known as the 'Army for the Liberation of South Vietnam'[68] and organised into core, regional and guerrilla forces. According to the 1 January 1961 directive issued by the Central Military Committee, the 'Army for the Liberation of South Vietnam' was a component of the VPA, and it was founded, developed, educated and led by the Party. It was to be both a fighting and a production army, and was expected to uphold the tradition of heroic struggle, the spirit of uprisings and service to the people. Its mission was to liberate the South from imperialist oppression and feudalism, and to achieve independence and freedom. However, the directive cautioned that, although this was an urgent task, it must be undertaken realistically depending on the circumstances and the existing practical capability of the army.[69]

By January 1961, the communists had dominated much of South Vietnam's 1st and 5th Military Regions, and most of the region from the jungle foothills of the High Plateau north of Saigon all the way south down to the Gulf of Siam. Thousands of communists had also infiltrated into the most productive parts of South Vietnam except for the Saigon-Cholon area and the narrow corridors protected by Diem's military and paramilitary forces.[70]

Directive of 31 January 1961

On 31 January 1961, the Politburo of the Lao Dong Party issued a directive that 'provided very important strategic guidance for the revolution in the South'. It observed that the North was gradually becoming more capable of defending itself as well as serving as a base area for the revolution to liberate the South. The revolution in the South was developing simultaneously along the path of a general uprising and there was no possibility that the revolution would develop in a peaceful manner. The strategy was to step up both the political and military struggles gradually. Recognising that their strength was not yet evenly distributed in the South, the Politburo called for the employ-ment of military struggle in the jungle and mountainous areas, a mix of military and political struggles in the lowland areas, and an emphasis on political struggle in the urban areas. According to the official North Vietnamese account, the 31 January 1961 directive pointed the way for the strategic direction of the revolution in the South.[71]

In a 7 February 1961 letter addressed to the comrades in the South, Le Duan underscored the importance of the 31 January 1961 directive. According to him, the revolutionary struggle at that point of time should not mimic the Chinese model of protracted armed struggle whereby rural forces would first descend upon and besiege the cities before the final liberation of the whole country by the military forces. Instead, in South Vietnam and in Laos as well, the strategy should begin with separate but co-ordinated uprisings with the objective of establishing base areas and employing guerrilla warfare tactics, culminating in a general mass uprising in the final stage. The most important aspect was to conduct political struggle supplemented by armed struggle to regain political supremacy for the masses.

In Le Duan's opinion, although the communists had the upper hand over the US-Diem clique in the political struggle, their armed forces were sorely lacking in numbers. For instance, they did not have sufficient troops to control the strategically important Central Highlands. Even if they had succeeded in capturing the cities, they would not be able to hold them. Le Duan was acutely aware that it was not merely the US-Diem clique that they were confronting but the Americans as well. Thus, while political struggle would continue to play the leading role at that stage, their immediate task was to build up the armed forces. He also reiterated in his letter the need to control the Central Highlands, an issue he claimed he had already discussed with the comrades of Inter-zone V. He was convinced that the Central Highlands was pivotal to the communist strategy as it was from this region that any attack against the enemy would be launched. It would also serve as a base area to build and protect the revolutionary forces. The countryside and the delta areas in the vicinity of the Central Highlands would be their main strategic targets, leaving the cities to the last. Before the year was out, the Party Central Committee would assist Inter-zone V and Nam Bo to establish 12 battalions. It would also help provide Nam Bo with enough cadres to form seven battalions.[72]

Developments in the VPA

On 25 February, the Politburo in Hanoi approved the military plan proposed by the Central Military Committee and the Ministry of National Defence. The plan identified four main tasks. The first was to increase the military strength of the VPA to effectively defend North Vietnam by establishing an air-defence force, laying the foundation for an air force and navy, and completing the regularisation and modernisation of the VPA. The second task was to build up the armed forces in South Vietnam. Infantry troops in the districts and provinces would be organised into platoons and companies and battalions, respectively. Ten to 15 regiments would be combined with a number of artillery units to take on the enemy's defence, tanks and aircraft. The third task involved assisting the Pathet Lao to train and fortify its armed forces, and to consolidate and develop the Pathet Lao liberated areas. North Vietnamese troops would be sent to Laos when required. The fourth task called for the re-organisation of the military command system in South Vietnam so as to improve the communication link between the Party Central Committee and the provincial and district committees right down the line to the village cells. The Military Regions in South Vietnam would be organised quickly. The Central Military Committee was entrusted with the task of supervising the military activities and developments in South Vietnam. At the Politburo meeting, Ho Chi Minh maintained that the VPA was a people's army, that the war was a people's war, and the army must always be closely associated with the people. While weaponry and technical skills must be constantly improved, the army should always live like the ordinary people.[73]

Soon after, in March, the General Staff of the VPA issued a new battle order: the 325th Division, 341st Brigade, and 244th Regiment would operate in Military Region IV while the 316th and 335th Brigades and 148th Regiment would operate in the Northwest Military Region. This was to ensure that troops were ready to move into Battlefield 'B' (that is, South Vietnam), and Battlefield 'C' (Laos), at short notice. The 338th Division was established as a special division for the training of all soldiers who were assigned to operate in South Vietnam. (In the years 1959–1963, the majority of the cadres and soldiers that fought in the South comprised those who had been recruited in the South or who were from the regrouped troops based in Inter-zone V, as well as those who had previous experience fighting in the South, armed only with rifles and a number of DKZ trench mortars.)[74]

In the same month, the Central Military Commission established a Committee led by Lieutenant-General Hoang Van Thai, a member of the Party Central Committee and Deputy-Chief of Staff, to review the overall strategy of the VPA. The Committee was to recapitulate and study the experiences of the armed struggle and the military strategy used in the resistance war against the French, and evaluate the role of the VPA in the dual missions of national construction and warfare.[75]

According to the *Lich Su Quan Doi Nhan Dan Viet Nam*, in the first five years in the development of the VPA (1955–1960), it had grown from several fragmented units of infantry equipped with inferior weaponry, to a regular and relatively modern army. Those were the foundation years. In 1961, the many new military commitments that the VPA had to undertake revealed the limitations of the VPA in the areas of organisation, weaponry, military science and strategy. The objectives of the 2nd Five-Year Military Plan, from 1961–1965, was therefore to develop a truly modern military that could fight effectively in the battlefields of Indochina as well as to accelerate the creation of military units in anticipation of the expansion of the war.[76] British intelligence reported that the VPA's military role was given more emphasis after March 1961.[77] However, its economic role was not ignored. The importance attached to it was reflected in the appointment of Nguyen Chi Thanh, the only other four-star North Vietnamese general, as head of the Ministry of Agricultural Co-operatives in 1961.[78]

Further developments in Laos

Meanwhile, the Vietnamese communists' revolutionary struggle to reunify Vietnam and the civil war in Laos were becoming increasingly inter-related. Pham Hung (the acting North Vietnamese Prime Minister and member of the Politburo) observed that the destinies of Laos and Vietnam were intertwined. Indochina formed a unified strategic arena. As such, the current problems were not contrived but a historical inevitability.[79] In early 1961, Hanoi sent a number of infantry, artillery and engineer battalions from the 316th and 335th Brigade (Northwest Military Region), the 325th Division and 271st Regiment (Military Region IV) into Laos. Some 12,000 North Vietnamese troops were in Laos as military advisers. Hanoi also helped the Pathet Lao to establish a military training school, transport supplies to southern Laos, and build revolutionary organisations along the Ho Chi Minh Trail.[80] From 1961, Hoang Van Hoan was put in charge of the secret CP38 Committee responsible for directing operations in Laos and Cambodia.[81] The opening of the North Vietnam-Laos border for trade after November 1960 further facilitated co-operation between the Pathet Lao and the North Vietnamese.[82]

In January 1961, the combined Pathet Lao-North Vietnamese force captured Tha Vieng and Tha Thom, the southern gateways of Xieng Khouang. They also captured Thabun, which controlled the approaches to Xieng Khouang and the Plaine of Jarres. In March, they captured Xala Phukhun, a strategic road junction north of Vientiane. It was at about the same time that Hanoi also directed Military Region V and Transportation Group 559 to extend their activities into the vicinity of Highway 9 and southern Laos.[83] The campaign, which began on 11 April, was under the command of the 325th Division and Group 559. Troops participating in the military operation included the 325th Infantry Division, the 19th battalion border defence troops in Military Region IV, and the 927th Battalion from Ha Tinh province.[84]

Despite the military activities in South Vietnam and Laos, Hanoi remained opposed to any escalation of the struggle that could lead to a full-scale war. Australian intelligence reported that the Pathet Lao with North Vietnam's assistance could probably have defeated Phoumi Nosavan but chose not to capitalise on the slow pace of Phoumi's advance.[85] In his letter dated 20 April 1961 addressed to the comrades in the South, Le Duan underscored the primary role of political struggle and the supportive role of armed struggle in the prevailing situation in the South. In his opinion, previous experience showed that uprisings would not be successful if the enemy's military was not defeated. He cautioned against underestimating the enemy's strength or despising the enemy. He pointed out that as the Diem regime planned to augment its armed forces with another 450,000 troops, the communist side needed to quickly bolster its armed forces. Finally, Le Duan stressed the need for the cadres to appreciate the fact that the struggle would be a long and difficult one, and hence each one must be psychologically prepared for the hardships and sacrifices ahead.[86]

By May 1961, the combined North Vietnamese-Pathet Lao force had gained control of the provinces of Sam Neua, Phong Saly, Xieng Khouang, extensive areas of Luang Prabang, the Plaine of Jarres and Highways 7, 8, 9 and 12. The following month they captured Ban Padong, a RLG base to the southwest of Xieng Khouang. Control of the highways was particularly important because Transportation Group 559 was operating within that vicinity.[87] Highway 7 was the principal supply route from North Vietnam to the Plaine of Jarres. Highway 9, just south of the 17th degree parallel, connected Savannakhet (where the Vietnamese had a storage depot) with Quang Tri Province. Also, any land link from Laos to Thailand and South Vietnam must pass through Highway 9. US intelligence reported in August that the communists controlled most of southern Laos, except for towns along the Mekong.[88] Denis Warner noted that the Pathet Lao by then held the entire interior trails and roads leading to South Vietnam and Cambodia and that 'it would require a considerable military campaign to dislodge them, especially since the area is vital to the success of any uprising in South Vietnam'.[89]

In October, the Nam Bo Central Committee held an enlarged conference in South Vietnam to review the political and military situation. The conference noted that despite their recent successes, they did not yet possess the military advantage over the Diem regime. It affirmed the primary importance of the political struggle and the supporting role of the armed struggle. However, they also realised that in order to reach the phase of general uprising, they would need to first push the armed struggle to an equal footing with the political struggle. The challenge was to find the correct calibration between armed and political struggle so as not to prematurely spark off a full-scale war. The US could instigate a pre-emptive war, or the communists, if they were not careful, could provoke one. As set out in the 31 January 1961 directive, the struggle would have to depend on the circumstances and the relationship of forces in the different regions. Whilst political and military struggle could be employed on an equal footing in the plains, political struggle alone should take precedence in the cities, and only military struggle in the mountainous region.[90]

By the end of 1961, although the communists were as yet not strong enough to hold any town or the coastal areas, they had strengthened their grip in the Central Highlands and in the Mekong Delta area, especially around Saigon. In broad daylight, it was no longer safe to travel anywhere outside the immediate vicinity of the large towns. By night, the dangers were heightened.[91] In response to Diem's recently launched 'strategic hamlet' strategy, in February 1962, the Politburo instructed the armed forces in South Vietnam to do their utmost to sabotage the programme and to be proactive in destroying the enemy. The Politburo recommended striking in small groups at the enemy's core forces, ranger-teams, military installations and aircrafts.[92]

The proposed International Conference on Vietnam

Readers would recall that a proposal was put forward in December 1960 to convene a conference on Laos. The International Conference on the Settlement of the Laotian Question finally convened on 16 May 1961 and concluded on 23 July 1962. Some time between March and April 1962, Sihanouk who was head of State of Cambodia, broached the idea of an international conference to resolve the question of South Vietnam.[93] In a private conversation with a 'delicate source', Sihanouk disclosed that he had been encouraged by the Chinese to raise the issue and the Russians had indicated they would support the idea.[94] From his early April conversations with Ambassador Abramov and Liu Chun, the charge d'affaires of the Chinese mission (in Khang Khay), Marek Thee found that both were receptive to the idea. Chen Yi, in a conversation with Andrei Gromyko, suggested that the Soviet foreign minister could remain as a permanent co-chairman. Beijing wanted the whole of Southeast Asia neutralised.[95]

At about the time when the idea of an international conference on Vietnam was being floated, on 13 and 14 April 1962, respectively, Hanoi and Beijing made public the resolutions of the 1st Congress of the NLFSV (which had taken place from 16 February to 3 March 1962). It was reported that the Congress had agreed that the responsibility of the front was to unite everyone to resolutely fight against American imperialism and the Diem regime so as to establish a democratic, free, neutral and independent South Vietnam.[96] On 1 July 1962, the NLFSV sent a memorandum to the co-chairmen of the 1954 Geneva Conference expressing its support for Sihanouk's proposal. The North Vietnamese press also expressed support for the memorandum. Meanwhile, Tran Van Huu had been encouraged by North Vietnamese officials to play the role of 'a neutralist Souvanna Phouma' in a future South Vietnamese coalition government.[97] On 23 July, Huu issued a statement welcoming the newly concluded Geneva Agreements on Laos and urged a similar conference to settle the Vietnamese problem.

Although many had expected that a conference on Vietnam would follow a few weeks immediately after the successful conclusion of the conference on Laos,[98] the idea of an international conference on Vietnam was suddenly dropped in late July 1962. Unfortunately, no one knows the reason why. Soon after the Geneva Conference, in a conversation with Bernard Fall, the respected French scholar of Vietnam, Pham Van Dong revealed that while Hanoi was prepared to negotiate, the situation was not yet ripe because the Diem regime had showed no intention to compromise.[99] On 1 August, Chen Yi also stated that perhaps the time was not ripe. A conference would become inevitable when the struggle had escalated to a certain stage.[100] By 20 August 1962, Sihanouk appeared to have completely lost interest in a conference on Vietnam. Instead, he appealed for an international conference on Cambodia.

Hanoi's position regarding Vietnamese communist strategy for the re-unification of the country in mid-1962 can be gleaned from a late July 1962 conversation of Bernard Fall with both Pham Van Dong and Ho Chi Minh,[101] and from a July 1962 letter by Le Duan to his comrades in the South.[102] Pham Van Dong informed Bernard Fall that Hanoi would not take any military action in the South that could give the Americans the pretext for military intervention in North Vietnam. According to Dong, the struggle in the South was progressing satisfactorily enough and that, given time and patience, American weariness would compel them to withdraw. Meanwhile, Hanoi would continue to publicise the American intervention and Vietnamese resistance. Ho said that Diem was in a very difficult position and lacked popular support. Both Dong and Ho agreed that it would be a protracted struggle. Fall went away from the meeting with the impression that in the interim, Hanoi was unlikely to risk its internal development by provoking American bombing of the North. Hanoi's short-term objective was not the re-unification of the country but a neutral South Vietnam that excluded Diem and any American military presence.

Le Duan's July 1962 letter to the South

The Vietnamese communists' strategy was clearly enunciated in Le Duan's July 1962 letter to his comrades in the South. He explained that although the revolutionary struggle in the South had made much significant progress in the last eight years, there were fresh obstacles. The Americans were determined to prevent South Vietnam from being drawn into the orbit of socialism and to make it their bulwark against the tide of socialism which threatened to engulf Southeast Asia. It was also their intention to use South Vietnam as a springboard to attack the North. Unlike Laos, South Vietnam did not share a common border with China. As such, the Americans might be more prepared to carry out a direct invasion of South Vietnam because the risk of clashing with China was smaller. He concluded that the most viable strategy was therefore to protect the peace in order that the North could carry out its socialist construction and at the same time to resolutely resist the Americans and their lackeys in the South. As the fates of both North and South Vietnam were intertwined, if they did not struggle in one accord against the Americans in the South, the stability and peace of the North could not be assured. Similarly, if they did not guard the peace to allow the North to complete its socialist development, the revolution would encounter even more difficulties. To those who were calling for the escalation of the military struggle, Le Duan urged them to evaluate fully and objectively their own capability. He cautioned against under-estimating the enemy, who was superior to them in all aspects – in numbers, in weaponry, transportation, and modern communication. Le Duan cited the successful struggle in Laos that had 'just temporarily ended' as an illustration of the correct line and strategy to adopt, · that is, to persistently struggle against the imperialists but knowing when to exercise restraint in order to avoid a war between the two opposing camps. In conclusion, Le Duan underlined the importance of combining both the political and military struggle, especially in countering Diem's 'strategic hamlet' programme. In his opinion, although it would be a long struggle, there was always the possibility that the enemy would 'throw in the towel' at some point when they realised that the cost far exceeded what they were prepared to pay, as exemplified in Laos and Algeria.

The military situation in the South

Between 15 and 30 August 1962, the communist forces in Ca Mau, My Tho, Bac Lieu, Soc Trang, Long An, Tay Ninh and Bing Duong thwarted *Operation 'Binh Tay'*, which comprised 5,000 enemy troops. Provincial forces of Binh Thuan attacked enemy reinforcements at the provincial capital Ham Tan, destroyed a company and another 150 soldiers. The 90th Battalion from

Quang Ngai defeated an enemy Ranger Battalion supported by helicopters in the Na Niu base area, Tra Bong district, and shot 13 helicopters in the encounter. In September 1962, the 514th Battalion from My Tho defeated the enemy along Route 4, killing 40 and captured a number of weapons. The Military Region V Command used four battalions of regular troops supported by regional forces to carry out an operation across the Tien River to destroy the strategic hamlets in Tien Phuoc, Que Son, Thang Binh, and Tam Ky. In October 1962, the 840th Battalion from Khanh Hoa, together with the 186th Battalion, incapacitated the enemy in the base area of B5 (Tuyen Duc). A company from the 514th Battalion from My Tho defeated a company of special mobile troops and shot down three planes. Two major military setbacks on the non-communist side not mentioned in the communist accounts were *Operation Morning Star* (October 1962), a major South Vietnamese effort to control Tay Ninh Province, and *Operation An Lac* (November 1962), which had aimed to gain control of the highland area in Darlac Province.[103]

Vietnamese communists' strategy remained unchanged despite the string of communist military successes from August to November. At a Politburo meeting (6–10 December 1962), the Hanoi leadership acknowledged that, in the previous two years, the revolution in the South had achieved a number of successes against the enemy. However, they also recognized that, although the armed forces had made rapid advancements, they were as yet unable to match that of the Americans. Political struggle amongst the masses was not fully developed yet, military education in many regions was still ineffective, and the liberated areas were still small and faced many difficulties. Also, they had not been able to defeat the enemy's mobility propelled by the use of armoured vehicles and helicopters. There was therefore the urgent need to further expedite the development of the military in the South in all aspects in order to out-manoeuvre the agility of the enemy as well as demolish its 'strategic hamlet' programme. To achieve this, the Politburo advocated the expansion of the guerrilla war in the South and closer coordination amongst the core, regional and guerrilla forces. Military Transportation Group 559 was assigned to facilitate the movements of more troops and resources into the South. Many local units were also tasked to study how they could counter the mobility of the enemy.[104]

According to a CIA assessment, the communists would need to progress gradually towards conventional warfare, but they were unlikely to be able to achieve that within a short time. Also, during that time, they were facing some very serious problems in the South. The Diem government had destroyed their food stores and there were increasing reports of low morale as a result of hunger and the lack of medical facilities, particularly in the Central Highland regions. In the view of the CIA, despite their increasing ability to shoot down helicopters, the communists found it difficult to concentrate and move troops in the face of greater South Vietnamese mobility. On balance, the war was at 'a slowly escalating stalemate'.[105]

The Battle of Ap Bac

The famous battle of Ap Bac must therefore be seen from the perspective of the above sequence of events and Vietnamese communists' strategy for the re-unification of the country. The details of the battle are well known[106] and only the broad outline needs to be highlighted here. South Vietnamese soldiers of the 7th Vietnamese Infantry Division, led by American military advisers and supported by planes, artillery and armour, and which out-numbered the communists by ten to one, refused to engage the communist forces at Ap Bac, a hamlet in Dinh Tuong Province on 2–3 January 1963. As a result, the US suffered its highest ever casualty of any battle in Vietnam at that time. Of the 14 US helicopters, 11 were shot at and five crashed. The battle became famous because of the public criticism by the US military advisers of the South Vietnamese soldiers, particularly the outspokenness of Lt. Col. John Paul Vann who was the senior military adviser of the 7th Division.[107]

It was only to be expected that the victory would bring about much jubilation and self-congratulation. The victory had 'important historical significance' as it 'signified the coming of age of the new revolutionary armed forces in the South' and 'opened the way for the bankrupting of the 'helicopter mobility' and 'armoured vehicle mobility' tactics, the trump cards of the US puppet forces in the "special war"'.[108] The victory boosted the morale of the Vietnamese communists who had been struggling against great odds for many years to re-unify the country. The fear of American helicopters and tanks was finally eradicated. In the words of Le Duan, 'After the Ap Bac battle, the enemy realised that it would be difficult to defeat us.'

Not surprisingly, the victory gave rise to a movement to study and emulate the success of Ap Bac,[109] from which they culled two important lessons. One was that the strategy of concentrating well-organised and well-equipped troops in the battlefield of South Vietnam was a correct one. The troops should also be well trained in both technical and tactical skills. They also learnt that the fighting force, well versed in the art of people's war and the political war, must work hand-in-hand. Only when all these factors were present, would it be possible to defeat the large-scale mopping-up operations, new tactics and weapons of the Americans. One of the most important developments which emerged from the Ap Bac experience was the decision to launch what was described as 'a combined campaign' involving both 'military' and 'political' forces which could simultaneously carry out armed struggle and political struggle.[110]

Despite the Ap Bac victory, American intelligence in April 1963 believed that the communist progress in the South had been blunted. The Vietnamese communists were in difficulties because of the strengthened capabilities and effectiveness of the South Vietnamese military. However, it concluded that there were as yet no persuasive indications that the communists had been grievously hurt.[111]

Modernisation of the VPA reviewed

In June 1963, the Central Military Committee met to review the progress of the regularisation and modernisation of the VPA, an exercise, which the readers would recall, first began in 1955 with the 1st Five-Year Military Plan (1955–1960). At the end of the first five years, in 1961, the leadership concluded that there was still much room for improvement in the areas of organisation, weaponry, science and military art. The target set in the second Five-Year Military Plan (1961–1965) was to accelerate the process so that the VPA would be ready to fight a war in Indochina, which the communist leadership expected to be imminent.[112] The meeting that Le Duan attended in June 1963 was therefore a mid-term appraisal. The Committee was satisfied with the progress and was confident that North Vietnamese troops were capable of assisting in the revolution in Laos. It also noted that the communist strength in the South had increased. However, the leadership still felt that a number of fronts needed to further hone their war-fighting skills and it was agreed that the training of cadres in the South should be accelerated. Finally, the committee adopted an action plan that included formulating a war plan, mobilising troops, expanding the armed struggle, and shifting the peacetime economy to a wartime economy. Le Duan who spoke at that meeting told the military that they must explore and employ new and fresh methods to defeat the enemy.[113]

Soon after the meeting, there was an increase in the movement of troops and equipment from the North to the South. Also, people's air-defence units were established in the North. According to North Vietnamese senior researcher, Luu Doan Huynh, Hanoi was already anticipating the bombing.[114] In October 1963, the Military Command of South Vietnam was established. Nguyen Van Linh, member of the party central committee as well as secretary of COSVN was concurrently appointed as its secretary. Lt. General Tran Van Tra, member of the party central committee and deputy Chief of Staff was appointed commander; and Major General Tran Do was appointed political commissar.[115]

Ngo Dinh Diem's death

According to Mieczslaw Maneli, in the spring of 1963 he was asked by Diem and Ngo Dinh Nhu to approach Hanoi to explore the possibilities of a peaceful resolution to the impasse. In the summer, Hanoi responded indicating that they would not press for an immediate reunification and that the process could be carried out gradually beginning with the development of postal, economic and cultural relations. Hanoi also posed the idea of a coalition government headed by Diem. It will never be known whether such an accommodation would have taken place had Diem not died.[116] Although the assassination of Ngo Dinh Diem on 2 November 1963 was only briefly mentioned and President Kennedy's death on 22 November 1963 was hardly referred to in the Vietnamese communist accounts of the war, the developments in the aftermath of Diem's death were very closely monitored. The North Vietnamese accounts noted that there were many changes in the situation in South Vietnam in the months before the end of 1963 but the conditions were as yet not conducive for peace. The various Saigon governments remained pawns in the hands of American imperialism. The dual mission of preparing to protect North Vietnam and fighting the 'special war' in the South remained unchanged. Seizing the advantage of the temporary disorientation in the aftermath of Diem's death, the communists intensified their military struggle by destroying even more strategic hamlets. But Hanoi was ever conscious of the fact that despite the significant progress made by the communist forces since the Ap Bac victory, in that short period of one year, they were as yet unable to fight the Americans in an expanded war.[117]

The CIA reported that the most notable communist success was the apparent unimpeded entry of a 300-man force into the US Special Forces civilian irregular training camp at Hiep Hoa in Hau Nghia province on 24 November, which resulted in a large number of casualties and weapon losses. Though the intensive communist activity failed to induce panic in the new regime, it demonstrated both a continuing and an enhanced capability for sustaining a high level of activity over several weeks. Even more serious was their growing capability against air-supported assault.[118] It was also reported that the southern communists had developed larger and better tactical units, including some of regimental size. These growing capabilities had been made possible with the infiltration of about 800 cadres from the North into the South in 1963. It was believed that this figure represented only a fraction of the actual numbers, which could be equivalent to, if not more than, the estimated 3,000 who entered South Vietnam in 1962.[119]

Chapter Three
The Armed Struggle Intensifies

The 9th Plenary Session of the Lao Dong Party

Soon after the unexpected deaths of Ngo Dinh Diem and Kennedy, the Lao Dong Party Central Committee convened its 9th Plenary Session. The Vietnamese communists considered this plenary session to be one of the landmarks in the party's history.[1] The exact date of the meeting is not known except for the fact that it was held in December 1963 and that it ended before the beginning of 1964. An editorial on the meeting was published in the *Nhan Dan* on 21 January 1964. A very recent official Vietnamese source disclosed that the plenary session was convened as early as November 1963.[2] If that was true, this would mean that it was convened soon after Diem and/or Kennedy's death and that it stretched into December. The *Lich Su Quan Doi Nhan Dan Viet Nam* indicated that it was a lengthy meeting with at least three sittings/sessions.[3]

The 1970 version of the 9th Plenary Session simply stated that it was convened to elaborate on the international line and tasks of the party. According to the 1977 version, after taking into account the world situation and the task of the international communist movement, the plenary session concluded that it was 'the responsibility of the party to partake in the struggle to safeguard the purity of Marxism-Leninism, contribute to the restoration and strengthening of unity in the socialist camp and the international communist movement ... and strengthen the unity and fighting strength of the party.'[4] The focus of these accounts was on the 'serious disharmony among some communist and workers' parties at the time'.[5]

The 1980 account[6] was more revealing. It reported that the plenary session was held to discuss a number of matters regarding the international and the revolutionary situations, as well as the missions in South Vietnam. With regards to the revolution in the South, the view was that there were three developmental stages: 'winning partial victories, advancing step by step, and advancing to a general offensive-general uprising'. The immediate and urgent task was to restrain and defeat the enemy's 'special war'. It was unlikely that there were any serious disagreement over that point. There were, however, differences in opinion on the issues of 'quick victory' versus 'protracted war' and the relative emphasis to be given to the political and military struggles. Bui Tin disclosed that Vo Nguyen Giap, who was the Minister for Defence, had been sidelined from 1962 onwards[7] Decisions on matters of politics, military and foreign affairs were concentrated in the hands of Le Duan, Le Duc Tho, Nguyen Chi Thanh, To Huu, Tran Quoc Hoan and Van Tien Dung[8] who all insisted that party members must 'fully understand (that) the motto of protracted conflict would also take advantage of opportunities to win victory in a relatively brief period of time', and that they must 'flexibly combine political struggle with armed struggle ... but with *military struggle playing the direct decisive role.*' (emphasis added).

According to the *Lich Su Quan Doi Nhan Dan Viet Nam*, the 9th Plenary Session reaffirmed that the struggle to liberate the South was both a political and an armed struggle, and that it was expected to be a long drawn-out one even though the inevitable victory would be decisive and relatively swift. Everyone in the North and the South was urged to play their part. Most importantly, the North must support and aid the South by expanding the size of its military force. The plenary session displayed a maturity in their debate on the appropriate strategy and organisational ability the Party should adopt in their fight against the Americans. The resolution that was passed at the end of the session called on all to remember the international responsibility of the Party, protect the North and to do their utmost to achieve victory in the South.[9] Immediately following the close of the plenary session, war preparations went into full swing in both North and South. There were three areas that required immediate attention: protecting the North, intensifying the struggle in the South, and supporting the Laotian revolution.[10]

During the US-Vietnam Dialogue in 1998, North Vietnamese senior researcher Luu Doan Huynh disclosed that Diem's assassination was viewed with alarm in Hanoi because it substantially raised the odds of a direct American intervention. Consequently, the 9th Plenary Session decided to try to win the war before the US could mount a successful intervention.[11] This corresponded with the account of North Vietnamese senior researcher Nguyen Khac Huynh, who revealed that Hanoi began sending combat troops to the South at the end of 1963 in an effort to achieve a quick victory after Diem's assassination before the American would be able to take over the war.[12] Bui Tin, in his memoir, also noted that the period of full-scale war began after the 9th Plenary Session.[13] He, with 11 other high-ranking cadres, was assigned by the top military leadership to make a reconnaissance trip at the beginning of 1964 to the South, where he spent almost ten months.[14]

Military preparations

The 2nd Five Year Military Plan (1961–1965) had provided for a peacetime and wartime army. The plan was to cap the regular army at approximately 170,000 during peacetime and at 260,000 when the country was in a state of war. Up to the end of 1963, North Vietnam maintained its troop strength at 173,500. But the target was adjusted to 350,000–400,000 for 1964–1965, and 500,000 for 1966–1967. The total strength of the regular army in the North stood at 300,000 in 1964.[15] The Central Military Committee and the Ministry of National Defence established a wartime outfit to coordinate all the activities of the military units and military regions.

In the South, at the beginning of 1964, Vo Chi Cong, a member of the party central committee and deputy secretary of

COSVN, was appointed secretary-cum-political commissar of Military Region V. In March, the military leadership put components of the air-defence and air force in the North on a war footing. On 1 May 1964, the Central Highland Front was established within Military Region V. Senior Colonel Nguyen Chanh, deputy commander of Military Region V and Senior Colonel Doan Khue, deputy political commissar of Military Region V, were appointed commander and political commissar of the Front, respectively. The Central Highlands was of strategic importance because control of communist infiltration depended on the control of the Highlands.[16]

Equipment and reinforcements were sent to the South through the Ho Chi Minh Trail as well as via the sea-route. Between the years 1961 to 1963, over 40,000 cadre-fighters trained to be regular soldiers in the North moved to the South; of these, 2,000 were commanders and technical personnel. The largest fighting unit of the regular troops in the South in 1964 was the regiment.[17] According to an American report of 2 March 1964, there was mounting evidence that the infiltration from the North into the South were of 'such proportions as to constitute an increasingly important factor in the war'.[18]

On 29 June 1964, the Politburo reiterated the need to increase the state of readiness to fight an imminent war. All North Vietnamese forces were exhorted to be ready to kill any enemy attempting to invade the North and to push on in their support of the South. At the end of June, Chief-of-staff General Van Tien Dung ordered the VPA on alert. Capability to take on US air power was considered a topmost priority. Much attention and energy were therefore focused on the readiness of the air-defence units. Air-defence training and preparation were stepped up, although the weapons and communication equipment in use were old and outdated.[19]

Developments in Laos and Cambodia

It is appropriate at this juncture to return again briefly to the events in Laos and Cambodia. The Vietnamese communist leadership had always considered the entire Indochina as a single battlefield. Despite the signing of the Geneva Agreements on Laos in July 1962, Hanoi never withdrew its forces from Laos. In the words of Roger Hilsman, 'the Viet Minh were the military backbone of the Pathet Lao and the shock troops in attack'.[20] The military situation in the strategic Plaine of Jarres continued to deteriorate and Pathet Lao-North Vietnamese forces were positioning themselves to control the Plaine. The Pathet Lao had since April 1963 broke ranks with neutralist forces led by Kong Lae, following the death of Quinim Pholsena. A CIA report of 1 November 1963 showed that key routes to Laos from North Vietnam had been re-opened and communist re-supply activities were detected along Highway 7 into the Plaine of Jarres, Highways 12 and 8 into central Laos, as well as various routes into the Tchepone region.[21] In February 1964, Pathet Lao-North Vietnamese forces advanced into central Laos. On 27 May 1964, the post-1962 Geneva Conference Laotian coalition government collapsed.[22] Cambodia, under the astute leadership of Sihanouk, was able to resist been fully drawn into the war during that period. Sihanouk was, however, unable to persuade the major powers to convene an international conference to guarantee the neutralisation of Cambodia. According to the US State Department, although there were numerous reports since 1956 about Vietnamese communist cells in Cambodia, there was no indication of any serious intensification of communist activities there.[23] Chu Huy Man, who was to lead the Pleiku campaign at Tay Nguyen (the battle of Ia Drang) later that year in November 1965, recalled that with the arrival of the US Marines and the 173rd Airborne Brigade in South Vietnam in May, the North Vietnamese military high command had to postpone its ambitious plan to seize control of the Central Highlands and attack down Route 19 to the coast. The problem was that the North Vietnamese communists had no previous experience fighting against the Americans, only the French. They therefore wanted to draw American units into contact in order to learn how to fight against them. According to Man, they decided to lure the American tiger out into the open by attacking the South Vietnamese military.[24]

Hanoi and the Sino-Soviet rift

Hanoi needed both material and political support from the Soviet Union and China to successfully carry out the war. Thus, in the midst of the military activities and preparations, Le Duan led a delegation, which included Le Duc Tho, To Huu and Hoang Van Hoan, to the Soviet Union, arriving in Moscow on 31 January 1964. The purpose of the visit was to inform the Russians of the decisions taken at the recent 9th Plenary Session and to enlist Russian support. The North Vietnamese communists viewed the growing rift between Moscow and Beijing as detrimental to their cause. Consequently, Hanoi tried very hard to avoid taking sides in the intensifying Sino-Soviet conflict and Ho Chi Minh did his utmost to persuade both sides to mend their differences. After the 22nd Congress of the CPSU (17–31 October 1961), Hanoi found it increasingly difficult to sit on the fence. It found itself sharing similar views with Beijing over a number of issues, such as Albania (October 1961), the Cuban Missile Crisis (October 1962) and the partial Nuclear Test-Ban Treaty (July 1963). The fundamental problem was that Khrushchev's strategy of peaceful coexistence with the West, specifically the US, could not be squared with Hanoi's reunification aspiration. As such, other than continued propaganda and moral support, the North Vietnamese delegation failed to obtain any material support from the Russians. Khrushchev told the North Vietnamese leadership very bluntly that unless Hanoi changed its position, there would be no prospects of concrete Russian assistance.[25]

The North Vietnamese delegation spent ten days in Moscow and returned to Hanoi after a brief stopover in Beijing. During that period both Hanoi and Beijing shared a common antagonistic attitude towards the non-communist countries. Most importantly, Beijing was sympathetic towards national liberation struggles. As noted earlier, in the summer of 1962, the Chinese began supplying guns of all types to the Vietnamese communists to be used for the guerrilla war in the South. In March 1963, a Chinese military delegation led by Luo Ruiqing, Chief-of-staff of the PLA, visited Hanoi. This was followed by

Liu Shaoqi's visit to Vietnam in May 1963. On both visits, the Chinese assured the Hanoi leadership that they would assist the Vietnamese communists in their military struggle. American sources reported that modern weapons of Chinese origin, such as recoil-less rifles and quadruple-mounted heavy machine guns, were being used by the Southern communists and these weapons were partially offsetting the South Vietnamese military's (ARVN) advantage of air mobility and armoured personnel carriers.[26] In October 1963, during a secret visit to Beijing by Kayone Phomvihane, secretary-general of the Laos Revolutionary Party, Zhou Enlai promised to assist the Pathet Lao[27] This contrasted sharply with Khrushchev's total disinterest in discussing Laos.[28]

Despite the ebb in Soviet-Vietnam relations during that period, Hanoi did not and never intended to 'burn its bridges' with Moscow. According to Nguyen Khac Vien, in 1963, the Lao Dong Party rejected a Chinese proposal to convene a meeting of 11 mainly Asian communist parties and also turned down Deng Xiaoping's proposal that China offer North Vietnam one billion yuan in exchange for Hanoi refusing all Soviet aid.[29] According to a Chinese source, apart from their (China's) differences with the Vietnamese over the handling of the 1956 agrarian debacle, the other significant point of divergence between them before 1965 was the reluctance of the Vietnamese communists to join them in denouncing the Soviet Union for deviating from Marxism.[30]

Special Political Conference (27–28 March 1964)

Although the Vietnamese communist leadership was in one mind on the goal of eventual re-unification, they continued to hold differing views on the pace to achieve the goal. There were personal rivalry and differences in opinion on the issue of the Soviet strategy of peaceful coexistence versus the Chinese strategy of supporting national liberation struggles in the colonial countries. Leaders such as Vo Nguyen Giap, Hoang Minh Chinh and Nguyen Kien Giang, all of whom advocated a more cautious pace, were crudely labeled as 'pro-Soviet' and unpatriotic to the national cause, whereas Le Duan and others who shared his view on speeding up the struggle became known as 'pro-China' and later re-labeled as 'pro-Soviet'.[31]

Readers would recall that despite the decision taken at the 9th Plenary Session of the Lao Dong Party Central Committee in November–December 1963, there were still differences within the leadership as to the degree and extent whereby the military struggle should be intensified at that stage. The disagreements were sufficiently serious for Ho Chi Minh to convene a Special Political Conference three months later on 27–28 March 1964 to re-affirm the December 1963 decision.

Ho Chi Minh's health was beginning to decline in 1964 and he no longer oversaw the day-to-day decisions, which were gradually being made by Le Duan and his associates. Ho, however, remained the powerful symbol of unity in the country.[32] The Special Political Conference (27–28 March 1964) convened by Ho Chi Minh should be seen as an extension of the 9th Plenary Session, which was perhaps the reason why that Conference, unlike the former, was not short-listed as a landmark in the party's history. On that occasion, Ho made use of his prestige in an effort to resolve the differences over the national struggle by re-affirming the decision made at the recent 9th Plenary Session. Over 800 officials and observers from various groups and strata attended the meeting. Ho prevailed on all in the party, the military, and everyone in the North and South to unite in order to defeat the Americans and unify the country.[33]

The Tonkin Gulf incident and its aftermath

The Tonkin Gulf incident in August was an important turning point in the Vietnamese communists' struggle. It stiffened the attitude of the Vietnamese communists towards the war[34] and inadvertently strengthened the position of the 'pro-escalation' lobby. On 2 August 1964, on the order of the site commander, North Vietnamese torpedo boats fired at the US destroyer Maddox that had ventured into the territorial waters of North

Vietnam during a reconnaissance mission. The Americans alleged that a second attack was launched on 4 August in international waters, thereby providing the pretext for US air strikes on North Vietnam and the passing of the Tonkin Gulf resolution. On 5 August, as a reprisal for the torpedo attack in the Tonkin Gulf, US aircraft destroyed an estimated 25 North Vietnamese PT boats, an oil storage depot at Phuc Loi as well as seven anti-aircraft installations at Vinh. It has been confirmed that the second attack did not take place as Hanoi had always maintained.[35] The false accusation and subsequent US actions convinced many communists that the US was plotting on destroying the North and on intervening directly in the war, thus confirming the fears of the 'pro-escalation' group.[36]

A week after the Tonkin Gulf incident, the Lao Dong Party Central Committee convened an extraordinary meeting to discuss the incident and the likelihood of the direct US intervention in the South. It was decided at that meeting that they would have to dispatch combat troops from the North to the South.[37] It was very likely that Le Duan made his trip to Beijing only after the said meeting and he met up with Mao Zedong on 13 August. The Tonkin Gulf episode also fueled the Chinese fear of the US threat and strengthened Beijing's support for the Vietnamese communists.[38] It also put pressure on Moscow, which hitherto had been strongly opposed to any escalation of the conflict, to reconsider its stance.[39] According to Ilya Gaiduk, the Tonkin Gulf incident marked a new turning point in Indochina. The most significant impact was undoubt-edly the conversion of the Kremlin whose support Hanoi needed just as much as that of the Chinese. Moscow finally recognised that both North Vietnam and the US were bent on resolving the problem by military means. The Kremlin had to support the Vietnamese communists if it wanted to hold on to its leadership status within the communist camp and if it did not wish to lose the prospects of strengthening Soviet influence in Southeast Asia.[40] Vietnam-Soviet relations gradually improved thereon.

From 25–26 September 1964, the Politburo met to evaluate the existing situation. They observed that after the Ap Bac battle of January 1963, the Americans had realised that the

South Vietnamese military would find it difficult to defeat the communists even with their (American) support. The only reason the Saigon regime was able to hold out all this while was because the communist main fighting force was still not ready to fight a conventional war. The Politburo was well aware that the US was hoping to achieve a breakthrough in the current impasse and had begun making preparations to fight in the South and to expand the war into the North. The Politburo hence decided to focus on developing its main fighting force in the quickest possible time. They estimated that the task would require at least 'a few years'. For the meantime, it was imperative that the war be kept at a level that would not give the Americans a pretext to transform the current 'special war' into a 'limited/local war' or worse still, to expand the war into the North. The Central Military Commission and the Ministry of Defence were tasked to draw up a military plan to foil any such American intentions. Meanwhile, in the South the COSVN had also taken note of the new developments. It advocated that the communists quickly defeat the 'special war' waged by the Americans, consolidate their area of control and seize the initiative by adopting what it described as an 'active offensive' strategy in order to fight the anticipated American-led large-scale counter-offensive.[41]

Soon after the Politburo meeting, Pham Van Dong and Hoang Van Hoan met with Mao Zedong on 5 October 1964 in Beijing to update him on the Politburo's decision. Mao's analysis, which the North Vietnamese concurred with, offered a further glimpse of how both Beijing and Hanoi read the situation. According to Mao, it was possible for the communists to eliminate the South Vietnamese military of several hundred thousand troops. His confidence was based on the premise that it was impossible for the US to send too many troops to South Vietnam because, out of the 18 US army divisions, nine had to be kept at home while the remaining half had to be divided between Europe and the Asia-Pacific. He also surmised that all the American soldiers in South Vietnam then were drawn from the navy which already had commitments elsewhere, and it would definitely overstretch the Americans if they invade North Vietnam. Nevertheless, the communists should avoid a head-on confrontation with the USA. A protracted war strategy was the recipe for success. Negotiations should only be conducted when the communists could defeat the US badly enough just as they did with the French.[42]

Preparations for the winter–spring 1965 offensive

On 11 October 1964, the Central Military Commission and the High Command of the VPA directed the communist forces operating in the South to carry out a series of offensives during winter/spring 1965. Three fronts of operation were identified: Eastern Nam Bo, Central Trung Bo and Tay Nguyen (Central Highlands). General Nguyen Chi Thanh was appointed commander of the military operations in the South. A number of senior military officers such as Major-Generals Le Trong Tan and Tran Do and Colonel Hoang Cam were also sent to the South to supervise the military preparations which began in earnest in November. Hanoi also dispatched the first complete North Vietnamese tactical unit, the 95th Regiment, to the South in October.[43]

In a top-secret letter of 19 November 1964 to Moscow, the Soviet ambassador to Hanoi reported that although both Hanoi and the NLF publicly declared their wish to achieve reunification peacefully, in reality they were expanding their military operations to first shore up their strength. According to him, Hanoi was confident that Beijing would give its support and Moscow would have to do the same.[44]

The Nam Bo Regional Command began urgent preparations for the offensive in winter/spring 1965, which was expected to be launched first in the Ba Ria-Long Khanh and Binh Long-Phuoc Long provinces, along Route 14.[45] The 1st and 2nd infantry regiments and a number of battalions started assembling in War Zone D (Phuoc Thanh area northeast of Saigon). At the beginning of November 1964, the 1st and 2nd infantry regiment, the 80th artillery detachment (comprising four battalions) and a number of other detachments moved from War Zone D across the Dong Nai river, and branched off in various directions before reaching Ba Ria province. On 20 November 1964, all the units arrived at a secret rendezvous. Participating in the offensive were the 500th and 800th battalions from the main force of Military Region VII[46] and 186th battalion from Military Region VI,[47] 445th company (Ba Ria province) and platoons from the Hoai Duc district (Binh Thuan province). The *Lich Su Quan Doi Nhan Dan Viet Nam* recounted the many difficulties and dangers faced by the cadres as they gradually moved closer into the vicinity of enemy-controlled Saigon.

The Nam Bo Regional Command established a sub-command under the charge of Tran Dinh Xu, with Le Van Tuong as political commissar, and Nguyen Hoa as deputy commander-cum-chief of staff. The mission was to destroy part of the enemy forces and the strategic hamlets in order to connect the bases in the eastern part of South Vietnam with Military Region VI. If that could be achieved, the movements of the communist main forces and the transportation of equipment and supplies by land and sea could be better protected.[48] By January 1965, Maritime Group 125 was able to deliver 50 tons of weapons to Ca Mau, Ben Tre, Ba Ria and Phu Yen.

Military offensive (I): The Binh Gia Campaign

The Vietnamese communists carried out three series of military offensives in 1965. The most well-known campaign of the first major military offensive of the winter/spring 1965 offensive was the *Binh Gia* campaign (2 December 1964–3 January 1965).[49] Amongst those involved in that campaign were the 1st, 2nd, 186th, 500th and 800th infantry regiments and the 80th artillery detachment. The campaign was led by Tran Dinh Xu with Nguyen Hoa as the deputy commander and chief-of-staff, and Le Van Tuong as the political commissar. According to the *Lich Su Quan Doi Nhan Dan Viet Nam*, the *Binh Gia* campaign was the first major battle in the war against the Americans, culminating in the defeat of the 'special war'. In the one-month campaign, the communist troops fought five battles at the regimental level and two at the battalion level in which they destroyed, amongst others, two enemy battalions, one reserve battalion and an armoured group. They also liberated Hoai Duc district and numerous strategic hamlets in Dat Do, Long Thanh and Nhon Trach districts along Routes 2 and 15. The Hat Dich base area (located in Ba Ria province and southern Binh Thuan province) was expanded in order to protect the sea transportation lines from North Vietnam into eastern Nam Bo and the extreme south of Trung Bo. Although the theatre of operation was small, to the communists it was significant as it opened a new phase of revolutionary war that combined guerrilla and regular war, military offensives and mass uprisings. The communists considered the *Binh Gia* campaign a victory. It showed that they could defeat the South Vietnamese military despite the latter's show of tanks, artillery and helicopters. In recognition of the particularly outstanding performance of the 1st infantry regiment in the campaign, it was bestowed the title '*Binh Gia regiment*'.[50] One major lesson that the communists learnt from the *Binh Gia* campaign was that they would have to accelerate the development of their regular and main forces to be able to engage the Americans in battle, and win the war. In his evaluation of the campaign, Le Duan noted that the war to liberate South Vietnam had made rapid leaps. From the Ap Bac battle, the enemy had recognised that the communists would be difficult to defeat. But after the battle of *Binh Gia*, the enemy realised that it would be impossible to defeat them.[51]

On 22 January 1965, a North Vietnamese military delegation visited China and met with Zhou Enlai. During the meeting, he advised them to continue with the elimination of the enemy main forces whenever they came out to conduct mopping-up operations so as to decimate their combat capacity. In Zhou's view, if the military should succeed in destroying all the strategic hamlets by the end of 1965, with the enemy's 'political bankruptcy', it would be possible to attain victory sooner than expected.[52] Following Zhou's advice and buoyed by the success of the *Binh Gia* campaign, in February 1965, the Central Military Commission decided to launch a second round of offensive.

Kosygin's visit to Hanoi

Meanwhile, on 7 February, the 409th battalion carried out a surprise attack on the airbase at Pleiku and Camp Holloway, injuring over a hundred soldiers and damaging 20 aircraft. Washington viewed the attack, which occurred when Soviet Prime Minister Alexi Kosygin was visiting Hanoi and when McGeorge Bundy was in Saigon, as a deliberate provocation from Hanoi. Moscow also shared the same view. In his memoir, Anatoly Dobrynin wrote, 'The North Vietnamese had done their unseemly bit by launching their offensive just when Kosygin was in Hanoi, without giving us advance notice. Indeed, they were doing their utmost to foster enmity between Washington and Moscow.'[53] Hanoi however claimed that it was the Pleiku Command that ordered the attack and hence it must be seen as part of a long-term offensive. Also, the Southern commanders were not aware that Kosygin and Bundy were in Hanoi and Saigon, respectively, nor did they discriminate between South Vietnamese and US soldiers.[54] It is perhaps worth mentioning that Kosygin stopped over in Beijing on 11 February and both sides were unable to agree on a coordinated plan to assist the Vietnamese communists. By 1965, the Sino-Soviet split had reached a point of no return.[55] In April, during a visit to Moscow by Le Duan and Vo Nguyen Giap, the Russians agreed to provide Hanoi with MiG fighters, surface-to-air missiles and other weaponry. Soviet pilots and specialists were also dispatched to North Vietnam.[56]

Hanoi's 4-point plan

In February 1965, soon after the launch of *Operation Flaming Dart*, the Hanoi leadership met to agree on a basic position with regards to an eventual negotiation with the US. The Foreign Ministry under the supervision of Prime Minister Pham Van Dong was tasked to produce a draft position in close consultation with Ho Chi Minh and Le Duan. It took almost two months before an agreed four-point position was drawn up towards the

end of March 1965.[57] Meanwhile, US bombing of North
Vietnam intensified. *Operation Flaming Dart* was followed by
Operation Rolling Thunder from 2 March 1965 to October 1968.
On 8 March 1965, two battalions of US marines landed on
Danang.

The draft position paper was probably discussed at the 11th
Plenary Session of the Lao Dong Party Central Committee
(25–27 March 1965).[58] At that session, the leadership rigorously
analysed the existing war against the Americans and their
relative strengths. They had evidently taken note of the ambi-
valence and divisions in the US regarding Vietnam. According
to their assessment, despite the show of American military
might, it had weak spots, particularly in the political area. There
was an apparent contradiction between US policy and strategy
as the US's direct military involvement in the war was being
seen by many in the international community as a manifestation
of neo-colonialism. The communists should therefore continue
with both their military and political struggles. The leadership
however noted that the military struggle was becoming more
important. Recognising their own military weakness vis-à-vis the
Americans, they felt that they (the communists) must hang on
tenaciously to the areas already under their control and must
never relinquish the initiative to the enemy. The leadership
concluded that the war had switched from a 'special war' to a
'limited war'. It was decided that North Vietnam had to be put
on a war footing, which meant that economic development had
to be redirected from peacetime to wartime production and the
VPA had to be rapidly expanded.

Meanwhile, in central Trung Bo and Tay Nguyen (Central
Highlands), the communists in Military Region V[59] and the
Central Highlands were positioning themselves in Quang Ngai,
north of Binh Dinh and west of Route 14 in the two provinces of
Kontum and Gia Lai, and between Routes 19 and 5. Troops
participating in that operation included the 320th infantry
regiment (comprising three infantry battalions drawn from
308th, 312th and 320th divisions) and a number of battalions.
The Rear Services Directorate provided the logistic support for
the main force in the Central Highlands. Transportation Group

559 was responsible for the delivery of 700 tons of weapons to the Central Highlands. Readers would recall that the first regular military unit from the North – the 95th regiment – had been dispatched to the South in October 1964. The 101st and 18th regiments followed soon after. All three regiments were components of the 325th division and were destined for the Central Highlands. On reaching the South, they were renamed the 10th, 11th and 12th regiments, respectively, and operated as independent regiments in the Central Highlands Front.[60]

Towards the end of March 1965, under the direction of the Military Region V Command, a combined regular force (comprising battalions and regiments) and local militia set out to destroy part of the enemy forces and strategic hamlets in the Central Highlands and in the delta region of Central Vietnam. Under the supervision of the Southern and Military Region V Commands, communist regiments also destroyed strategic hamlets along Routes 7, 14, 19 and 21 and expanded the liberated areas in the northern and southern part of Tay Nguyen. On 30 March 1965, the 101st and 320th regiments attacked a number of enemy military outposts along Route 14 in the provinces of Pleiku and Kontum, and ambushed two battalions of special mobile troops and the 42nd battalion at Dac Long. In the spring of 1965, the 325th B Division, 21st, 22nd, 23rd, 33rd, 42nd, 66th and 88th infantry regiments, special force battalions, artillery and other troops passed through the Truong Son range into the main battlefield in the South. The Rear Services Directorate provided logistical support. Bicycle battalions were organised and Group 559 was directed to improve the mechanised vehicles to facilitate the transfer of weapons, rice and other essentials into Military Region V, Tay Nguyen and Nam Bo.

On 8 April 1965, at a National Assembly meeting, Pham Van Dong finally announced Hanoi's Four-Points condition which was to be used as the basis for the peaceful resolution of the conflict. The four points were: (1) Recognition of the basic rights of the Vietnamese people – peace, independence, sovereignty, unity and territorial integrity. The US must remove its troops from South Vietnam and must stop its acts of war – i.e. the bombing against North Vietnam. (2) Pending the peaceful reunification of Vietnam, the military provisions of the 1954 Geneva Agreements on Vietnam must be strictly respected. All foreign troops must leave the country. There must be no military alliances between the Hanoi government or the Saigon government with any external powers. (3) The internal affairs of South Vietnam must be settled by the South Vietnamese people themselves in accordance with the programme of the NLF without foreign interference. (4) The peaceful reunification of Vietnam should be settled by the Vietnamese people in both zones, without foreign interference. Both Hanoi and Washington were unable to reach an understanding on the Four-Points.[61] In early May 1965, when McNamara, Maxwell Taylor and Westmoreland met in Honolulu, they decided to send to South Vietnam an additional 40,000 American soldiers to operate on the area within 50 miles of the American enclave on the Vietnamese coast.

A letter from Le Duan to Nguyen Chi Thanh in May 1965 provided additional information on the thinking of the communist leadership at that time. The content of the letter revealed that Le Duan and Thanh were in basic agreement on the mission, strategy and tactics applied in the South. Perhaps alluding to those who were still unconvinced about the merits of intensifying the military struggle, Le Duan assured Thanh that a change in the stance and guiding principles that were already defined and adopted was out of the question. The challenge was to apply the guiding principles in an appropriate manner in order to counter the new US tactics. In Le Duan's view, should the US bring in an additional 100,000 to 150,000 troops into South Vietnam, it would merely be for the purpose of strengthening their defence and hence would not necessarily indicate a shift to the offensive. It was still a 'special war' with elements of a 'local war'. However, should they began moving in 200,000 to 350,000 troops, that would be a definite indication that the war had changed from a 'special war' to a 'local war'. He felt that the US was still hesitant to extend the war to the North, but neither were the communists strong enough to deal a fatal defeat on the Americans. Finally, Le Duan concluded that if the communist forces could quickly bring about the disintegration of the South

Vietnamese military and launch a general offensive and insurrection, it would reduce the possibility of the US sending in more troops and turning the war into a 'local war'. The North would however continue to prepare for the worst-case scenario.[62]

It is however worth mentioning that beneath the 'calm', the policy of political struggle within the framework of Sihanouk's regime implemented by the senior leaders of the Workers' Party of Kampuchea and which was in line with Hanoi's policy was gradually being challenged by Pol Pot (Saloth Sar) and his group who advocated a militant struggle against Sihanouk.

Military offensive (II): (a) The Dong Xoai Campaign

Meanwhile, in the South, after the *Binh Gia* battle, the communist main forces (regiments) in eastern Nam Bo retreated back to War Zone D to recapitulate the experiences and the lessons learnt from *Binh Gia*. A new regiment – the 3rd regiment – was formed. All the battalions in Military Region VII were re-organised into a new 4th mobile regiment. After more than two months of consolidation and training, in May 1965, part of the main Southern force (1st, 2nd and 3rd regiments) and parts of Military Region VII (4th regiment), including two additional infantry battalions and the 80th artillery detachment in combination with the local troops, moved into action. Together with the Rear Services of Military Region VI, the 81st and 83rd were the two most active units that provided the logistic support for the military operation. A new command was formed to direct the second round of offensive. Major-General Le Trong Tan (deputy commander of the Southern Command) was appointed commander-in-chief, while Major-General Tran Do (deputy political commissar of the Southern Command) was appointed political commissar and Lieutenant Colonel Hoang Cam was made the chief-of-general-staff.[63]

The main battleground for the *Dong Xoai* campaign (11 May–22 July 1965)[64] was the two provinces of Binh Long and Phuoc Long. A subsidiary theatre of operation was the five mountainous and economically backward provinces of Lam

Dong, Binh Thuan, Ba Ria, Long Khanh and Bien Hoa. The mission was to destroy part of the enemy forces and to eliminate the strategic hamlets so as to enlarge the liberated areas. On that occasion, the objective was to link all the communist bases there with those in the southern part of the Central Highlands in order to facilitate the movements of troops and equipment from North Vietnam to Nam Bo and southern Trung Bo.

On the night of 11 May 1965, the 1st battalion of the 2nd regiment with the support of an artillery regiment exposed and destroyed the enemy's defence positions at Phuoc Long. On the same night, the 1st battalion of the 1st regiment with the support of the 840th battalion (of the main force of Military Region VI) and a special force platoon seized a number of strategic targets in the towns in Phuoc Long. On 9 June 1965, the 2nd regiment with a number of infantry battalions from the 3rd regiment attacked the enemy at Dong Xoai and took control of the region, compelling the enemy to carry out a rescue operation. The 1st and 3rd regiments destroyed three enemy battalions, one of which was the 7th parachute battalion. The Dong Xoai victory exceeded the expectations of the Southern Military Command. After the *Dong Xoai* battle, the 2nd regiment was conferred the title '*Dong Xoai* regiment'.

The *Dong Xoai* battle was one of the earliest large conventional battles that the Vietnamese communists fought and among the Vietnamese communist veterans, it is still also one of the best known and controversial. A first-person Vietnamese communist account of the battle is described in David Chanoff's oral history of the Vietnam War. The last part of the battle is worth quoting in full: '*Reports of heavy casualties kept coming in . . . By 5pm, the fighting had become sporadic. In the relative quiet, a call came in from Q762 reporting that they totally controlled Dong Xoai. When he heard that, Colonel Nam shouted, 'We've won!' Shortly afterwards, the telephone rang and the message that a relief column had been ambushed in Q761, just as we planned. Suddenly, there were explosions all over the place. At the phone, Nam said, 'My God! It's brutal, brutal.' A fleet of jets had come in to bomb the whole area. The bunker was shaking, its lights swaying back and forth. Colonel Nam said, 'Oh my God, what's happened to 761?'*'[65]

According to the analysis in the *Lich Su Quan Doi Nhan Dan Viet Nam*, the combined forces would have destroyed more of the enemy had they not come under US air attack. After more than two months of fighting, they had killed 4,459 enemy soldiers (of which 73 were Americans); captured 1,652 weapons of all sorts; and destroyed 28 armoured vehicles, five tanks and 35 planes, amongst others. The communists gained much fighting experience from the military campaign involving the infantry, artillery and the Special Forces.

Military offensive (II): (b) The Ba Gia Campaign

The other major military campaign in the second round of offensive was the *Ba Gia* campaign (19 May–20 July 1965). It was launched on the occasion of Ho Chi Minh's 75th birthday on 19 May 1965. This was the first major battle to take place in the Quang Ngai area (Ba Ria, Tra Bong, Binh Son and Son Tinh) or Military Region V. The slogan for the campaign was 'search out the Americans, pursue and kill them'. Preparations for the campaign began at the beginning of 1965 when Tran Kien (permanent member of the regional committee and chairman of the Rear Services in Military Region V) and other senior committee members of the region began organising human transportation and establishing warehouses in the area. Huynh Huu Anh (deputy chief of general staff of Military Region V) was responsible for area reconnaissance and the air-defence plan. In May 1965, the 1st regiment of regular forces in the South under Le Huu Tru moved from Quang Nam into northern Quang Ngai to join with the local troops at Ba Gia. The campaign was led by Major-General Chu Huy Man (commander and political commissar of Military Region V) and involved the 1st regiment and the 45th battalion (from Military Region V), two artillery platoons and local troops. On 25 May, a platoon from the Son Tinh district attacked an outpost at Phouc Loc and destroyed a US battalion (1st battalion of the 51st regiment) from Go Cao (Ba Gia). On 28 May 1965, local troops in Quang Nam province almost killed a whole company of naval personnel at Nui Thanh.

The communist forces also set out to destroy part of the US 25th Division in Quang Ngai.

There were two long stretches of fighting. The first took place from 10–25 June 1965 when the combined 1st regiment and local troops liberated five villages of 15,000 inhabitants in Quang Ngai. The other was from 4–20 July 1965 in Ba Gia where three villages strategically located between Tra Bong and Ba Lanh were liberated. During the period of fighting, the 1st regiment, under Military Region V Command destroyed the enemy and liberated 20,000 people in 29 villages in six districts (Son Tinh, Binh Son, Tra Bong, Nghia Hanh, Tu Nghia and Duc Pho). The communists also killed 2,054 enemy soldiers, captured 973 weapons, and destroyed 15 military vehicles and one plane. It was the first military campaign in South Vietnam in which the communists were able to destroy large components of the enemy main force and in the process disrupted the American plan to turn it into an expansive war. It also showed the vulnerability of the South Vietnamese military when faced with a large and flexible communist force.

The 4th regiment (of Military Region VII) and the local militia also fought many battles along Routes 1, 2, 13, 15, and 20 in order to divide and disrupt the enemy's military operations, as well as to assist in the destruction of the strategic hamlets. The communist forces were able to liberate 56,000 out of a total of 67,000 people living in Phuoc Long, thereby enlarging the eastern Nam Bo-south Tay Nguyen liberated zone. The communication lines from North Vietnam to Nam Bo and the southern part of Trung Bo were further developed and strengthened in the process.

The *Lich Su Quan Doi Nhan Dan Viet Nam* noted that the battles of *Binh Gia, Ba Gia* and *Dong Xoai* raised the war to a new level, that is, the concentration of regular troops and forces in the battlefield, departing from the 'special war' strategy of the previous years. The communist launched another military operation from 15–22 July 1965. The most outstanding victories of that operation included the ambush of one infantry battalion and an armoured unit of the enemy's 2nd battalion at Bau Bang, and the destruction of the ranger training centre at Bu Dop by the 840th battalion of the main force of Military Region VI supported by part of the 3rd regiment.[66]

Considering the urgency and shortage of time to properly train their soldiers, it was not at all surprising that the combat effectiveness of the communist forces varied widely, ranging from battle-tested veterans to poorly trained recruits or new draftees with minimal, little or no combat experience. But according to US assessment, despite this constraint, the Vietnamese communists could mount even larger scale operations than what they were conducting then. The ARVN was already having difficulty fighting against the communist forces at the current magnitude.[67] US intelligence concurred that the communists were winning at that stage.[68] In June 1965, General Westmoreland reported that the ARVN was experiencing difficulties in coping with the increased communists capability. In his view, reinforcement by either US military or a third country was the only remedy to the situation.[69] In late July 1965, Washington finally decided to reinforce the 90,000 American soldiers already in South Vietnam by another 100,000 before the end of 1965. Meanwhile, on 20 July 1965, Ho Chi Minh declared that regardless of whether the war would go on for another five, ten, 20 years or even longer, the people must fight to achieve total victory.

Developments in the VPA

In the North, soon after the 11th Plenary Session of the Lao Dong Party Central Committee, Ho Chi Minh issued a decree in April 1965 regarding military service. The decree stated that the length of military service was expected to be long and dependent on the circumstances of the war. On 5 May 1965, Ho issued an order for a partial call-up of the reserves. All military personnel were recalled to attend a three-month training course at the respective military schools. Over 290,000 people were mobilised to join the military of which ten per cent were party members and 50 per cent were from the Lao Dong Youth Group. Seventy per cent of those mobilised were between the ages of 18 and 25.

The most active month was May 1965 when over 150,000 were called up. The highest number (200,000) was mobilised in Military Region III (which was the area east and west of Hanoi).

The VPA thus expanded from 195,000 at the beginning of 1965 to 350,000 in May 1965, and by the end of the year, it had reached 400,000. There were ten divisions – 304th, 308th, 312th, 316th, 320th, 324th, 325th, 341st, 330th and the 350th, six regiments and a number of battalions. Some of the regiments that went into South Vietnam had had wartime experience fighting the French. The strength of the artillery units doubled that of 1964 and two armoured regiments were also established. The Special Force (communication and reconnaissance) units also increased threefold.

The strength of the people's self-defence force also grew from 1.4 million in 1964 to 2 million in 1965. More than 3,000 air-defence teams equipped with rifles, heavy machines guns, anti-aircraft guns were formed to protect the North. A number of organisations and enterprises formed self-defence companies or battalions. Many of the cooperatives and collectives also formed platoons and companies. A number of villages on the border of Military Region IV[70] organised artillery units to bombard American vessels. The number of the local militia also increased to 28,000; they were organised into 16 battalions, 32 infantry companies and a number of air-defence artillery and military engineers, primarily to protect the coastal region.

One area that Hanoi focused much attention on was the development of the air-defence capability. Defeating the US air war was one of the three pre-requisites for a successful negotiated settlement of the conflict. Indeed, one key reason for the failure to reach a negotiated settlement despite the many attempts at negotiation between April 1965 and 1967 was the issue of American bombing of both North and South Vietnam.

Although the communist leadership had expected the US to bomb North Vietnam as early as in 1963, it was the US bombing reprisal in the aftermath of the August 1964 Tonkin Gulf incident which brought home the urgency of putting in place an effective air defence. At that time, the only weaponry they had were very basic and old cannons, machine guns and rifles. On the day after the US air attack, on 6 August, the 921st air force regiment, which had been training overseas returned to North Vietnam.[71] According to the *Lich Su Quan Doi Nhan Dan Viet Nam*, that was the first time the North Vietnamese military had ever possessed a squad of modern planes. In the same month, the 212th anti-aircraft artillery regiment was formed. Also established in August 1964 were a number of anti-aircraft artillery battalions as components of the 308th, 312th, 320th and 325th infantry divisions which had been assigned to West Military Region IV.[72] In November 1964, the 3rd company of an air-artillery battalion belonging to the 325th infantry division tasked with the responsibility of protecting the transport line in Cha Lo (West Quang Binh) shot down three enemy aircraft.

The US bombing of North Vietnam code-named '*Operation Rolling Thunder*' began on 2 March 1965 and lasted until October 1968. The air-defence artillery units of the communists expanded from 12 regiments and 14 battalions at the beginning of 1965 to 21 regiments and 41 battalions, of which eight were mobile units forming a network of layered air defence. On 1 May 1965, after a period of training and difficulty, the first rocket/missile unit was established (236th regiment also known as the Song Da unit). The following month, another regiment (238th) was formed. The first cadres of these two units were veterans who had fought against the French as well as Americans. A number of them had also received their training in the former Soviet Union. Those selected to man the two missile regiments included cadres with background in science and engineering, university and high school students. The training under the Russian specialists, which was planned to consist of 37 sessions over one year, became a three-month crash course due to the exigencies of war. According to a Soviet report, 2,600 Vietnamese were sent to the Soviet Union for pilot and air-defence training in 1966.[73]

The air force was also expanded from one regiment to three. In 1964, there were two radar regiments belonging to the air-defence artillery units. This increased to four in 1965. Both the air force and the navy had five radar battalions each. Between 1964 and 1965, the number of soldiers in the air-defence/air force grew two and a half times. At the end of 1964, it was 22,500. By the end of 1965, it had grown to 52,700, which was 16 per cent of the total strength of the VPA. The *Lich Su Quan Doi Nhan Dan Viet Nam* noted that that was the first time the North Vietnamese military had a comprehensive capability to fight in the air. One particular episode it cited was the battle on 3–4 April 1965 to protect the Ham Rong bridge in Thanh Hoa. In May 1965, US intelligence reported the construction of air-defence sites in and around Hanoi. Visitors to Hanoi in June reported that anti-aircraft sites surrounded the city and the population was busy constructing bomb-shelters. The first indication that Soviet weaponry was being used was on 24 July 1965 when Soviet surface-to-air-missiles shot down one US F4C.[74] The *Lich Su Quan Doi Nhan Dan Viet Nam* further recorded that between February and June 1965, the air-defence units of Military Region IV shot down more than 300 US planes. By the end of 1965, they had shot down a total of 834 American aircraft.[75]

As the war progressed, the availability and security of transportation and communication lines became one of the central concerns of the leadership. For the successful prosecution of the war, lines of communication needed to be established especially to facilitate movements of troops (particularly from the North to the South). The lines of communication also required protection. According to a directive issued by the Party Central Committee in October 1965, 60 per cent of the air-defence resources in the North were devoted to ensuring the security of the transportation lines.

Much energy and resources continued to be channeled to the development of an effective air-defence strategy. In June 1966, the General Staff ordered that all the air-defence units be merged into five divisions – 361st, 363rd, 365th, 367th and 369th. Each division would have three to five air-defence artillery regiments (57mm and 100mm). The 367th, comprising four regiments of air-defence artillery plus a missile regiment, was a mobile air-defence unit which saw action in July 1966 in the Thai Nguyen region and along Route 1 (which linked Ninh Binh and Thanh Hoa) in September 1966. Besides air-defence, improvements were also made in coastal defence of which the artillery units formed the backbone. The enhanced defences paid off and succeeded in foiling many of the American maritime operations. Apparently, only four out of the 34 American cross-beach missions carried out against the communists in 1966 were successful.

On 26 April 1965, the Central Military Committee established a transport headquarters (headed by Colonel Nguyen Danh Phan who was also the political commissar) as a component of the Rear Services Directorate that would support Military Transportation Group 559 and the war in Laos. The transportation system was re-configured into six relay stations spreading out from the northern border and the port of Haiphong terminating at southwestern Military Region IV (where Group 559 was based). Every relay station had a motor vehicle battalion, motor repair facility, medical facility and an anti-aircraft artillery battalion. In the inventory of the transportation force were boats and railway lines. The quantity of equipment that was moved into South Vietnam in 1965 via the route developed by Group 559 was almost equivalent to that from 1959–1964. Also, in 1965, nearly 50,000 cadres and fighters – organised into seven regiments, 20 infantry battalions, combat engineers, special force and others – moved into the South. This was equivalent to the number that went South between 1959 and 1964.[76]

A conversation between Ho Chi Minh and Mao Zedong on 16 May 1965 in Changsha (Hunan) revealed that there was an urgent demand for more human resources to be sent to the South and Laos during this period. During the meeting, amongst others items, Ho requested for Chinese assistance to build some roads near the border with China, specifically roads from Sam Neua to Xieng Khoang, and from Xieng Khoang to Lower Laos, and to the south of Vietnam. According to Ho, Chinese assistance would enable Hanoi to send 30,000 more people to the South.[77] In the following month, Chinese troops were dispatched to North Vietnam to take over the air defence of areas north of the 21st parallel, operate two railway lines between Hanoi and China, construct defence works along the northeast coast and in the Red River delta, and build highways linking north and northwest Vietnam. Beijing also increased its supply of weapons and ammunitions to the North Vietnamese.[78]

In June 1965, the Rear Services Directorate established the 665th detachment to study the logistics involved in moving troops from the North into the South as well as the evacuation of injured soldiers back to the North for medical treatment. Group 559 also worked very closely with about 1,500 workers from the Ministry of Transportation and 7,600 assault and shock troops (volunteers). One regiment, four battalions, 53 companies and 17 platoons were assigned to open new roads and repair damaged ones. Military Transportation Group 559 (then under the command of Major-General Phan Trong Tue, member of the Party Central Committee and Minister of Transportation) created a sub-group to open new transportation and communication lines into South Vietnam and Lower Laos. The purpose was to facilitate the movement of troops to and from the Pathet Lao liberated zones west of Truong Son. In October 1965, in the South, a committee headed by Pham Hung was established to coordinate and regulate the traffic of troops and equipment.[79]

By the end of 1965, the strength of Group 559 had grown to 24,400. It had six battalions of motor vehicles, two battalions of bicycles, one battalion of boats, 18 battalions of combat engineers, four battalions of anti-aircraft artillery and guard units. It also controlled 45 relay stations. There were also one regiment of combat engineers and four battalion of anti-aircraft artillery on the Truong Son route that was under the direct supervision of Group 559.

Military preparations in the South

In the winter of 1965, the Central Military Committee and the Ministry of Defence decided to establish five divisions and an artillery division in the South. On 2 September 1965, the 9th Infantry Division was established in the Binh Long base area (eastern Nam Bo). The division consisted of the 1st regiment (also known as the Binh Gia regiment), 2nd regiment (also known as Dong Xoai regiment) and 4th regiment (recently formed from the local forces in the Cuu Song River delta region). On the same day, the 3rd infantry division was established in Binh Dinh base area (Military Region V) comprising the 2nd regiment from the main force of Military Region V and the 12th and 22nd regiments that arrived from North Vietnam. On 20 October 1965, the 2nd infantry division was established in the Quang Nam base area comprising the 1st regiment (also known as the Ba Gia regiment) from the main force of Military Region V and the 21st regiment from the North. On 23 November 1965, the 5th infantry division was established in the Ba Ria base area. It comprised the 4th regiment (also known as the Dong Nai regiment) from the main force of Military Region VII and the 5th regiment (recently created out of the local troops in the Nam Bo region). On 20 December 1965, the 1st infantry division was established at Tay Nguyen comprising the 320th, 33rd and 66th regiments, which had arrived from the North at the end 1964 and in 1965. The 80th artillery detachment, under the Southern Command, was reinforced and elevated to a unit at the divisional level. Renamed the 66th artillery detachment, it was also known as the Bien Hoa artillery detachment. The military leadership also allocated one regiment to Military Region IX,[80] two battalions to Military Region VIII,[81] five battalions to the Saigon-Gia Dinh Military Region, one battalion to Military Region VII, one regiment and one battalion to Tri Thien, and one regiment to the southern part of Trung Bo.[82]

Major strides were also made in the development of the Special Forces in the South. There were four such battalions – 407th, 408th, 487th and 489th – operating in Military Region V; the 12th battalion in Tri Thien; and nine battalions (3rd to 11th) and two detachments (A.20 and A.30) operating in Saigon-Gia Dinh. As for the rear/logistic services, the Southern Command established two additional units – the 85th and 86th – in eastern Nam Bo. Towards the end of 1965, the North sent 42,906 weapons of all types to the Nam Bo and southern Trung Bo battle zones.

Military offensive (III)

The third major communist offensive in the South in 1965 consisted of three military campaigns. The first was the *Pleiku* campaign at Tay Nguyen (19 October–26 November 1965), which involved the 33rd, 66th and 320th regiments, 952nd Special Force battalion, 200th artillery battalion and the 32nd anti-aircraft battalion. Led by Chu Huy Man with Nam Ha as political commissar, the campaign showed that the communists were able to destroy American battalions, counter US air-mobility and fight in the 'limited war'. The second military campaign took place in the Bau Bang-Dau Tieng area in eastern Nam Bo. Led by Le Trong Tan with Hoang Cam as deputy-commander and chief of staff, the battle involved the 9th division and a number of battalions of local troops from the Binh Duong province. In two particular battles – at Bau Bang on 12 November and at Dau Tieng on 27 November – the communists managed to inflict heavy casualties on the US 3rd brigade of the 1st division thereby boosting their confidence to further beat the Americans. The third and final military campaign of 1965 was the *Dong Duong* campaign that took place in the districts of Que Son, Thang Binh, Tam Ky and Tien Phouc in Quang Nam province. The commander was Nguyen Nang (commander of 2nd division) with Vo Minh Thanh (secretary of the Quang Nam Regional Committee) as the political commissar and Le Huu Tru as the chief of staff. The 2nd infantry division (incomplete), 70th infantry regiment (independent), 72nd infantry battalion (from Quang Nam), one special force battalion, one mortar battalion (120mm and DKZ), one anti-aircraft battalion and local loops participated in the campaign. Within a period of one month, the communists killed or captured 6,184 enemy soldiers (of which 1,142 were Americans), shot down 62 planes, captured 809 weapons, and liberated 43,500 people.

By the end of 1965, the Vietnamese communists had 174,000 more soldiers than their opponents in the South. There were 80,000 regional troops organised into battalions in the provinces and into platoons in the districts. A number of the provinces had two battalions. A number of battalions, platoons and local militia were banded together to form four regiments of regular troops. In addition, the North sent seven fully-equipped infantry regiments, as well as artillery, Special Forces, military engineers, and communication specialist units, to the South. The total troop strength at the end of 1965 was nearly 92,000 organised into 18 infantry regiments and a number of people's units. The Vietnamese communists had also managed to put firmly in place three contingents of regular mobile forces, one each in eastern Nam Bo, Military Region V and Tay Nguyen. For the first time, they were able to prosecute the war at the divisional level.[83]

A November 1965 letter from Le Duan to COSVN threw some light on the communist leadership's thinking of the war in South Vietnam at that stage. The purpose of the letter was to elaborate on some of the issues discussed at a recent Politburo meeting to assess the situation and to issue a resolution on the South. According to the letter, the introduction of 150,000–200,000 US troops to the South had brought about new problems. Nevertheless, Le Duan was confident that the communists would be able to check the Americans in the South. The Politburo continued to believe that the current fighting contained elements of both 'special' and 'local' wars. The operational target of the communists in the South was both the US and the South Vietnamese (and other puppet) troops. The annihilation of American troops was seen as necessary if the communists wanted to hold the initiative in the war. Le Duan however reminded COSVN that they should, as a general rule, attack the puppet troops first because they were weaker than the American troops. The exception was in the mountainous battlefields of Military Region V where the US troops were actively involved. In the plains of Nam Bo, the most important operational target was the 'puppet troops'. The letter also dealt with the critical question as to whether the conditions to win a decisive victory still existed given the presence of such a large number of American troops. In the Politburo's assessment, if they continued to adhere to the guideline of fighting a protracted war, they still had the possibility of achieving a decisive victory in a short time. The communist leadership was of the view that the US could not fight a long drawn-out war. If the Americans chose to fight a protracted war, it could only end in victory for the communists.[84]

Developments in 1965 reviewed

On 27 December 1965, the 12th Plenary Session of the Lao Dong Party Central Committee meeting, chaired by Ho Chi Minh, was convened to review the developments over the past year.[85] In the leadership's analysis of the situation, although the US was economically and militarily the strongest power in the imperialist camp, it was restrained by both international as well as American domestic opinion from bringing its full power to bear. The enemy was therefore politically weak even if it was economically and militarily strong. On the other hand, the communists had been able to strengthen their armed forces on every front, laid a strong foundation, and were able to hold the initiative in launching the war. Thus, even though the US had sent an expeditionary force consisting of ten of thousands of troops into South Vietnam, the basis of the communists' and the enemy's strengths could not be simply compared. The leadership affirmed that the communist strategy was to fight a protracted war but the tactic should be to concentrate the armed forces to exploit any opportunity to achieve a decisive victory in a relatively short period. The North must defeat US air power, protect and construct socialism, and assist in the liberation of South Vietnam. At the same time, it must positively prepare to fight on all fronts in the event that the enemy expanded the war throughout the country. The meeting advocated the need to focus on both enhancing the quality and increasing the number of troops in the armed forces. Great importance was also attached to the development of local and regional troops and guerrillas in the many important regions.

The Hanoi leadership also foresaw that the Americans would launch more offensives in the mountain and adjoining regions in the 1965–1966 dry season to force the communists into a position of passive defence, which was precisely what the communists had been trying to avoid since 1964. Indeed, immediately after the autumn/winter 1965 series of offensives, preparations began for the anticipated spring/summer offensives in 1966. Many meetings and conferences at all levels were held to distill the experiences gathered from the recent military encounters.

Responding to the US counter-offensive

Soon after the 12th Plenary Session, the war went into full swing.[86] As anticipated, in January 1966, the US launched its first major counter-offensive in South Vietnam. From January to May 1966, the enemy conducted 450 sweeping operations in eastern Nam Bo and the plains in Military Region V, of which 20 were major operations. These were mainly around northeast and southeast Saigon, particularly in the Duong Minh Chau base area, Boi Loi, Cu Chi, Long Nguyen, War Zone D, Xuyen Moc and Hai Dich. The objective was to search and destroy the communist 5th and 9th Divisions. One such well-known military operation was *Operation Crimp* during which the existence of the Cu Chi tunnels was discovered. In response, the Southern Command ordered the communist forces not to allow the enemy to concentrate their forces in any one direction.

On 16 January 1966, a meeting of senior cadres from the party, government and military was convened to discuss the resolutions of the 12th Plenary Session. Ho Chi Minh noted that there were then 200,000 American soldiers in South Vietnam and that the US had the capacity to send another 30,000 or 40,000 or even 50,000 more soldiers. Nevertheless, he believed that eventually the communists would win. He reminded his audience, however, that victory was not God-given. The whole party, the military and everyone in the country must be united in order to win. At the same time, they must not forget their 'international responsibility' in the communist camp.

On the same day, the Military Region V Command directed its armed forces to counter-attack whenever and wherever the enemy attacked and to make immediate preparations in the places where the enemy had yet to reach. At the end of January 1966, the US with 50 battalions swept through central Trung Bo focusing on southern Quang Nam, north of Binh Dinh and south of Phu Yen. The objectives were to search and destroy the communist 2nd and 3rd Divisions and to carry out the pacification of the region. At the end of January, they also concentrated troops on Route 19 (linking Quy Nhon and Pleiku) in Binh Dinh province. An offensive was launched into Tay Nguyen.

In order to counter the large enemy force, the Military Region V Command established a separate Front in Binh Dinh under Colonel Giap Van Cuong (commander of the 3rd Division) with Hai Lam (secretary of the provincial committee) as political commissar. Three regiments (from Hoai Nhon, An Lao and Kim Son districts) of the 3rd Division formed the backbone of this new Front. On 7 February 1966, the Saigon-Gia Dinh Command held a meeting to identify the lessons that could be learnt from their war-fighting experiences in Cu Chi. The lessons identified were : (1) Every communist regardless of size could and must beat the Americans using any kind of weapons and means; they could do so singly or in a group, anywhere and everywhere and at any time (2) Every enemy counter-attack was an opportunity to kill them. (3) They should confuse the enemy and keep them on their toes by attacking the enemy in the front, rear and everywhere; it was easier to kill the enemy this way.

The Central Military Committee also met in February 1966 to consider General Nguyen Chi Thanh's report on the situation in the war zone. The Central Military Committee advocated holding on to the initiative and broadening and intensifying the offensive against the Americans in the South. The Committee made the following recommendations: (1) Conduct a 'war of concentration' by launching as many campaigns, in as many locations as possible through the use of the main force. (2) Raise the standard of guerrilla warfare, ensuring that the guerrillas, local troops and the main force were effectively coordinated. (3) Destroy the rear areas/logistic and support bases of the enemy. (4) Develop the transportation and communication lines. (5) Concentrate on the harmonisation of the military and political struggles based in the cities, towns and border regions. (6) Combine the political and military struggles with military actions.

The Central Military Committee also identified three strategic battlegrounds – Eastern Nam Bo, Tay Nguyen and Tri Thien. In all three, there was the need to continue building up the military strength, the transportation/communication lines as well as accumulate weapons in preparation to fight the enemy. The military strength in the Nam Bo delta region and in Trung Bo was considered to be still too weak. In the Central Highlands and Lower Laos, there was the need to coordinate with allies to protect in particular the communication lines. There was also the need to protect and exploit the many 'economic and political potentials' in Cambodia. Finally, the Central Military Committee felt that the military forces in the South must be strengthened more quickly. It was decided that in 1966, the North would send 27,000–30,000 more soldiers comprising 30 regiments of regular troops and 51 battalions of local troops to the South. The North would also assist in the development of the guerrilla force throughout the South. As for the North, further improvement would be made in the areas of air-defence and transport-cum-logistics. The Politburo and the Central Military Committee sent many senior cadres to the South to ensure that the resolutions passed at the 12th Plenary Session could be swiftly disseminated and also to assist in the upgrading of the Southern military command apparatus. The journey from the North to the South was a long and arduous one. According to the *Lich Su Quan Doi Nhan Dan Viet Nam*, the route to the South passing through the Truong Son range of mountains was over 2,000 kilometres long. Many sections of roads between Tay Nguyen and Nam Bo had still not been fully opened and each soldier had to carry 30–40 kilograms of equipment and supplies. Out of the 2,800 soldiers (or 52 regiments) that started the arduous journey to the South, only about 1,200 reached their final destination.[87]

In the South, from 20 February–20 April 1966, a military campaign was waged in western Son Tinh (Quang Ngai). The commander was Nguyen Nang and Nguyen Minh Duc was the political commissar. Participating in the campaign were the 2nd infantry division (incomplete), one Special Force battalion (incomplete), one mortar battalion (120mm and DKZ.75), one anti-aircraft battalion, the 48th and 83rd battalions, one Special Force company (from Quang Ngai province), six companies of local troops from Son Tinh and local guerrilla units. The combined force managed to destroy two battalions, four companies of US marines, 12 enemy companies and 22 enemy platoons. It also shot down 112 planes, 27 motorised vehicles and captured 823 weapons of all kinds. Meanwhile, fighting also broke out in Cu Chi in January/February 1966. On 24 February 1966, at the battle at Nha Do-Bong Trang (Thu Dau Mot), elements of the 9th division in a counter-offensive destroyed two infantry battalions and one armoured battalion killing a number of field commanders. Fighting also occurred in Vung Tau on 12 March 1966, in Tay Nguyen and Tri Thien, amongst other places.

In March, COSVN met to recommend ways to implement the resolutions of the 12th Plenary Session and to carry out the February instructions of the Central Military Committee. The meeting directed the military to carry out a three-step offensive – draw out the enemy, stretch them thin, and enter/infiltrate into the enemy lines. The regional committees and commands, and especially Military Region V, were directed to hasten the development of the military force and quickly make other war preparations.[88]

Fighting and negotiating

Despite the intensification of the military struggle, the communist leadership did not ignore the value of the political and diplomatic struggle. Numerous secret negotiations to find a peaceful settlement were being pursued through various channels even as the fighting was going on.[89] However, Hanoi's attitude towards negotiation (which Beijing strongly encouraged) was that it was an inevitable phase that they would have to deal with at some stage but the timing then was not yet conducive.[90] Moscow, on the other hand, had all along been nudging Hanoi to negotiate, without much success. Anatoly

Dobrynin recalled that many Soviet Politburo members privately cursed the Americans, Chinese and Vietnamese for their unwillingness to seek a compromise solution and Brezhnev's remark that he did not wish to 'sink in the swamps of Vietnam'.[91]

In a letter to Nguyen Chi Thanh in March 1966, Le Duan wrote, '... With regard to struggle, we stand for joint political and armed struggle, that is to say, the armed struggle must be simultaneously conducted with the political one. Heavy emphasis is to be given to the political or diplomatic struggle 'which is of prime importance'. As a consequence, the strategy on war and negotiation must be properly used to efficiently serve the political and military aims of our strategy on pitting the weak against the strong'. He cited examples from Vietnamese and Chinese history to illustrate the 'fight-and-negotiation' policy. He concluded that negotiations then were premature since the Americans were trying to impose its own settlement on the communists.[92] General Nguyen Van Vinh made the same point when he addressed a congress of NLF cadres in April 1966. According to Vinh, the future situation might lead to negotiations. But even then, negotiations would have to be conducted simultaneously with even more vigorous fighting because, at the end of the day, the decisive factor lies in the battlefield.[93]

In the following month, the Central Military Committee established the Tri Thien Military Region (B4) as part of Military Region V. Major-General Le Chuong was named commander and political commissar. Comprising the 6th infantry regiment and supplemented by a number of other local units and four battalions (804th, 808th, 810th and 814th) from Quang Tri and Thua Thien provinces, B4 would work in tandem with the forces fighting in central and lower Laos. In May 1966, the Southern Command decided to establish a Rung Sat Special Military Region (in Nam Bo and southern Trung Bo) called 'Group 10' to more effectively oversee the military and other developments in the Rung Sat base area. The following month, the Route 9-north Quang Tri Front (B5) was established with Senior Colonel Vu Nam Long as commander and Major-General Nguyen Xuan Hoang as political commissar. B5 was to check the enemy force in the delta of the Cuu Long River.[94]

On 13 June 1966, the Southern Command created the 7th Infantry Division comprising three regiments (141st, 165th and 52nd) at Phuoc Long base area (eastern Nam Bo). The 5th and 9th Divisions, which had been operating in the Nam Bo region, were reinforced with a machine gun battalion each. Also joining the military force in the region were 84A missile (DKB) regiment (formerly known as 72A). Reinforcing the 69th artillery battalion was the 20th artillery battalion (75mm and 120mm). The Tay Nguyen Front (B3) was also strengthened by the arrival of the 24th regiment (originally the 42nd regiment of 304th Division), 88th regiment (of the 308th Division), 95th B and 101st B regiments (of the 325th B Division), 68th artillery (105mm) regiment and the 95th and 96th mortar battalions (120mm). Military Region V (B1) was strengthened by the 20th regiment (originally the 18th B regiment), 31st regiment (originally the 64th A regiment of 320th division), 368th B missile/rocket regiment (DKB) and the 19th missile (A.12) battalion. The forces in Nam Bo and the extreme south of Trung Bo regions were reinforced by the 141st and 165th regiment (from the 312th division), the 16th regiment (originally the 101st regiment transferred from the Tay Nguyen Front), 84th A missile/rocket (DKB) regiment and four battalions of 102mm mortar and air-defence artillery.

Ho Chi Minh

In 1966, Ho Chi Minh's health was beginning to deteriorate. It improved somewhat in April but failed again soon after. Ho subsequently went for treatment at Guangzhou where he spent his 77th birthday, returning to Hanoi only on 1 July 1966.[95] A conversation between Ho Chi Minh and Jean Sainteny on 5 July 1966 showed Ho's strong resolution to unify the country. Ho believed that the US, like all past invaders of Vietnam, would become weary of the conflict. At the same time, he was convinced that the Vietnamese communists would be able to endure the burden of the war to its end. Asked by Sainteny whether that would change if the Americans should raise the stakes by increasing their military forces in Vietnam, Ho replied that he and his colleagues were aware that the US could wipe out all the principal towns if they wanted to. They had anticipated it and were prepared for the eventuality but they remained determined to fight to the end.[96]

In the same month, a meeting of the highest ranking defence officials in the North was held in Hanoi under the chairmanship of Ho Chi Minh to be apprised of a report on the war situation and the achievements of the military in the North and South. The meeting affirmed that the communists must strengthen their struggle against the enemy's new round of offensive. On 17 July 1966, Ho said that the war might drag on for another five, 10, 20 years or longer. Hanoi, Haiphong and other cities might be destroyed in the process. But he called on all not to be intimidated and to be willing to make the sacrifices because there was nothing more precious than independence and freedom.[97] In response to Ho's appeal, in the summer of 1966, nearly 200,000 youths, both male and female, from the North and thousands from various part of South Vietnam joined the military. There were 460,000 soldiers in the North and 230,000 in the South. The establishment of the Rear Services Directorate increased by six times, the amount of equipment increased by 3.3 times, warehouse/storage space increased by 2.7 times and many groups responsible for training and for guiding the soldiers into the South were formed. As a further reinforcement, in the second half of 1966, two new divisions – the 324th and 325th – were formed comprising four infantry regiments, one missile (DKB) regiment, one missile (A.12) battalion, four anti-aircraft battalions and a number of other smaller units. This was six times more than the number of reinforcemenst in 1965. By the end of 1966, there was a total of over 690,000 troops in the South – 600,000 regular troops and 93,000 regional troops.

Stalemate

A series of post-mortem meetings took place in South Vietnam in the months of August and September 1966. COSVN and the

Southern Command convened a second conference to discuss the political task of the armed forces in the South. The main message that emerged from the conference was that in the face of the uncertainties in the new war situation, the leaders must be flexible, nimble and remain positive in their outlook. They must also hold on to the offensive spirit. The conference also acknowledged the units that had performed well in both their political and military tasks, such as the 9th and 5th divisions (which were the main forces in Nam Bo), the 2nd and 3rd Divisions (Military Region V), the regional troops in Long An, Binh Duong and Quang Nam provinces as well as the local troops and guerrillas in the districts of Cu Chi (Saigon-Gia Dinh), Duc Hoa (Long An), Ben Cat (Thu Dau Mot), Chau Thanh (My Tho), Mo Cay (Ben Tre), Phung Hiep (Can Tho), amongst others. In Military Region V, Hoang Van Thai (secretary of the regional committee and political commissar of Military Region V) presided over a conference to review the experiences gained from the fighting from spring 1965 to summer 1966. The conference discussed many new matters related to the art of war, tactics and political tasks. In Nam Bo and southern Trung Bo, the Southern Command also organised a meeting to distill and disseminate their experiences. In September 1966, another similar meeting was jointly organised by COSVN and the various Military Regional Committees.[98]

The Politburo, which met in October 1966, noted that the previous six months or so was an important period in the war where maximum strength was used against the Americans to save the country. In the Politburo's view, the communists had achieved very significant victories, both military and political, but especially military. Many valuable experiences were gained which had helped to further their understanding of the laws of national liberation. In the assessment of the communist leadership, by mid-1966, they had managed to defeat the first American counter-offensive in the South.[99] However, the leadership noted that even though the enemy had been continuously defeated, the Americans kept on increasingly its military strength and expanding the war in the hope of solving the Vietnam problem between 1967 and 1968. They envisaged that 1967 would be a critical year. The Politburo resolved to give its best effort to defeat the enemy's second counter-offensive.[100]

Indeed, the communists were finding it more and more difficult to fight the Americans after the middle of 1966. According to one account, in August 1966, the headquarters of Military Region V was bombed three times by B-52s and the number of deserters amongst both the officers and men grew. The communists were also being defeated in almost every battle they were engaged in. To replace the number of deaths and deserters, Hanoi sent the 325th, 324th, 308th and 330th Divisions to the South but the communists continued to lose the battle.[101]

From October 1966, the US military launched a second wave of counter-offensive that continued till April 1967. Reinforced by 100,000 more soldiers, this counter-offensive targeted the Duong Minh Chau war zone (located in eastern Nam Bo). The objective was to halt the communists' movements throughout South Vietnam – from Tri Thien to Quang Ngai, in the highlands in Trung Bo, the delta region in Military Region V and in the Cuu Long River delta. The Americans also implemented a tight defence cordon on the Route 9 Front to check the movements of the communist main force. From a 'search and destroy' strategy, the Americans now adopted a two-pronged strategy of 'search and destroy' and 'pacification'. Two major campaigns in the early months of that phase were '*Operation Attleboro*' in Tay Ninh Province (14 September–25 November 1966), considered the largest US military operation at the time, and *Operations Thayer I and II* in Binh Dinh Province (13 September–6 December 1966). By the end of 1966, there were nearly 360,000 American soldiers involved in the war. The number increased to 535,000 in 1967. Despite all the firepower and military activities, there was no sign that the Vietnamese communists were capitulating or considering to capitulate, but they were not winning either.

Chapter Four

Breaking the Stalemate

Military situation in early 1967 reviewed

By the end of 1966, the US military had carried out over a dozen major search-and-destroy operations and many smaller scale ones in South Vietnam. US air attacks on North Vietnam escalated and expanded into the Hanoi-Haiphong area as well as the demilitarised zone along the 17th Parallel. There were also air attacks in eastern Laos where the Ho Chi Minh Trail(s) were located. US forces were also involved in the fighting on both the eastern and western borders of Cambodia, where the Vietnamese communists were believed to have their sanctuaries. Despite all the firepower and military activities, there was no sign that the Vietnamese communists were capitulating or even considering it. They were not winning either.

In January 1967, the US military launched another two major search-and destroy operations – *Operation Deckhouse V* in the Mekong River Delta, and *Operation Cedar Falls* in the 'Iron Triangle' (or War Zone D, the area 20 miles north-west of Saigon), which was then the largest offensive of the war. It was during this time that the 13th Plenary Session of the Lao Dong Party Central Committee was convened from 23 to 26 January 1967.

At the meeting, the Party surmised that the situation was very complex. While the Americans were not winning the battle, they had the potential to expand the war. On the other hand, while the communists had successfully managed to withstand US military power, they were not able to achieve a decisive victory. They set themselves to continue pursuing the goal to win a decisive victory in a relatively short time. At the same time, they also braced themselves for the possibility of a prolonged war that could be expanded throughout the country, and the need to make contingencies for such an eventuality. They were particularly concerned about the US aerial bombing of North Vietnam. The meeting decided that, until the US unconditionally ceased their bombing of the North, no official talks would take place.

The meeting agreed that there were essentially three 'struggles' to be carried out simultaneously – military, political and diplomatic, of which the military and political struggles should serve as 'the basis for victory on the diplomatic front'. The basic premise was that one could only win at the conference table what one had already won on the battlefield. At the same time, it was also felt that the 'diplomatic struggle could not merely reflect the struggle on the battlefield'. The diplomatic struggle played an 'important', 'positive', 'active' and 'innovatory' role.[1] According to Luu Van Loi, although the leadership had thought of 'fighting while negotiating' since late 1965, it was only in 1967 that diplomacy was considered a front.[2] How the three strands of struggle should be reconciled in practice must have been actively debated at the plenary session, but the problem was apparently not resolved then.

Soon after the plenary session was Tet 1967. The Tet cease-fire lasted from 8 to 12 February. Ten days later, the USA launched *Operation Junction City* (22 February–14 May 1967), which was on an even larger scale than *Operation Cedar Falls*. The mission was to destroy War Zone C near the Cambodian border. In the words of Vietnamese historian Nguyen Khac Vien, 'Never before had the US military effort in South Vietnam been so great, while the bombing raids on the North were intensified.'[3] It was during *Operation Junction City* that the US Military Command in Saigon on 18 March made public photographs they had seized of Generals Nguyen Chi Thanh, Tran Van Tra and Tran Do leading Vietnamese communist troops in the South.[4]

In April 1967, in the thick of *Operation Junction City* and amidst reports of General Westmoreland's intention to request a troop increase in South Vietnam, a high-level North Vietnamese delegation, which included Pham Van Dong and Vo Nguyen Giap, visited Beijing and Moscow to ascertain the views of their two allies regarding the war. The Chinese position was that the Vietnamese communists must persist in the military struggle to the very end. After Beijing, Dong and Giap went on to Moscow to persuade the Soviet Union to provide the Vietnamese communists with all necessary aid for the military struggle, which was expected to escalate. Moscow, however, recommended a diplomatic solution to the war.

From the exchanges at the meeting, the Russians realised that the Vietnamese communists were not in favour of a negotiated settlement. Although the Vietnamese communists depended more heavily on Soviet than Chinese military equipment, Moscow was unable to induce the Vietnamese communists to negotiate because 'a refusal ... to provide support to the DRV ... (would) jeopardise Soviet positions in Vietnam which were always precarious because of Chinese influence there'.[5] According to Russian researcher Ilya Gaiduk, after the April meeting and despite Soviet appeals, Hanoi remained adamant on its refusal to maintain contact with the USA.

The *Lich Su Quan Doi Nhan Dan Viet Nam*[6] revealed that in April 1967, an analysis of the military scenario was carried out on all fronts with the objective of obtaining a better appreciation of the on-going military-political situation in order to formulate an appropriate strategy. The Politburo and Military Central Commission subsequently met to consider the reports. Although they decided that a strategy to win a decisive victory was required, the means whereby that 'decisive victory' was to be achieved was apparently not clearly articulated at that meeting, and was to be the subject of discussion during the subsequent three months. Meanwhile, the VPA General Staff started to identify detachments of cadres in the South and making logistical preparations.

The meeting also led to a major re-organisation of its military command structure in the South, in particular Military Region V and the Tri-Thien-Hue Region. Military Region V was formed in 1960 and at that time included Southern Trung Bo, the Central Highlands, and the northern most provinces of Quang Tri and Thua Thien. It came under the direct control of the North Vietnamese High Command. The northern and southern most parts were subsequently re-grouped as sub-regions. In May, following the April 1967 deliberations, another re-organisation in Tri Thien (Quang Tri and Thua Thien) was carried out. The Northern sub-region, that is Quang Tri and Thua Thien Provinces, was elevated to full region status and given the new name, Tri-Thien-Hue Region. The provincial committees and military detachments were dissolved. The district committees came under the direct control of the regional committee and all military detachments came under the direct control of the Regional Military Command. Military Group 4 (comprising the 804th B Infantry Battalion and two battalions of combat engineers) was responsible for the communication route between south of Phu Loc and north of the Hai Van Pass. Military Group 5 (comprising the 804th A, 810th and 845th Battalions, 2 battalions of special forces, K1 and K2, and 14 teams of special mobile troops) was responsible for Hue and its three surrounding districts. Military Group 6 (the 6th Infantry Regiment) was responsible for the two districts of Phong Dien and Quang Dien (in Thua Thien Province). Military Group 7 (comprising the 9th Infantry Regiment of the 304th Division – which at the end of 1967 was replaced by the 2nd Regiment of the 324th Division, 808th and 814th Infantry Battalions, a Special Forces Battalion – the K10, and two companies of local troops) was responsible for the two districts of Trieu Phong and Hai Lang in Quang Tri Province.

Nguyen Chi Thanh and the Tet Offensive proposal

In May 1967, the Central Office of South Vietnam (COSVN) held its 5th conference chaired by General Nguyen Chi Thanh, which affirmed the need for vigorous, continuous attacks to destroy and expel the enemy forces, and to build up the momentum to a stage amounting to a general offensive and general uprising.[7] One communist veteran fighter recalled that the Chinese had calculated that it would require one Vietnamese communist division to destroy one US battalion. Thanh countered that, if that was the case, the Vietnamese communists might as well quit fighting because they would never have enough men to do that. Thanh was convinced that the Vietnamese could fight the Americans one on one. The COSVN proposal was relayed to Hanoi and in June 1967 it was accepted by the Politburo in principle. The Politburo surmised that a prolonged or protracted war strategy would only lead to a further increase in US military strength and hence there was the urgent need to win the war in a relatively short period, ideally in 1968.[8]

General Nguyen Chi Thanh, Secretary of COSVN, Political Commissar and Commander-in-Chief of the communist forces in the South, as well as the principal brainchild of the 'COSVN proposal', (subsequently dubbed by the west as the '*Tet Offensive*' and by the Vietnamese as 'General Offensive General Uprising'), was summoned to Hanoi to explain in person the 'COSVN proposal'. Thanh made his circuitous way to Hanoi by first travelling to Phnom Penh, where he obtained Chinese travel documents. From Phnom Penh, he took a commercial flight to Hong Kong and from there slipped into China, and finally from China to Hanoi. It was not known when he left R Base on the Vietnam-Cambodia border (where COSVN was located) and when he reached Hanoi.[9] But he must have arrived in Hanoi by the beginning of July 1967 as it was recorded in the *Lich Su Quan Doi Nhan Dan Viet Nam* that, in July 1967, the Politburo and Military Central Committee met to listen to a report by the VPA General Staff on the strategy of the 'General Offensive General Uprising'. At that meeting, General Nguyen Chi Thanh explained that the proposed strategy involved amassing both military and political strength to carry out a series of surprise attacks in places where the enemy least expected (specifically Saigon, Hue and Danang) and drawing out and striking at US forces in the mountainous regions of Tri Thien, Tay Nguyen (Central Highlands) and in the south-east region. For the plan to succeed, it was essential that it be kept top-secret. The Military Central Committee would direct and supervise preparations, paying special attention to raising the capability of the main force to annihilate the enemy.[10] The meeting ended on 6 July with two farewell parties, one hosted by the Politburo and the other by the Military Central Committee. General Nguyen Chi Thanh was scheduled to return to the South to carry out preparations for the plan the next day. But on the night of 6 July, Thanh, who had a heart problem, died of a heart attack after having drunk too much at the parties.[11]

Thanh's sudden demise was a great loss to the Vietnamese communists' struggle in the South. The *Lich Su Quan Doi Nhan Dan Viet Nam* described him as a man of 'courage, energy, fortitude and perseverance'[12] Although the plan was not abandoned, preparations must have been delayed for the leadership to consider and appoint Thanh's replacement(s), presumably not an easy task, considering the need to find someone to match his experience and ability. The Politburo and the Military Central Committee had to carry out a major reshuffle in the Southern communist leadership. It was significant that Pham Hung, deputy Prime Minister, was appointed Secretary of COSVN and Political Commissar while Lieutenant-General Hoang Van Thai, deputy Chief of the PAVN General Staff and Commander and Political Commissar of Military Region V, was appointed Commander-in Chief of the Southern Forces. Thai's responsibilities in Military Region V were taken over partly by Vo Chi Cong and Major-General Chu Huy Man, both members of the Central Committee. Cong was appointed Secretary and Political Commissar and Man was appointed Military Region V Commander. In Tay Nguyen, Major-General Hoang Minh Thao was appointed Commander and Senior Colonel Tran The Mon became Political Commissar.[13]

With Thanh's death, direct responsibility for overseeing the 'General Offensive General Uprising' was assumed by Defence Minister Vo Nguyen Giap. Contemporary American intelligence reports which have shaped much of the writings on the *Tet Offensive* highlighted Giap's opposition to Thanh's strategy for a quick and decisive victory, and his preference for the continuation of the protracted war strategy. The reports had based their conclusions on analysing the contents of the various speeches of Thanh and Giap, an approach which was useful then but inadequate today. There is no new evidence to prove or refute the Giap-Thanh disagreement. It would appear from this reconstruction of events that American intelligence had perhaps accentuated the seriousness of their differences.[14] In the event, while the *Tet Offensive* was largely Thanh's idea, what took place after 6 July 1967 was Giap's responsibility. It would not be possible to assess how far Giap had adhered to or deviated from the original idea until Thanh's blueprint for the *Tet Offensive*, hitherto unpublished, is made public.

Ho Chi Minh's health

At this juncture, it is timely to look at the role played by Ho Chi Minh during this period. Chinese sources[15] revealed that from 1966 onwards Ho had been in ill health. In early 1967, China twice sent medical doctors to Hanoi. Ho recovered sufficiently to visit the sapper combat arm on its 'tradition day' on 19 March,[16] but soon after he suffered a relapse and in April went to Guangxi for medical treatment.[17]

Readers would recall that a very high-level Vietnamese delegation, which included Pham Van Dong and Vo Nguyen Giap, was in China in April. No details are available on the visit but it was probable that the delegation met and consulted with Ho. It is not known when Ho returned to Hanoi, but, according to Van Tien Dung, Ho presided over the Politburo meeting in May 1967 when the 'COSVN proposal' was discussed.[18] He was definitely in Hanoi by 24 July because, for 50 minutes that afternoon, he met with M. Aubrac, then with the FAO, and also a personal friend. Aubrac was struck by how Ho, dressed in a Chinese gown and walking with the aid of a cane, had aged. Aubrac noted that his intelligence was unimpaired and his eyes still had their old sparkle. He seemed to enjoy playing the role of a grandfather-figure and was not concerned with details. After Ho left the meeting, Pham Van Dong disclosed to Aubrac that, as far as was possible, they had tried to spare Ho many details which might vexed him as they wanted him to live long enough to see Vietnam unified.[19]

In an interview with Pham Van Dong in summer 1967, David Schoenbrun learnt that doctors had advised Ho to stay away from Hanoi during the summer (May to September) to avoid the heat.[20] However, against doctor's advice, Ho remained in Hanoi for much of the summer of 1967. He must have felt the need to be around during the crucial months when the key decisions regarding the *Tet Offensive* were debated. It could also be because of a purge, carried out by Le Duan and Le Duc Tho during this time, of a number of people who did not share their views, of which perhaps the most prominent was Hoang Minh Chinh. However it is difficult provide more details of this or of Ho's role, if any, from the somewhat sketchy samizdat sources.[21] In September, however, he was again in Beijing for medical treatment, and he remained there till late December 1967. Although he was unwell, Ho continued to be very concerned about developments in Vietnam and the world, and exchanged views with the Chinese leaders.[22] Reports confirmed that he had returned to Hanoi by 20 December in time to address a Hanoi rally for the anniversaries of the VPA and the anti-French struggle.

Preparations for the Tet Offensive

Preparation for the eventual Offensive was set in motion at the end of July 1967. Most of the second half of 1967 was spent mobilising and making preparations for the 'General Offensive General Uprising' while at the same time coping with the continuing American bombing in the North and the fighting in the South.[23] The Military Central Commission started a class to train 150 senior and middle-ranking cadres of the Central Bureau, Military Regions, as well as representatives from VPA and the militia, to study the situation and educate them on the responsibilities pertaining to the task of annihilating the Americans. At the end of the training session the officers were expected to return to their units and departments to conduct similar sessions with their subordinates. A number of training manuals originating from the VPA General Staff were compiled with titles such as 'Company, Battalion and Regiment fight enemy in firm and stable defence' and 'Notebook for Company Commanders'[24] In the same month, Military Region V under the command of Major-General Chu Huy Man established the 4th Front (comprising three infantry battalions and the 575th Artillery Regiment), which was entrusted with the responsibility for military operations in Danang. In order to raise the quality of the troops, the Regional Committee and Command convened several meetings and conferences in August to train them in both military tactics and political work. A letter (Number 98) dated 9 September, despatched by the VPA General Staff to COSVN and the Military Commission of the communist forces in the South, listed the requirements and other matters relating to the effort to raise the fighting capability of the main force.[25] Also, in September 1967 in Military Region V, the Vietnamese communist troops launched a series of attacks in Hoi An, Tam Ky, Quang Ngai, Tuy Hoa, and others. According to the *Lich Su Quan Doi Nhan Dan Viet Nam*, those military operations taught the Military Region V Command many valuable lessons about command and control, as well as helped them identify their shortcomings in the area of military preparation. In October, a conference was organised to recapitulate the lessons of the past on guerrilla warfare in the plains and highlands.

The *Lich Su Quan Doi Nhan Dan Viet Nam*[26] recorded that in October the Politburo ordered the dissolution of Military Region VII and the Saigon-Gia Dinh Military Region. It was replaced by a 'special region' consisting of Saigon and a number of neighbouring provinces divided into six sub-zones. Nguyen Van Linh, deputy Secretary of COSVN, was appointed Secretary, and Vo Van Kiet his deputy.[27]

Every region or zone had to build up a force of two to four infantry battalions equipped with light weapons. Their objective was to infiltrate Saigon and join up with the special forces already in place there to take control of key targets. Sub-region 6 (which consisted of districts within Saigon) had 11 special force detachments and a special mobile unit, which together formed an Eastern, a Southern and a Northern group.

In Tay Nguyen, the 88th Regiment was bolstered by the 568th Regiment, six infantry battalions, two artillery battalions, as well as four regiments of mortars from North Vietnam and a few units of combat engineers, signallers, Special Forces and artillery. All this was done in preparation for the eventual assault into the north and northwest and the plains of Saigon. To supervise the operation, COSVN established two Vanguard Commands – Vanguard Command I, to be responsible for operations in the east, north and the main force; and Vanguard Command II, to be responsible for operations in the west, south and the armed forces within Saigon

Military Regions VI, VIII, IX and X were required to mobilise guerrilla forces in the villages and recruits to form a number of companies and battalions in the provinces. Many conferences were organised – for instance, in Military Region V, in August 1967, the Military Command of the South Vietnamese Forces held a conference to study the political tasks of the armed forces, and in October 1967, it organised another conference to study the application of guerrilla warfare strategy in the delta and mountain regions.

Vo Nguyen Giap's *Big Victory, Great Task*,[28] which was serialised in the *Nhan Dan* and *Quan Doi Nhan Dan* from 14 to 16 September 1967, should be seen in the context of the ongoing military preparations, as part of the leadership's effort to indoctrinate, educate and imbibe the masses with the 'correct' perspective and understanding of the struggle to reunify the country.

It is difficult to determine the extent of Chinese aid to North Vietnam in 1967. China was in the midst of the Cultural Revolution. A Chinese source described the three-month period from July to September 1967 as 'the worst turmoil China was to experience through the Cultural Revolution'[29] It is worth noting that the Chinese publications on China's role in the Vietnam War contain hardly any information on Chinese assistance to Vietnam in 1967.[30] But, estimates by the US Department of Defense showed that Chinese aid in 1967 was only US$250 million while Russian and Eastern European aid amounted to US$750 million. It was also estimated that small arms in general and 50 per cent of the anti-aircraft ammunition used by the Vietnamese communists were Chinese-made.[31]

According to Chinese sources as well as the account of Hoang Van Hoan, at a meeting between Ho Chi Minh and Mao Zedong in China in late 1967, Mao had suggested that the Vietnamese communists should consider a strategy of annihilation. Ho felt that the suggestion was logical and reasonable. After confirming with Zhou Enlai that he had noted down Mao's proposal correctly, he sent it back to the Lao Dong Party Central Committee in Hanoi for its consideration.[32]

Sources also revealed that North Vietnamese deputy Prime Minister, Le Thanh Nghi, Hoang Van Hoan and Ly Ban (deputy Minister for Trade) were in China at the end of September 1967 and in early October. (Prior to the visit, Nghi had been in China on 5 August 1967 where he signed an economic and technical aid agreement.) On that occasion, Le Thanh Nghi was leading a delegation from the North Vietnamese Political Affairs Department at the same time as the visit of the NLG's combat hero, Huynh Van Danh. On 5 October, the North Vietnamese delegation met Mao Zedong. As noted earlier, Ho Chi Minh was also in China during that time. A trade agreement was signed between the North Vietnamese and Chinese on 5 October.[33]

In September, Le Thanh Nghi led a North Vietnamese economic delegation to Moscow to request supplementary aid. According to the communiqué issued after the talks, the Russians agreed to provide items 'necessary for the further enhancement of the DRV defence capability and the development of the people's economy of the DRV'. The communiqué mentioned specifically that aircraft, anti-aircraft weapons, artillery, firearms, ammunition and other military supplies would be delivered in 1968.[34] Ilya Gaiduk observed that it was not usual for the Russians to publicise their aid package in such detail. At the end of October, Le Duan, Vo Nguyen Giap and Nguyen Duy Trinh visited Moscow to attend the 50th anniversary of the October Revolution. There, Le Duan met with Leonard Brezhnev, Alexei Kosygin and Nikolai Podgornyi but as yet no information is available on the exchanges which took place during that meeting.

The CIA assessment of the capabilities of the Vietnamese communists for fighting in South Vietnam, based on information available as of 1 October 1967, was that Hanoi's control and share of the burden of the war in the South had grown substantially. The communists, however, faced problems of declining manpower, recruitment, morale and quality of the troops in the South. While the problems had not yet affected their overall military effectiveness, the CIA was of the view that the communists would face increasing difficulties. However, it estimated that the communists still retained sufficient capabilities to sustain a protracted war of attrition for at least one more year.[35]

In Hanoi, in October, the Politburo met to evaluate the military and political situation, the ongoing military preparations, and to review their strategy. It was at that meeting that the decision to launch the 'General Offensive General Uprising' on Tet in 1968 was taken. Major-General Le Trong Tan, Deputy Chief of the VPA General Staff, and Senior Colonel Le Ngoc Hien, Head of the Warfare Department, were chosen to travel to the South to convey the decision of the Politburo and also to supervise the preparations.[36] Military preparations for the Offensive, which were already underway, were intensified. In October 1967, the main military force (68th Artillery Regiment of the 304th Division) in Military Region V was expanded to include the 577th Artillery Regiment. The 401st Special Forces Regiment (comprising the 406th and 409th Battalions) was also formed under the Military Region V Command. At the same time, the 403th Battalion arrived from North Vietnam to bolster its strength.

On 1 November 1967, the Province Party Standing Committee issued a directive to the district and local party organs explaining the rationale for the decision to launch the General Offensive, and describing how it should be conducted and the preparations to be carried out.[37] However, it was only in December 1967 that the Politburo issued the resolution moving the revolution in the South into a new phase – 'the phase of winning decisive victory'.[38] According to the resolution, the 'General Offensive General Uprising' was expected to be complex and violent. The Nam Bo region and the Saigon-Cholon area were to be the most important and decisive battlefields. *The Route 9-Tri Thien-Quang Da stretch was second in importance* (emphasis added). The three critical targets for the offensive were the cities of Saigon, Hue and Danang.[39] Finally, the whole operation was to be as secret as possible with the aim of creating an all round effect to exploit to the fullest the element of surprise.

On 6 December 1967, the Military Central Commission established the Party Committee and Military Command for the Route 9-Tri Thien Front, in which Khe Sanh came under. Brigadier-General Tran Quy Hai (alternate-member of the Party Central Committee and assistant Head, PAVN General Staff) was appointed Commander while Brigadier-General Le Quang Dao (member of the Party Central Committee and assistant Chief of the General Political Directorate, PAVN) was appointed the Political Commissar. The Front was under the direct supervision of the High Command of the VPA and the Military Central Commission.[40] The mission was 'to create the environment' for a direct attack on Tri Thien and Hue.[41] The Route 9-Tri Thien Front was one of the fronts of the 'General Offensive General Uprising' created for the purpose of drawing out American troops for destruction, thus giving support to other battlefields, foremost of which was Saigon-Hue-Danang, and most directly that of Hue.[42]

The North Vietnamese military strength for the Route 9-Tri Thien Front included the following: 304th, 320th, 324th and 325th Divisions; 1 regiment of infantry (270th Regiment); 5 artillery regiments (16th, 45th, 84th, 204th and 675th); 3 regiments of anti-aircraft artillery (208th, 214th and 228th); 4 battalions of tanks; 1 battalion of combat engineers; 1 battalion of combat communication specialists; and a number of units of local troops/militia.[43] Military Group 31 (comprising two infantry battalions under the military command of the Route 9-Tri Thien Front) was put in charge of the area from Route 9 to the DMZ. The main military force of the Military Region V was also expanded to include three more infantry regiments – 9th (of 304th Division), 2nd (of 324th Division) and 8th (of 325th Division).[44]

According to Van Tien Dung,[45] from September 1967 and in the period between December 1967 and mid-January 1968, the Hanoi leadership ordered all the battle fronts in Nam Bo – Military Region V, Central Highlands, Tri Thien and Route 9 – to submit regular reports and hold discussions on the developing situation. Representatives from COSVN submitted three situation reports. Both Ho Chi Minh and Le Duan participated actively in the discussions.[46]

In the midst of the military preparations, North Vietnam's foreign minister, Nguyen Duy Trinh, announced in a speech on 29 December 1967, that Hanoi would hold talks with the Americans 'on all questions concerned' once the bombing of North Vietnam and other war operations against the North were stopped unconditionally.[47] Mai Van Bo, North Vietnam's representative in Paris subsequently reaffirmed the pronouncement on 1 January 1968[48] and again in an interview on 16 January.[49] We can now confirm that these statements were a ploy to divert the enemy from the preparation for the forthcoming military offensive. As Truong Cong Dong, a member of the NLF mission in Hanoi said, 'The talks will begin when the Americans have inflicted a defeat on us or when we have inflicted a defeat on them. Everything will be resolved on the battlefield.'[50]

The Tet Offensive (or 'General Offensive General Uprising') – Phase I

In early January 1968, at the 14th Plenary Session of the Party Central Committee, the December 1967 resolution of the Politburo was passed.[51] After the 14th Plenary Session, Le Duan issued a letter, dated 18 January 1968, to the Vietnamese communist comrades in the South.[52] The letter summed up the leadership's thinking on the 'General Offensive General Uprising' strategy as spelt out in the December 1967 resolution. The following points were covered in the letter: (1) The leaders were certain that the American war efforts in Vietnam had reached its climax and was in a 'strategic stalemate', with the Vietnamese communists holding the initiative and advantage. The situation thus presented 'a strategic opportunity' to shift the revolutionary war to a period of winning a decisive victory. (2) The Central Committee predicted three possible outcomes of the 'General Offensive General Uprising'; the communists would either (a) win in the 'major centre' (Saigon-Gia Dinh City), or (b) succeed in a number of cities and rural areas, but not in Saigon, or (c) achieve some victories as before but not sufficiently to expel the American forces. The first outcome would be the most desirable, but should events unfold according to (b) or (c), the communist forces would still not be weakened; it would only mean that the war would be reverted to a protracted struggle. (3) The primary objective of the 'General Offensive General Uprising' was to 'deal him (the enemy) thundering blows so as to change the face of the war, further shake the aggressive will of US imperialism, compel it to change its strategy and de-escalate the war'. (4) The policy was to stretch the enemy throughout the Southern battlefield. Although one of the main thrusts of the Offensive was the cities, the communists would not launch all their main force against the big cities as the enemy forces were numerous and well-equipped. The primary aim was to take control of the countryside. (5) It was Ho Chi Minh's intention to visit the South to provide encouragement to the comrades, but the Politburo had persuaded him to postpone the trip on account of his health. The goal was for them to win 'the greatest victory to welcome Uncle Ho in the South'.

Considering that the December 1967 Resolution had emphasised the holistic and secretive nature of the Tet Offensive, it is significant that none of the North Vietnamese accounts explained why the Khe Sanh siege was launched on 20 January 1968, ten days earlier than scheduled. Van Tien Dung revealed that it was only on 21 January 1968 (that is, one day after the Khe Sanh operation had begun) that the decision was taken to launch the 'General Offensive General Uprising' on the eve of the 1968 Lunar New Year of Mau-Than.[53] Apparently, the Tet Offensive was brought forward from 5 February 1968 to 31 January.[54]

There is the possibility (although this is nowhere explicitly stated in the Vietnamese communists' official histories) that the Khe Sanh siege might have been inadvertently forced upon the North Vietnamese by Westmoreland's preemptive actions. According to the Official history of the US Marines in Vietnam, the North Vietnamese had since August 1967 successfully severed Route 9 west of the Marine outpost of Ca Lu isolating the Marines at Khe Sanh and permitting resupply on by air.[55] Vietnamese sources noted that towards the end of December 1967, the Americans discovered the North Vietnamese communist build-up around the region of Khe Sanh and the bases around Saigon, and got wind of the increased activities of the Military Transportation Group 559.[56] This event was indeed captured in the American intelligence reports and mentioned by General Westmoreland.[57] North Vietnamese intelligence noted that the American military responded by increasing the number of units defending Saigon, sending 12 battalions of the 1st Cavalry Division, the 101st Airborne Division and a Marine Corps Division to the Route 9 area.[58] Westmoreland had unleashed a combined US Air Force, Navy and Marine air assault – *Operation Niagara* – on 14 January 1968. And on the afternoon of 20 January, a North Vietnamese lieutenant defected and provided the Americans with detailed information of the communist build-up.[59]

The *Lich Su Quan Doi Nhan Dan Viet Nam* briefly revealed that the communists were not ready for the *Khe Sanh* operation and that preparations had to be carried out in a hurry, with the consequence that on the Route 9 Front there was much hardship and it was difficult to follow orders. Senior Lt. General Tran Van Quang also revealed that when those in Tri Thien was apprised of the decision regarding the offensive, they feared that there might not be sufficient time to make the necessary preparations.[60] There was indeed much that needed to be done, which included 'setting the operation and battle plans; organising military, political, and proselytising forces; readying the battle-field; positioning the troops, organising the material supplies; and disseminating instructions and giving ideological guidance. . . .'[61] Tran Van Tra, who played a key role in the *Tet Offensive* in the South, recalled in his reflections on the preparation for the 1968 offensive, that 'it was too short a time for such a colossal and complex undertaking'.[62]

Another communist veteran fighter spoke of the 'the substantial conflicts' between the military command and the regional party committees. The military, according to him, had good knowledge of local situations whereas the regional party officials would get its orders from the central command and would often execute orders without consulting the local units. Many of the military cadres did not agree with the *Tet Offensive* at all but as it was the Party's order, they had to carry it out. The Party believed that there would be strong support from the people but most of the military did not believe that. Before the Offensive began, there was a lot of confusion, he recalled.[63]

It is perhaps also worth mentioning that almost all the North Vietnamese communist accounts of the critical months of December 1967 to January 1968 placed more emphasis on the military developments taking place in Northern Laos than on Khe Sanh. According to these accounts, Laotian forces under the direction of American advisers were incrementally taking over Pathet Lao controlled areas. In July 1966, they took control of Nam Bac and were developing a defence line north of Luang Prabang, thereby threatening Pathet Lao territory. In order to pre-empt this, in December 1967, both the Central Committees of the Neo Lao Hak Xat (Lao Patriotic Front) and the Vietnamese Communist Party jointly decided to launch a military offensive in Nam Bac. To this end, they sent the 316th infantry Division to Laos. The 147th and 148th Regiments were involved in the fighting that apparently took place between 12–27 January 1968 before Nam Bac was finally 'liberated'.[64] All the extra effort channelled into the operation make one wonders if the Hanoi leadership had considered the *Nam Bac* military campaign more significant or successful than *Khe Sanh*.

According to Senior Lt. General Tran Van Quang,[65] the confusion as to whether the *Khe Sanh* siege was meant to be primarily a diversionary tactic was a reflection of the considerable differences of opinion between the policy-makers and those 'on the ground' regarding both strategy and tactics. He recalled that those in Tri Thien were initially uncomfortable with the lack of time to prepare for the offensive but subsequently accepted the decision when they interpreted their mission as a diversion to draw the enemy away from Saigon. According to Van Tien Dung, the leadership's decision was that the Route 9-Khe Sanh Front was to be one of the many fronts of the 'General Offensive General Uprising' with the objective of either destroying or surrounding part of the US forces. The most important targets were Saigon, Hue and Danang.[66]

The North Vietnamese communists also did not plan to re-stage another 'Dien Bien Phu' at Khe Sanh. The *Lich Su Quan Doi Nhan Dan Viet Nam* noted that it was the Americans who were worried that Khe Sanh would be 'the second Dien Bien Phu' and that President Johnson vowed to protect Khe Sanh at all costs.[67] Van Tien Dung recalled that the objective of Khe Sanh as well as the other battles along Route 9 on 20–21 January 1968 was both to draw out and to confine and hold up the enemy in one location. It was the Americans who, on witnessing the strength of the Vietnamese communists in Khe Sanh, had thought that it was a potential Dien Bien Phu in embryo. In Dung's view, given the ferocity of the fighting at Khe Sanh, and specifically the American bombings, the fighting was indeed reminiscent of the battle at Dien Bien Phu.[68]

According to the *Lich Su Quan Doi Nhan Dan Viet Nam*, the communist forces in the 170 days siege eliminated 17,000 enemy (of whom 13,000 were Americans), destroyed 480 planes of all types, and immobilised 32 battalions (of which 26 were American; they estimated that this number would amount to a quarter of all American forces in South Vietnam). American withdrawal from Khe Sanh (in April) was seen as a heavy political and military defeat that increased the doubts and contradictions within the American leadership. The siege showed that the Vietnamese communist forces had the ability to take on a large and powerful enemy with superior air power in a strategic position and over an extended period of time. But there were also shortcomings which required attention such as the need for improvements to command and control, as well as 'the movement to contact'.[69]

The 'General Offensive General Uprising' was launched on 30 January and ended on 31 March 1968 with simultaneous uprisings all over South Vietnam, most notably in Hue and the Saigon-Gia Dinh vicinity. During that period, the Vietnamese communists continued to reiterate their willingness to enter into talks with the US. While Beijing condemned U Thant, the Vietnamese drew attention to the United Nations Secretary-General's support of the Vietnamese position on the talks. On 22 March, Mai Van Bo reiterated that Hanoi was seriously ready to take part in peace talks with the US after the unconditional cessation of the bombing of the North.[70]

The decision to negotiate

On 31 March 1968, President Johnson made several pronounce-ments: (1) He was restricting air strikes to the area below the 20th degree parallel, thus sparing most of North Vietnamese territory. (2) He had authorised Averell Harriman to open negotiations whenever the Vietnamese communists were ready. (3) He would not seek another term as president. However, he was silent on whether he would resume the bombing or increase American forces in Vietnam should the talks failed. On 3 April, Hanoi issued a statement declaring that, although the US government had not fully met its demands, it was prepared to meet the Americans for preliminary discussions.

According to Hoang Van Hoan, it was Le Duan who was responsible for making the decision which had led to the statement. The decision, however, did not win unanimous support. Ho Chi Minh was not consulted as he was then recuperating in Beijing.[71] Luu Van Loi recalled that Johnson's announcement was very significant as 'it marked a great change in the US strategy, from intensification of the war to de-escalation, from refusal of negotiations to acceptance of probing negotiation'. In Loi's view, the public would not have supported a rejection of Johnson's proposal. On the other hand, it was not expedient to accept the proposal immediately as it was too early to begin negotiations. The Politburo was of the view that contacts should be made but, above all, complete cessation of US bombing of North Vietnam must be insisted upon. Discussion of related matters could only follow the cessation of bombing. Secret probing discussions could be held but no negotiations would commence.[72]

The *Nhan Dan* and *Quan Doi Nhan Dan* editorials of 4 April expressed support for the decision. According to the editorials, the decision to meet the Americans 'conformed to the aspirations of the world people, who cherished independence, peace and justice, and would surely receive widespread approval and support in the world'. But the editorials also stressed that the Vietnamese communists were determined to fight till total victory was theirs.[73]

Hanoi spared no time in stepping up the diplomatic offensive. In an interview with the Japanese writer Seicho Matsumoto on 6 April, Pham Van Dong disclosed that Hanoi had already appointed its representative to meet the Americans.[74] On 8 April, during a CBS interview, Nguyen Duy Trinh appealed to the American people for support.[75] Pham Van Dong also sent a message to the American public through CBS in which he called upon the American people to join the Vietnamese in the common objective of bringing the war to an end by demanding that the US withdraw its troops form Vietnam.[76] Hanoi was clearly trying to exploit the split within the US in the aftermath of the *Tet Offensive* to advance its cause.

The Tet Offensive – Phase II

Having agreed to negotiate, Hanoi then needed a clear military victory, otherwise they would not be able to negotiate successfully on their terms. The *Tet Offensive* had not achieved the goals set but had resulted in heavy losses on the communist side. The Politburo on 24 April decided to carry out another military offensive with the objective of securing a clear victory. The Nam Bo Regional Command created five new battalions of mobile Special Forces (3rd, 4th, 5th, 7th and 8th). Phase 2 of the *Tet Offensive* began on 4 May 1968 and lasted until 17 August 1968. The communists attacked 31 cities, 58 districts, 30 airfields and 20 operation staging bases chiefly in Saigon and Gia Dinh; they suffered high casualties in the process. On 12 June, they withdrew from Saigon.[77]

The first session of the peace talks involving the North Vietnamese and the Americans was eventually held in Paris on 13 May. On 7 May, enroute to Paris, Xuan Thuy, North Vietnam's representative at the talks, made a stopover at Beijing. It seemed that Mao Zedong had refused to meet him. Xuan Thuy had a brief meeting with Zhou Enlai, who was reported to have told him that Hanoi's agreement to the Paris talks was a major tactical and diplomatic mistake and that Hanoi had fallen into an American trap.[78]

The Tet Offensive – Phase III

The failure of the second phase of the *Tet Offensive* led to a third phase. In August, the Politburo met again. Although the leadership was becoming increasingly less optimistic than they were in December 1967 and in April 1968, they decided to continue the military offensive 'to win a decisive victory'. Phase Three of the *Tet Offensive* began on 17 August and continued until 30 September 1968. They warned of the need to be 'prepared to defeat the US should they prolong or expand the war'. This contrasted sharply with the view held in December 1967 when they had considered it was unlikely that the US would increase its forces and expand the war. In this third phase, the communists attacked 27 cities and towns, 100 districts and military posts and 47 airfields. The *Tay Ninh-Binh Long* campaign which involved the 5th, 7th and 9th infantry divisions began on 17 August and ended on 28 September. The third phase of the *Tet Offensive* also did not achieve the desired results. Instead, the losses piled up.[79] In the analysis of the Politburo, the initial success of the 'General Offensive General Uprising' had undergone 'complicated changes'.[80]

By September 1968, it was obvious that the Vietnamese communists had to live with the second of the three possible courses of development that they had predicted in December

1967. The decisive victory desired did not materialise. Although the Americans did not expand the war during this period, it did not augur well for the Vietnamese communists because the entire*Tet Offensive*, which lasted for the better part of 1968 and had consumed much human and material resources, only brought about another stalemate in the struggle. American intelligence in 1968 calculated that the communists lost 85,000 out of about 195,000 troops in the *Tet Offensive*. By the end of 1968, the number had grown to 280,000, which was more than 100% of their total military strength.[81] Although the exact figures are not known, the more recent Vietnamese accounts acknowledged that it was inconclusive and they suffered heavy losses. By the end of 1968 and in the beginning of 1969, the communists had lost both ground and support. Many of their grassroots organisations were smashed and their activities in the liberated areas curtailed. The enemy had pacified 9,200 hamlets and about 16 million people, out of a total of 12,395 hamlets with a population of 17,500 million. Although their main forces remained numerically strong, they did not have the capability to mount moderate and large offensives until 1970.[82]

According to Bui Tin, in retrospect, it was a mistake to launch the second and third phases of the offensive. The communist forces in the South were almost wiped out by the fighting in 1968 and it was not till 1971 that the communists were able to recover their strength. American withdrawal in 1969 thus inadvertently provided them a respite.[83] Tran Van Tra's *Vietnam: History of the Bulwark B2 Theatre, Volume 5: Concluding the 30 Years War*, which the Vietnamese banned soon after its publication in 1982, was perhaps the first to admit publicly that the *Tet Offensive* was less then the unmitigated success it was made out to be by the Vietnamese. A case can however be made for the decision to launch the second and third phases of the offensive. Tran Van Tra opined that, while on hindsight the second and third phases should not have been carried out because of the damage it inflicted on the southern revolution-aries in 1969 and 1970, the second phase of the offensive forced Washington and Saigon to join the peace talks, and it was during the third phase that Johnson finally ordered the unconditional cessation of the bombing of North Vietnam and announced that a four-party conference which included both the NLF and Saigon would be convened.[84] One should not over-exaggerate the communist losses. Although it was true that the communists were severely mauled by the military campaigns in 1968, they were not completely destroyed. Ngo Vinh Long in his case study of the strategic province of Long An showed that the NLF was able to rise like a phoenix out of the ashes in the post-Tet period as a result of popular support from the ground.[85]

On 31 October, Johnson unilaterally halted all bombing of North Vietnam. On 6 November 1968, Richard Nixon was named the new President of the United States. Nixon had promised to end the war and achieve peace with honour. On 25 January 1969, after more than half a year of wrangling the peace talks which included the United States, North Vietnam, South Vietnam and the NFL finally materialised.

The military situation in 1969

In 1969, the communists carried out two rounds of military offensives. The first was in spring from 22 February 1969 to 30 March 1969 in the Dong Du (Cu Chi) Thu Dau Mot region), and another in the summer from 11 May to 23 June (*Kontum and Long Khanh* campaigns). According to Van Tien Dung, although they killed many enemies, they were unable to make any changes in the balance of strength worth mentioning. The destruction in 1968 made it difficult to carry out the missions satisfactorily.[86] Luu Van Loi recalled that after the 1968 *Tet Offensive*, the communists were slow in changing the orientation of the offensive. Consequently, their control of the rural areas were considerably weakened which created conditions for the enemy to carry out pacification campaigns and to recapture all the rural areas the communists had controlled causing them great difficulties and big losses.[87]

In April 1969, in between the two offensives, the Politburo met and passed the resolution to mobilise both the power of the military and the people in both North and South Vietnam to

develop an offensive strategy in order to defeat the 'Vietnamisation' policy in the South. The goal was to force the
Americans to retreat, achieve a decisive victory and end the
war. The leadership admitted that the failure of the *Tet
Offensive* could be attributed as much to the opponent's strength
as to the many shortcomings and errors committed by the
leadership during that period. The Vietnamese communists
were not sufficiently responsive to the changing circumstances,
they did not have a good understanding of strategy, there was
weakness in the party leadership, and there were also
organisational weaknesses. The Politburo noted that the
transfer of a large proportion of their forces from the countryside to the town and cities inadvertently aided the success of
the opponent's Pacification programme. They were also slow to
recognise and react to the opponent's Pacification strategy and
thus had failed to concentrate their strength to destroy the
Pacification programme. As for the 'Vietnamisation' policy
introduced by Nixon, they thought that it was a crafty policy
replete with contradictions and could not succeed. According
to the Politburo, 'Vietnamisation' was a policy of the defeated
and showed that the US was in decline.[88]

Following the April resolution, the Central Military Committee ordered all forces to quickly put in order their organisations
to enable them to effectively carry out the goals spelt out by the
leadership. Top priority was given to air-defence and efforts were
made to expand and protect the transportation lines between the
North and the South. More cadres were posted to all the units in
the southern Military Region IV and along the routes that Group
559 operated. The General Staff transferred two regiments, 12
battalions and six companies of combat engineers from the
southern part of Military Region IV to assist Group 559 build the
'20 July route' from the Thach Ban cross-road to join Route 9.
Group 500 and components of the Rear Services Directorate of
southern Military Region IV were placed under the control of
Group 559. The 367th air-defence division was moved from Ha
Tinh to the western Quang Binh-Vinh Linh area. The number of
soldiers in the training establishments and institutes was reduced
in order to increase the number posted to the war-zone. Thirteen

thousand and two hundred cadres and fighters were sent to replenish the battlefields. Units with sufficient troops and equipment were sent to the strategic eastern Nam Bo region. These included a number of main infantry units from Tay Nguyen and Military Region V – 1st infantry division, comprising three regiments (95th C, 101st C and 209th) as well as the 33rd, 174th, 10th and 20th regiments. From the North, ten battalions and 100 companies and regiments were sent to the South to replenish troops lost in 1968. Slowly and gradually, the Nam Bo command rebuilt the strength of the Special Forces and other services in the South.[89]

COSVN Resolution Number 9 (dated July 1969) directed the communists to preserve their strength in order to prolong the war. Large units were instructed to be broken down into smaller ones, while provincial local force units were to split into smaller cells. The objectives were to hit US troops and installations to pressurise US troops to withdraw as well as disrupt pacification and destroy Saigon's control of the population.[90] It was a difficult period as the re-organisation had to be carried out whilst the war was on.

One communist veteran fighter recalled that from the second half of August 1968 to the second half of August 1969, they had to constantly avoid the enemy, build new installations, and search for food. As a result, their health and fighting ability deteriorated. Indeed, many Vietnamese communists remembered 1969 to be a particularly difficult year. The hardship was to an extent alleviated by the 'true heroism of the peasants', many of whom risked their lives to provide food for the guerillas and soldiers.[91] Another factor which helped was the fact that the US was withdrawing its troops in 1969 which convinced the communists that the Americans could not last and would eventually withdraw altogether. In the words of one veteran, '... We knew that even though we faced tremendous difficulties, so did they. They had terrible problems, especially at home. We don't think their government could stand it in the long run. That gave me heart.'[92]

Differences within the Hanoi leadership

It was mentioned earlier that within the Vietnamese communist leadership, there had long been prolonged tension between those who supported and those who were against the escalation of the armed struggle in the South, described as the 'North-first' or the 'South-first'. Many southerners, rightly or wrongly, believed that Hanoi, especially members of the National Assembly, placed the long-term interest of the North before the liberation of the South.[93] After the *Tet Offensive* debacle, a variation of the dichotomy developed. The policy debate during that period is still unclear. Apparently, there was one group (represented by Le Duan and his followers) who supported the 'fight-and-negotiate' strategy. They believed that in order for the 'fight-and-negotiate' strategy to succeed, the fighting must be sustained and intensified to make an impact on the negotiation. Coming up against this group were others like Truong Chinh and Hoang Van Hoan, who held the view that, given the heavy losses already incurred, a 'protracted war' strategy was the more appropriate choice. The most notable effort from this camp was a speech made by Truong Chinh on 5 May 1968 to commemorate the 150th anniversary of the birth of Karl Marx. The speech was said to have generated much heated debate and was only published on 23 August 1968, almost four months after it was delivered. In that speech, Truong Chinh made the following key points: (1) The correct revolutionary strategy should combine armed struggle and political struggle. (2) The task of building and consolidating socialism in the North was both urgent and crucial. (3) There was the need to restore and strengthen the solidarity of the international communist and workers' movement on the basis of Marxist-Leninist principles and proletarian internationalism. (4) The war in the South was likely to be protracted and therefore ought to be fought on the basis of 'self-reliance' and guerrilla tactics until such time as another offensive could be successfully launched.[94]

However, it would appear from the events in 1968 and 1969 that Le Duan and those who shared his view had the upper hand in determining policies.[95] A July 1969 communist document, which summarised the 9th COSVN Conference (1969), labeled those who held the retreating back to a 'protracted war' view as 'skeptical', 'lacking resolution and 'absolute determination' when confronted with difficulties. They were said to have 'an erroneous conception of the transitional nature of the General Offensive and Uprising, now thinking it is a one-blow affair and consequently lacking vigilance against the enemy plots, now thinking it is a period of protracted struggle and consequently lacking boldness and a sense of urgency; worse still, they become right-leaning and shrink from action'.[96]

Hanoi and Sino-Soviet relations

The differences within the Vietnamese communist leadership on the appropriate strategy to adopt mirrored the differences in views held by Beijing and Moscow, and had implications for North Vietnam's relations with China and the Soviet Union. Beijing was for 'protracted war' and opposed negotiations. It was with great reluctance that the Chinese supported the escalation of the armed struggle in 1959 and the 1968 *Tet Offensive* and they continually reminded the Vietnamese that 'perseverance means victory' and that the final victory could only be achieved through protracted struggle. In 1979 the Vietnamese disclosed that Beijing had on 9 October 1968 continued to pressure them to break off their negotiations with the US, and to sever relations with the Soviet Union as well. It seemed that, on 17 October 1968, the Chinese went so far as to threaten to sever ties with the Lao Dong Party if the Vietnamese refused to accede to the Chinese demands. If these claims were true, the Chinese did not carry out their threat. On 19 October, after 26 sessions of the peace talks, the Chinese for the first time took official notice of the meetings. In its report on the Paris talks, the NCNA quoted a number of positive Western news reports on the ongoing talks.[97] However, Beijing began to withdraw its troops from North Vietnam in November 1968. By March 1969, it has withdrawn all its anti-aircraft artillery units and by July 1970, all its support troops had returned to China.[98] Moscow, on the other hand, had from the very beginning advocated negotiation and a peaceful settlement of the conflict.

1969 was a particularly stressful year in the communist camp. On 2 March 1969, armed clashes between Soviet and Chinese frontier guards took place along the River Ussuri on a small uninhabited island, known to the Chinese as Zhenbao Island and to the Russians as Damansky Island. This incident could possibly explain the Chinese recall of its anti-aircraft artillery units from North Vietnam in March. More significantly, the incident marks the nadir of Sino-Soviet relations and the beginning point in Beijing's rapprochement with the US, and was to have serious consequences for the Vietnamese communists and its relations with China.

Ho Chi Minh's final months

The rest of this study will focus on the last four months of Ho Chi Minh's life. According to Ho's secretary, Tuu Ky, Ho's heart had begun to fail in early 1969.[99] Chinese sources revealed that Ho had taken ill in February 1969, and a team of doctors from Beijing was sent to attend to him. The doctors only returned to Beijing when he appeared to have recovered in the latter part of June.[100] Various monitored reports of his activities showed that Ho was in Hanoi in February and early March. Readers would recall that he was recuperating in Beijing on 3 April when he heard the news that Hanoi had agreed to Johnson's call for talks. He would have returned to Hanoi by 28 April as he was reported to be 'healthy and smiling' as he chatted with some polling station officials and voters after casting his vote at the polls for the election of the People's Council.[101] Ho was most active in the month of May. On 2 May, he attended a May day meeting in Hanoi. On 10 May, he completed the revision of his will. From Ho's will, it can be conjectured that, in May 1969, the war was not going too well for the Vietnamese communists and Ho did not expect the war to end in the near future. It can also be inferred from his will that there were differences within the Party, and he was particularly concerned about the matter. The divisions in the international communist movement also troubled him.[102]

On 11 May, Ho addressed a big and important high-level military conference on the subject of the change of the nature of the struggle and the use of the military in the newly developed situation. In his closed-door speech, Ho said that from Tet to the present, the war against the Americans had entered a new phase. The Americans had clearly lost out in the struggle but they were not yet defeated. The communist troops must not fear making sacrifices and facing difficulties head-on for the people could not expect to experience peace and real freedom until after the Americans had been completely defeated and South Vietnam completely liberated. In order to realise the dream of the joyous day when North and South Vietnam would be united as one, everyone must put their best foot forward, correct their shortcomings and complete the responsibility entrusted by the Party. He cited the Vietnamese hero Tran Hung Dao to illustrate his point that what the military needed was not numerical might but intelligence.[103]

Ho celebrated his 70th birthday on 19 May. It was reported that he was 'in good health'. On 23 May, he received a group of high-ranking cadres of the army. It was again reported that he was 'in good health and had a ruddy complexion'.[104] The Chinese media reported the meeting at length.[105] At that meeting, Ho exhorted the army to continue the struggle against the Americans. He spoke of the need to 'economise on human and material resources' even while continuing the struggle and the consolidation and strengthening of the North.

On 6 June, Ho was briefed by Xuan Thuy on the ongoing peace talks.[106] On 13 June, he received the PRGSVN delegation led by Nguyen Van Tien, which was a clear indication that the formation of the PRG in early June had his support.[107] August was a particularly complicated month on the communist side and there is little information available on what happened then. The Hanoi leadership apparently gave the go-ahead for a secret meeting between Xuan Thuy and Henry Kissinger, which took place on 4 August[108] It was unfruitful and both agreed to meet again. Ho must have been ill in August as he did not meet the delegation from the Vietnam Alliance of National Democratic and Peace Forces when they were in North Vietnam from 16–20 August. On 16 July 1969, Nixon had sent a letter to Ho through Jean Sainteny, urging both sides to settle the war at the conference table. The negotiations in Paris were not making any headway. Sainteny passed the letter to Xuan Thuy on 19 July. Kissinger was informed by Xuan Thuy on 4 August that the letter had been forwarded to Hanoi. Ho's uncompromising reply, dated 25 August, only reached the American President on 30 August 1969.[109] According to Tuu Ky, by late August Ho could no longer work.[110] Chinese sources further revealed that in August Ho's illness had worsened, and in late August he fell into a coma.[111] On the morning of 2 September, Ho passed away.

Ho's death did present one final opportunity for the North Vietnamese to play a small but significant role in helping to make possible a three and a half hour meeting between Zhou Enlai and Kosygin at Beijing airport on 11 September. This meeting helped diffuse the high tension between China and the Soviet Union because of the border clash earlier in the year.[112] But signs of anti-Chinese feelings in Hanoi began to emerge not long after Ho's death.[113] According to Truong Nhu Tang (former Minister of Justice of the Provisional Revolutionary Government of South Vietnam), the Lao Dong Party had decided to ally itself with Moscow and a move in that direction began in 1969. Ho's death opened the way for formalising the decision.[114]

Although Ho was unsuccessful in closing the Sino-Soviet rift, he remained the most powerful source of unity for the communists in both North and South Vietnam and was respected in both Beijing and Moscow.[115] When he was alive, the divisions in the international communist movement had troubled him, and his continued pleas for unity indicated that he had tried to guard against any split within the Vietnamese communist leadership and strived to restore the unity of the movement. At the very least, he would not allow Vietnam to contribute to deepening the existing dissension. His untimely death weakened the solidarity of the Vietnamese communist leadership and Hanoi's finely calibrated relations with Moscow and Beijing and would have consequences for the subsequent years.

The Vietnam War did not come to an end until 1975. The sequel to this study will focus on the negotiations in Paris and show how events and decisions made between 1969 and 1975 on the communist side continued to shape the outcome of the war.

Notes

Introduction

1 Ngo Vinh Long, 'South Vietnam' in Peter Lowe (ed.), *The Vietnam War* (London: Macmillan Press, 1998), pp. 62–94; David Hunt, 'Images of the Viet Cong' in Robert M. Slabey (ed.), *The United States and Vietnam from War to Peace* (Jefferson: McFarland, 1996), pp. 51–66.

2 R.B. Smith, *An International History of the Vietnam War, Volume III: The Making of a Limited War, 1965–66* (London: Macmillan, 1991), p. 10.

3 *Ibid.*, p. 10

4 'How Armed Struggle Began in South Vietnam' in *Vietnam Courier*, Number 22, March 1974, pp. 19–24.

5 Wilfred Burchett, *My Visit to the Zones of South Vietnam* (Hanoi: Foreign Languages Publishing House, 1966), p. 17; For a more detailed account of the situation in South Vietnam during this period, see Carlyle Thayer, *War by Other Means: National Liberation and Revolution in Vietnam 1954–60* (Sydney: Allen and Unwin, 1989), Chapter 7.

6 Memorandum from the Director of the Defence Intelligence Agency (Carroll) to the Secretary of Defence (McNamara), 13 December 1963, *Foreign Relations of the United States* (hereafter cited as *FRUS*), Vietnam 1961–1963, Volume IV, pp. 707–710.

7 PRO: FO 371/170097, Hanoi to FO, 1 March 1963; PRO: FO 371/170107, Saigon to FO, 5 September 1963 cited in Fredrik Logevall, *Choosing War: The Lost Chance for Peace and the Escalation of War in Vietnam* (Berkeley: University of California Press, 1999), p. 10, 426, ftn. 24; 'The DRV in 1962' in *China News Analysis*, Number 460, 15 March 1963.

8 Mao Zedong and Pham Van Dong, Hoang Van Hoan (Beijing, 5 October 1964) in *New Evidence on the Vietnam/IndoChina Wars* (Cold War International History Project hereafter cited as *CWIHP*).

9 Robert S. McNamara, *Argument Without End: In Search of Answers to the Vietnam Tragedy* (New York: Public Affairs, 1999), pp. 226–227.
10 See Ang Cheng Guan, 'Decision-making Leading to the Tet Offensive (1968) – The Vietnamese Communist Perspective' in *Journal of Contemporary History*, Volume 33, Number 3, July 1998, pp. 341–353.
11 For details of the in-fighting within the Hanoi leadership, see Bui Tin, *op. cit.*, pp. 44–46, 54–56.

1 Prelude to the Armed Struggle

1 *Lich Su Quan Doi Nhan Dan Viet Nam, Tap II – Quyen Mot*, (Hanoi: Nha Xuat Ban Quan DoNhan Dan, 1988), p. 11–12; For a brief account of the 6th Plenary Session which apparently included a closed session, see 'Mot Vung Chien Khu Xua' in *Nhan Dan*, 28 August 1993; Cao Van Luong, *Lich Su Cach Mang Mien Nam Vietnam: Giai Doan 1954–1960*, (Hanoi: Nha Xuat Ban Khoa Hoc Xa Hoi, 1991), p. 160. Cao Van Luong recounted that Ho's view was reiterated at the 8th Plenary Session in August 1955.
2 *Lich Su Quan Doi Nhan Dan Viet Nam*, p. 12. (hereafter cited as LSQDNDVN)
3 *Ibid.*, p. 14.
4 Guo Ming (ed.), *Zhongyue Guanxi Yanbian Shishi Nian*, (Guangxi People's Publisher, 1992), p. 65.
5 See *Socialist Republic of Vietnam Foreign Ministry White Book on Relations with China*, (Hanoi Home Service, 6 and 11 October 1979, SWB/FE/6238 and 6242). For the replies of the Chinese government and Hoang Van Hoan, see *Beijing Review*, 23 November 1979, 30 November 1979, 7 December 1979, also see, Mao Zedong and Pham Van Dong, Beijing, (17 November 1968) in 77 Conversations Between Chinese and Foreign Leaders in Indo-China, 1964–1977 (CWIHP), Working Paper Number 22, May 1998.
6 Hoang Van Hoan, *A Drop in the Ocean: Hoang Van Hoan's Revolutionary Reminiscences*, (Beijing: Foreign Languages Press, 1988), p. 324.
7 *Zhongguo Junshi Guwentuan Yuanyue Kangfa Douzheng Shishi*, (Beijing: Jiefang Jun Chubanshe, 1990), p. 141–142.
8 *Confidential United States State Department Central Files* (hereafter cited as CUSSDCF): 751 G. 00/2–1156, 2743, 11 February 1956, State Department to Saigon (Secret).
9 Aleksandr Kaznacheev, *Inside a Soviet Embassy: Experiences of a Russian Diplomat in Burma*, (Philadelphia: J.B. Lippincott Company, 1962), Chapters 10–11 and 17. Kaznacheev was based in Rangoon from 1957–1959.

10 For the full text of Khrushchev's report on 'The International Position of the USSR', see Proceedings of the 20th Congress of the CPSU (14 February–25 February 1956, *SWB/SU/16* February 1956), Supplement No. 1, p. 3–24.

11 Hoang Van Hoan, *A Drop in the Ocean*, (Beijing: Foreign Languages Press, 1988), p. 324.

12 Hoang Van Hoan, *op. cit.*, p. 324; Guo Ming (ed.), *Zhongyue Guanxi Yanbian Shishi Nian*, (Guangxi Renmin Chubanshe, 1992), p. 65.

13 Author's correspondence with Han Suyin: Private conversation between Wang Bingnan and Han Suyin. Wang was the Chinese ambassador to Poland from April 1955 to 1964 and also the Chinese representative at the Sino-US ambassadorial talks from 1955 till 1964.

14 Han Suyin, *Eldest Son: Zhou Enlai and the Making of Modern China, 1898–1976*, (London: Jonathan Cape, 1994), p. 260. The Chinese version of this book was published in the PRC as *Zhou Enlai Yu Ta De Shiji 1898–1998*, (Beijing: Zhongyang Wenxian Chubanshe, 1992).

15 See *CUSSDCF*: 751 G. 00/2–2856, 3498, 28 February 1956, from Saigon to State Department (Secret); *CUSSDCF*: 751 G. 00/4–1656, 334, 16 April 1956, from Saigon to State Department: Country Team evaluation of Vietminh subversive capability in Free Vietnam and the government's ability to counter this continued threat to its stability (Secret); The weakness of the Vietnamese communist forces in the South during this period is confirmed by Le Duan in '*Duong Loi Cach Mang Mien Nam*'. For the full text, see *Race Document Number 1002*.

16 *CUSSDCF*: 751 G. 00/3–1556, 302, 15 March 1956, from Saigon to Foreign Office.

17 For an account of the impact of Diem's 'denounce the communists' campaign on the communists in South Vietnam, see 'How Armed Struggle began in South Vietnam' in *Vietnam Courier*, Number 22, March 1974.

18 United States Department of State '*Working Paper on North Vietnam's Role in the War in South Vietnam*' (27 May 1968), Appendices, Item 19 (Translation of a document found on the person of a political officer with communist forces in Zone 9 of the Western Inter-zone on 27 November 1956), Item 31 (An intelligence report from an agent of the GVN who had contact with Vietnamese Communist Party members in Saigon area in 1956) and Item 204 (Document purportedly issued probably in late spring 1956 by Lao Dong Party Central Committee for guidance of senior cadres in GVN zone).

19 See United States Department of State '*Working Paper on North Vietnam's Role in the South*' (27 May 1968), Appendices, Items 19, 31 and 204.

20 United States Department of State *'Working Paper on the North Vietnam's Role in the War in South Vietnam'* (27 May 1968), Appendices, Item 31.

21 *Voice of Vietnam*, 27 April 1956, SWB/FE/557, p. 58; *Ho Chi Minh: Selected Works*, Volume IV, (Hanoi: Foreign Languages Publishing House, 1962), p. 153–156.

22 *Vietnam: The Anti-US Resistance War for National Salvation 1954–1975: Military Events*, (JPRS 80968, 3 June 1982), p. 16–17.

23 *Hanoi Home Service*, 17 August 1956, SWB/FE/589, p. 41–42.

24 *LSQDNDVN*, p. 77; *Vietnam: The Anti-US Resistance War for National Salvation 1954–1975: Military Events*, (JPRS 80968, 3 June 1982), p. 16–17; 'A Party History' (JPRS 75579), Translations on North Vietnam, Number 2185 cited in William J. Duiker, *The Communist Road to Power*, (Colorado: Westview Press, 1981), p. 359, ftn.17; Cao Van Luong, *Lich Su Cach Mang Mien Nam Vietnam: Giai Doan 1954–1960*, (Hanoi: Nha Xuat Ban Khoa Hoc Xa Hoi, 1991), p. 88.

25 *LSQDNDVN*, p. 36; *Ho Chi Minh: Selected Works*, Volume IV, (Hanoi: Foreign Languages Publishing House, 1962), p. 157–161.

26 *LSQDNDVN*, p. 77–78.

27 Janos Radvanyi, *Delusion and Reality: Hoaxes and Diplomatic One-Upmanship in Vietnam*, (Indiana: Gateway Publishers, 1978), p. 24.

28 *LSQDNDVN*, p. 14.

29 United States Department of State *'Working Paper on the North Vietnam's Role in the War in South Vietnam'* (27 May 1968), Appendices, Item 301: *CRIMP Document*, p. 2. The *CRIMP Document* is believed to be a notebook of a high level political cadre written some time around 1963, recording his impressions of communist policies during the early years of the revolutionary struggle against Diem. Allied forces captured it in early January 1966 during *Operation CRIMP* north of Saigon.

30 *LSQDNDVN*, p. 78; Cao Van Luong, *Lich Su Cach Mang Mien Nam Vietnam: Giai Doan 1954–1960*, (Hanoi: Nha Xuat Ban Khoa Hoc Xa Hoi, 1991), p. 89. According to Cao, Le Duan's thesis was completed by August 1956. The original text is catalogued as Number 1002 in the Race Collection deposited in the Centre for Research Libraries. A summary of the thesis can be found in Jeffrey Race, *War Comes to Long An: Revolutionary Conflict in a Vietnamese Province*, (Berkeley: University of California Press, 1973), p. 75–81; Carlyle A. Thayer, *War by Other Means: National Liberation and Revolution in Vietnam, 1954–60*, (Sydney: Allen and Unwin, 1989), p. 106–109; Gareth Porter, *Vietnam: The Definitive Documentation of Human Decisions*, Volume II, (London: Heyden and Son Limited, 1979), p. 52–53.

31 Vo Tran Nha (chu bien), *Lich Su Dong Thap Muoi*, (Hanoi: Nha Xuat Ban Thanh Pho Ho Chi Minh, 1993), p. 190.

32 'A Party Account of the Situation in the Nam Bo region of South Vietnam from 1954–1960' (undated document captured by US forces in Phuoc Long

Province in April 1969) cited in William J. Duiker, *The Communist Road to Power in Vietnam*, (Colorado: Westview Press, 1981), p. 180.

33 *Duong Loi Cach Mang Mien Nam* (Race Document Number 1002).

34 Tran Van Tra, *Nhung Chang Duong Lich Su Cua B2 Thanh Dong, Tap 1- Hoa Binh Hay Chien Tranh*, (Hanoi: Nha Xuat Ban Quan Doi Nhan Dan, 1992), p. 153.

35 See Carlyle A. Thayer, *op.cit.*, p. 100–111; Thayer's source for this plenary session is an article entitled, 'Tang Cuong Doan Ket, Nang Cao Tinh To Chuc Va Boi Duong Chi Khi Dau Trong Toan Dang' in *Hoc Tap*, November–December 1956, Number 11; also see *SWB/FE/ Economic Supplement*, Number 250 for some details of the economic issues discussed at the session.

36 For the 6th session of the DRV National Assembly, see *SWB/FE/629*, p. 21; *SWB/FE/633*, p. 24–26.

37 *Vietnam: The Anti-US Resistance War for National Salvation 1954–1975: Military Events*, (JPRS 80968, 3 June 1982), p. 20; Tran Van Tra, *Nhung Chang Duong Lich Su Cua B2 Thanh Dong, Tap I – Hoa Binh Hay Chien Tranh*, (Hanoi: Nha Xuat Ban Quan Doi Nhan Dan, 1992), p. 153; 'Tu Nghi quyet lich su den Duong Ho Chi Minh' in *Su Kien Va Nhan Chang*, Number 4 (17 January 1994), p. 4.

38 Tran Van Tra, *Nhung Chang Duong Lich Su Cua B2 Thanh Dong, Tap I – Hoa Binh Hay Chien Tranh*, (Hanoi: Nha Xuat Ban Quan Doi Nhan Dan, 1992), p. 153.

39 Hoang Van Hoan, *op.cit.*, p. 107; also Tran Van Tra, *op.cit.*, p. 152; *Black Paper: Facts and Evidences of the Acts of Aggression and Annexation of Vietnam against Kampuchea* (Department of Press and Information of the Ministry of Foreign Affairs of Democratic Kampuchea, September 1978) noted that in 1957 (no date given), Le Duan was in transit through Kampuchea.

40 Hoang Van Hoan, *A Drop in the Ocean*, (Beijing: Foreign Languages Press, 1988), p. 307.

41 Thanh Tin, *Hoa Xuyen Tuyet (Hoi Ky)*, (California: Saigon Press, 1991), p. 139–140. A slightly different account was that Ho was afraid that the charisma of Giap as the Hero of Dien Bien Phu would outshine his own, and therefore he listened to other voices especially that of Le Duc Tho.

42 Hoang Van Hoan, *A Drop in the Ocean*, (Beijing: Foreign Languages Press, 1988), p. 326.

43 Vo Nguyen Giap, 'Arm the Revolutionary Masses and Build the People's Army' in *Vietnam Documents and Research Notes*, Document 106, Part II, June 1972.

44 Hoang Van Hoan, *op. cit.*, p. 38–39; *Vietnam: The Anti-US Resistance War for National Salvation 1954–1975: Military Events* (JPRS 80968, 3 June 1982), p. 21–22.

45 Vo Nguyen Giap, *op. cit.*
46 *LSQDNDVN*, p. 38–44.
47 *Ho Chi Minh: Toan Tap,Tap 7 (July 1954-December 1957)*, (Hanoi: Nha Xuat Ban Su That, 1987), p. 674–677; *Ho Chi Minh: Selected Works*, Volume IV, (Hanoi: Foreign Languages Publishing House, 1962), p. 231–234.
48 *Ho Chi Minh: Toan Tap,Tap 7 (July 1954-December 1957)*, (Hanoi: Nha Xuat Ban Su That, 1987), p. 710–712.
49 *LSQDNDVN*, p. 60–61.
50 VNA, 2 September 1957, *SWB/FE/696*, p. 55–58; *Ho Chi Minh: Selected Works*, Volume IV, (Hanoi: Foreign Languages Publishing House, 1962), p. 238–247.
51 'How Armed Struggle Began in South Vietnam' in *Vietnam Courier*, Number 22, March 1974, p. 19–24.
52 VNA, 29 April 1958, *SWB/FE/764*, p. 27–28.
53 For the full text of the 1957 Moscow Declaration, see G.F.Hudson, et al.(documented and analysed), *The Sino-Soviet Dispute*, (China Quarterly, 1961), p. 46–56; *SWB/SU/Supplement*, 25 November 1957 contains the full texts of the 12-Party Declaration and the 64-Party Peace Manifesto.
54 *LSQDNDVN*, p. 49.
55 *LSQDNDVN*, p. 85–86.
56 *Hanoi Home Service*, 17 January 1958, *SWB/FE/735*, p. 33–34.
57 *LSQDNDVN*, p. 50–51.
58 *Hanoi Home Service*, 20 March 1958, *SWB/FE/755*, p. 32–35; VNA, 26 March 1958, *SWB/FE/754*, p. 32–35.
59 For details of the domestic policies of the Diem regime from January 1957-December 1958, see Carlyle A. Thayer, *War by Other Means: National Liberation and Revolution in Vietnam 1954–60*, (Sydney: Allen and Unwin, 1989), Chapter 6.
60 Guo Ming (ed.), *Zhongyue Guanxi Yanbian Sishi Nian*, (Guangxi Renmin Chubanshe, 1992), p. 66.
61 Hoang Van Hoan, 'Distortion of Facts about the Militant Friendship between Vietnam and China is Impermissible' in *Beijing Review*, 7 December 1979, Number 49, p. 15.
62 Zhang Xiaoming, 'Communist Powers Divided: China, the Soviet Union, and the Vietnam War' in Lloyd C. Gardner and Ted Gittinger (ed.), *International Perspectives on Vietnam*, (College Station: Texas A&M University Press), p. 82.
63 'How Armed Struggle Began in South Vietnam' in *Vietnam Courier*, Number 22, March 1974, p. 19–24; *Vietnam: The Anti-US Resistance War for National Salvation 1954–1975: Military Events* (JPRS 80968, 3 June 1982), p. 24.
64 'Tu Nghi quyet lich su den Duong Ho Chi Minh' in *Su Kien Va Nhan Chung*, Number 4 (17 January 1994), p. 4 and 32.

65 *LSQDNDVN*, p. 86–87; *Vietnam: The Anti-US Resistance War for National Salvation 1954–1975: Military Events*, (JPRS 80968, 3 June 1982), p. 25–26.

66 *An Outline History of the Vietnam Workers' Party (1930–1975)*, (Hanoi: Foreign Languages Publishing House, 2nd Edition, 1978), p. 81; VNA, 8 December 1958, *SWB/FE/827*, p. 53–54.

67 George Carver, 'The Faceless VietCong' in *Foreign Affairs*, Volume 44, Number 3 (April 1966); United States Department of State '*Working Paper on North Vietnam's Role in the South*' (27 May 1968), Appendices, Item 36: Interrogation of a Vietcong infiltrator captured on 4 April 1964; Janos Radvanyi, *Delusion and Reality: Gambits, Hoaxes and Diplomatic One-Upmanship in Vietnam*, (Indiana: Gateway Editions, 1978), p. 23; Carlyle Thayer's interview with Phan The Ngoc from My Tho province, who was Le Duan's escort officer during part of his trip in late 1958 in Carlyle Thayer, *War by Other Means: National Liberation and Revolution in Vietnam 1954–1960*, (Sydney: Allen and Unwin, 1989), p. 222, ftn 85.

68 *Race Document Number 1025: Tinh Hinh Va Nhiem Vu 59* (no date). The document was seized in July 1959.

69 *NCNA*, 11 January 1959, *SWB/FE/836*, p. 10.

70 *LSQDNDVN*, p. 89.

71 Cao Van Luong, *Lich Su Cach Mang Mien Nam Vietnam: Giai Doan 1954–1960*, (Hanoi: Nha Xuat Ban Khoa Hoc Xa Hoi, 1991), p. 120.

72 'Tu Nghi quyet lich su den Duong Ho Chi Minh' in *Su Kien va Nhan Chung*, Number 4 (17 January 1994), p. 32.

73 Tran Van Tra, *Nhung Chang Duong Lich Su Cua B2 Thanh Dong*, Tap I – *Hoa Binh Hay Chien Tranh*, (Hanoi: Nha Xuat Ban Quan Doi Nhan Dan, 1992), p. 153.

74 United States Department of State '*Working Paper on North Vietnam's Role in the South*' (27 May 1968), Appendices, Item 301: CRIMP Document.

75 *LSQDNDVN*, p. 89–91; Cao Van Luong, *Lich Su Cach Mang Mien Nam Vietnam: Giai Doan 1954–1960*, (Hanoi: Nha Xuat Ban Khoa Hoc Xa Hoi, 1991), p. 120–123.

76 *LSQDNDVN*, p. 98.

77 *LSQDNDVN*, p. 74–76.

78 *LSQDNDVN*, p. 93.

79 FO 371/144404, DV 1041/5, 27 January 1959, from Saigon to Foreign Office.

80 *LSQDNDVN*, p. 91–92.

81 *Vietnam: The Anti-US Resistance War For National Salvation 1954–1975: Military Events*, (JPRS 80968, 3 June 1982). p. 28–29.

82 Janos Radvanyi, *Delusion and Reality: Gambits, Hoaxes and Diplomatic One-Upmanship in Vietnam*, (Indiana: Gateway Edition, 1978), p. 22–24.

83 United States Department of State '*Working Paper on North Vietnam's Role in the South*' (27 May 1968), Appendices, Item 301: CRIMP Document.

84 Janos Radvanyi, *op.cit.*, p. 22–24. According to Truong Nhu Tang, Nguyen Hun Tho was then held in detention in Tuy Hoa in South Vietnam by the Saigon regime

85 'How Armed Struggle Began in South Vietnam' in *Vietnam Courier*, Number 22, March 1974, p. 19–24.

86 See *Fascist Terror in South Vietnam: Law 10–59*, (Hanoi: Foreign Languages Publishing House, 1961); 'How Armed Struggle Began in the South' in *Vietnam Courier*, Number 22, March 1974, p. 19–24.

87 Le Duan, 'We will surely be victorious, the enemy will surely be defeated' (no date given) cited in *LSQDNDVN*, p. 88.

88 Tran Huu Dinh, 'Qua Trinh Hinh Thanh Luc Luong Vu Trang va Can Cu Dia O Nam Bo Trong Nhung Nam 1954–1960' in *Tap Chi Nghien Cuu Lich Su*, 6(277)(XI-XII), 1994, p. 5–6.

89 *VNA*, 13 May 1959, *SWB/FE/27/A3/1–3*.

90 *VNA*, 14 May 1959, *SWB/FE/28/A3/3*.

91 The following account is from *LSQDNDVN*, p. 93–96; *The Ho Chi Minh Trail*, (Hanoi: Foreign Languages Publishing House, 1982); Interview with General Vo Bam in *The Economist*, February 1983, p. 70; Brigadier-General Vo Bam, 'Opening the Trail' in *Vietnam Courier*, Number 5, 1984, p. 9–15; David Chanoff and Doan Van Tai, *Portrait of the Enemy: The Other Side of the War in Vietnam*, (London: I.B. Tauris and Co. Ltd, 1986), p. 147–148; 'Chuyen xoi duong dau tien' in *Su Kien Va Nhan Chung*, Number 4 (17 January 1994), p. 6–7.

92 *Vietnam: The Anti-US Resistance War for National Salvation 1954–1975: Military Events*, (JPRS 80968, 3 June 1982), p. 32.

93 'Tu Nghi Quyet lich su den Duong Ho Chi Minh' in *Su Kien Va Nhan Chung*, Number 4 (17 January 1994), p. 32.

94 United States Department of State 'Working Paper on the North Vietnamese Role in the War in South Vietnam' (27 May 1968), Appendices, Item 73: Interrogation of a Senior Sergeant, 5th Military Region, captured in 1964 in Tra Bong District, Quang Ngai Province.

95 *The Ho Chi Minh Trail*, (Hanoi: Foreign Languages Publishing House, 1982), p. 13.

96 *LSQDNDVN*, p. 93–96.

97 *CUSSDCF*: 751 J. 00/8–1059, 271, 10 August 1959, from Vientiane to State Department (Secret).

98 Paul F. Langer and Joseph J. Zasloff, *North Vietnam and the Pathet Lao: Partners in the Struggle for Laos*, (Cambridge: Harvard University Press, 1970), p. 67–70, 236.

99 Joseph J. Zasloff, *The Pathet Lao: Leadership and Organisation*, (Toronto: Lexington Books, 1973), p. 15.

100 *Vietnam: The Anti-US Resistance War for National Salvation 1954–1975: Military Events*, (JPRS 80968, 3 June 1982), p. 33–34.

101 'Bieu Tuong Cua Tinh Doan Ket Chien Dau Ba Nuoc Dong Duong' in *Su Kien Va Nhan Chung*, Number 4 (17 January 1994), p. 6.
102 Tran Van Tra, *Nhung Chang Duong Lich Su Cua B2 Thanh Dong,Tap I – Hoa Binh Hay Chien Tranh*, (Hanoi: Nha Xuat Ban Quan Doi Nhan Dan, 1992), p. 160–162.
103 The facts of the case: On 1 December 1958, a large number of prisoners died from food poisoning in Phu Loi prison in Thu Dau Mot province, 33 kilometres from Saigon. Hanoi claimed that among the incarcerated population of over a thousand political prisoners, the Saigon authorities had intentionally poisoned the inmates who were either communists or communist-sympathisers. However, according to reports from the British Embassy in Saigon, the deaths from food poisoning were either accidental, the results of negligence on the part of the prison authorities, or both; it was not a massacre and the death toll did not approach the scale alleged by Hanoi
104 For text of Khrushchev's report at the 21st CPSU Congress, see G.F. Hudson, et al.(documented and analysed), *The Sino-Soviet Dispute*, (China Quarterly, 1961), p. 56–57; for a discussion of the report and its implications for Sino-Soviet relations, see Donald S. Zagoria, *The Sino-Soviet Conflict 1956–61*, (New York: Princeton University Press, 1962), Chapter 9.
105 Janos Radvanyi, *op.cit.*, p. 26–27..
106 FO 371/144391, DV 1016/28, 3 August 1959, from Hanoi to Foreign Office.
107 Tracy B. Strong and Helene Keyssar, 'Anna Louise Strong: Three Interviews with Chairman Mao Zedong' in *China Quarterly*, Number 103, September 1985; Han Suyin's interviews with Anna Louise Strong in 1964 and 1969 in Han Suyin, *Wind in the Tower: Mao Tsetung and the Chinese Revolution 1949–1975*, (London: Jonathan Cape, 1976), p. 169–170.
108 *Mao Zedong Sixiang Wansui (Long Live Mao Zedong Thought)(1969)*: Speech to co-operative heads, 30 November 1958, p. 255 and Speech at 16th enlarged session of the Supreme State Conference, 14 April 1959, p. 289.
109 Janos Radvanyi, *op.cit.*, p. 26.
110 Han Suyin, *Zhou Enlai Yu Ta De Shiji 1898–1998*, (Beijing: Zhongyang Wenxian Chubanshe, 1992), p. 363; *Eldest Son: Zhou Enlai and the Making of Modern China, 1898–1976*, (London: Jonathan Cape, 1994), p. 277, see also, Qiang Zhai, China & the Vietnam Wars, 1950–1975 (Chapel Hill: The University of North Carolina Press, 2000) p. 82.
111 VNA, 13 May 1959, SWB/FE/27/A3/1–3.
112 Hoang Van Hoan, *A Drop in the Ocean: Hoang Van Hoan's Revolutionary Reminiscences*, (Beijing: Foreign Languages Press, 1988), p. 324.
113 Wang Xiangen, *Yuanyue Kangmei Shilu*, (Jinan Chubanshe, 1992), p. 18.

2 The Armed Struggle Begins

1 *Vietnam: The Anti-US Resistance War for National Salvation 1954–1975: Military Events*, (JPRS 80968, 3 June 1982), p. 34; 'Cuoc Dong Khoi Tra-Bong (28–8–1959)' in *Nghien Cuu Lich Su*, Number 138, May–June 1971, pp. 19–27.
2 *The Pentagon Papers as published by the New York Times* (London: Routledge and Kegan Paul, 1971), Chapter 2; *Vietnam: The Anti-US Resistance War for National Salvation 1954–1975: Military Events* (JPRS 80968, 3 June 1982), pp. 34–35.
3 Vo Tran Nha (chu bien), *Lich Su Dong Thap Muoi* (Hanoi: Nha Xuat Ban Thanh Pho Ho Chi Minh, 1993), p. 196.
4 Department of State '*Working Paper on North Vietnam's Role in the South*' (27 May 1968), Appendices, Item 301: *The CRIMP Document*.
5 *Vietnam: The Anti-US Resistance War for National Salvation 1954–1975: Military Events*, (JPRS 80968, 3 June 1982), p. 34.
6 Tran Huu Dinh, 'Qua Trinh Hinh Thanh Luc Luong Vu Trang va Can Cu Dia O Nam Bo Trong Nhung Nam 1954–1960' in *Tap Chi Nghien Cuu Lich Su*, 6(277)(XI–XII), 1994, p. 4.
7 Le Duan, 'Under the glorious Party banner, For Independence, Freedom, and Socialism, Let us advance and achieve new victories' (14 February 1970) in *Vietnam Documents and Research Notes*, Document Number 77, April 1970.
8 *LSQDNDVN*, pp. 107–115. For a first-person account, see Mai V. Elliot (transl.), *No Other Road to Take: Memoirs of Mrs. Nguyen Thi Dinh* (Data Paper Number 102, Southeast Asia Programme, Department of Asian Studies, Cornell University, June 1976), pp. 59–77.
9 *LSQDNDVN*, p. 114.
10 'Special Report on Current Internal Security Situation in Vietnam' (7 March 1960), in US Department of Defence, *United States-Vietnam Relations 1945–1967* (Washington, 1971), pp. 1254–1275.
11 Gareth Porter, *Vietnam: The Definitive Documentation of Human Decisions*, Volume II (London: Heyden and Son, Ltd., 1979), pp. 59–70. Porter's source is *Race Document 1044*. An English translation of the same document is in United States Department of State '*Working Paper on the North Vietnamese Role in the War in South Vietnam*' (27 May 1968), Appendices, Item 34.
12 VNA, 27 March 1960, *SWB/FE/296/B/1*.
13 Le Duan, 'Leninism and Vietnam's Revolution' in *On the Socialist Revolution in Vietnam*, Volume I, (Hanoi: Foreign Languages Publishing House, 1965), p. 9–56.
14 FO 371/152746, DV 1016/16, 9 April 1960, from Hanoi to Foreign Office.

15 *Vietnam: The Anti-US Resistance War for National Salvation 1954–1975: Military Events*, (JPRS 80968, 3 June 1982), pp. 40–41.
16 FO 371/152745, DV 1016/5A, 11 January 1960, from Hanoi to Foreign Office.
17 FO 371/152745, DV 1016/13, 8 April 1960, from Hanoi to Foreign Office.
18 VNA, 1 May 1960, SWB/FE/323/A3/2.
19 NCNA, 13 May 1960, SWB/FE/333/A3/1.
20 *Vietnam: The Anti-US Resistance War for National Salvation 1954–1975: Military Events*, (JPRS 80968, 3 June 1982), pp. 44–45.
21 Guo Ming (ed.), *Zhongyue Guanxi Yanbian Sishi Nian* (Guangxi Renmin Chubanshe, 1992), p. 67.
22 Hoang Van Hoan, 'Distortion of Facts about the Militant Friendship between Vietnam and China is Impermissible' in *Beijing Review*, 7 December 1979, Number 49, p. 15.
23 *Zhonghua Renmin Gongheguo dui Wai Guanxi Gaishu* (Shanghai Waiyu Jiaoyu Chubanshe, 1989), p. 89.
24 Huang Guoan, et al., *Zhongyue Guanxi Jianbian*, (Guangxi Renmin Chubanshe, 1986), p. 209; Guo Ming (ed.), *Zhongyue Guanxi Yianbian Shishi Nian* (Guangxi Renmin Chubanshe, 1992), p. 69; Wang Xiangen, *Yuanyue Kangmei Shilu* (Jinan Chubanshe, 1992), p. 18; *Dangdai Zhongguo Waijiao* (Beijing: Zhongguo Shehui Kexue Chubanshe, 1990), p. 159; 'On Hanoi's White Book' in *Beijing Review*, No.47, 23 November 1979; Hoang Van Hoan, 'Distortion of Facts about Militant Friendship between Vietnam and China is Impermissible' in *Beijing Review*, No.49, 7 December 1979.
25 In December 1964, the Americans captured Chinese communist-manufactured weapons and ammunition in Chuong Thien province and subsequently in the four Corp areas of South Vietnam as well. These weapons included the 7.62 semi-automatic carbine, 7.62 light machine gun and 7.62 assault rifle, all manufactured in China in 1962. See *United States Government 'White Paper': Aggression from the North: The Record of North Vietnam's Campaign to Conquer South Vietnam* (US Department of State Publication 7839; Far Eastern Series 130)(Washington D.C., February 1965) reproduced in Gettleman, Marvin E. (ed.), *Vietnam: History, Documents and Opinions on a Major World Crisis* (Middlesex: Penguin Books, 1966), pp. 300–334. There was no report of Chinese weapons captured in the 1961 'White Paper', *A Threat to Peace: North Vietnam's Efforts to Conquer South Vietnam* (US Department of State 7308; Far Eastern Series 110)(Washington D.C., December 1961).
26 Zong Huaiwen (compiled), *Years of Trial, Turmoil and Triumph – China from 1949 to 1988* (Beijing: Foreign Languages Press, 1989), p. 102.
27 VNA, 9 July 1960, SWB/FE/382/A2/2.
28 Hoang Van Hoan, 'Ho Chi Minh's Last Will Was Tampered With' in *Beijing Review*, Number 37, 14 September 1981; Hoang Van Hoan, A

Drop in the Ocean: Hoang Van Hoan's Revolutionary Reminiscences (Beijing: Foreign Languages Press, 1988), p. 314.

29 Nikita Khrushchev, *Khrushchev Remembers* (London: Andre Deutsch, 1971), pp. 444–445.

30 'The Sino-Soviet Dispute and Its Significance' CIA, 1 April 1961, TS #142274-b (Top Secret) cited in Allen S. Whiting, 'The Sino-Soviet Split' in John Fairbank and Roderick MacFarquhar (eds.), *Cambridge History of China*, Volume XIV, (Cambridge: Cambridge University Press, 1989), p. 518.

31 For full text of the 1960 Moscow Declaration, see G.F. Hudson, et.al., *The Sino-Soviet Dispute* (China Quarterly Publication, 1961), pp. 177–205.

32 Brigadier-General Vo Bam, 'Opening the Trail' in *Vietnam Courier*, Number 5, 1984, pp. 9–15.

33 *LSQDNDVN*, p. 152–153; FO 371/159812, DF 1015/2, 1 January 1961, from Washington to Foreign Office; FO 371/159824, DF 1015/243, 10 February 1961, from Vientiane to Foreign Office (Secret).

34 'Memorandum of Conference on 19 January 1961 between President Eisenhower and President-elect Kennedy on the subject of Laos in United States Department of Defence' in US Department of Defence, *United States-Vietnam Relations 1956–1960*, pp. 1360–1364; *The Pentagon Papers*, Volume II, (Senator Gravel Edition) (Boston: Beacon Press, 1971), pp. 635–637.

35 FO 371/159811, DF 1011/1, 23 June 1961, from Vientiane to Foreign Office.

36 Arthur J. Dommen, *Conflict in Laos: The Politics of Neutralisation* (London: Pall Mall Press, 1964), pp. 129–133.

37 FO 371/152328, DF 1015/144, 13 April 1960, from Vientiane to Foreign Office.

38 FO 371/152335, DF 1015/265, 25 May 1960, Record of Conversation between Lord Lansdowne and Prince Khammao, Laotian Ambassador to the United Kingdom; FO 371/152339, DF 1015/321, 30 June 1960, from Foreign Office to Vientiane (Secret).

39 *Vientiane home service in French* (0515h GMT), 9 August 1960, SWB/FE/406/B/1.

40 *Vientiane home service*, 9 August 1960, SWB/FE/407/B/2.

41 FO 371/152353, DF 1015/563, 3 September 1960, from Vientiane to Foreign Office.

42 FO 371/152359, DF 1015/685, 5 October 1960, from Vientiane to Foreign Office.

43 *Vietnam: The Anti-US Resistance War for National Salvation 1954–1975: Military Events*, (JPRS 80968, 3 June 1982), p. 44.

44 FO 371/152379, DF 1015/1057, 27 December 1960, from Hanoi to Foreign Office.

45 *Documents relating to British Involvement in the IndoChina Conflict 1945–1965* (Cmnd. 2834), p. 26.

46 US Department of Defence, *United States-Vietnam Relations 1956–1960*: Memorandum of Conference on 19 January 1961 between President Eisenhower and President-elect Kennedy on the subject of Laos in United States Department of Defence, pp. 1360–1364.

47 FO 371/159846, DF 1015/734, 4 May 1961, from Bangkok to Foreign Office.

48 FO 371/150425, FC 10338/83, 30 November 1960, from Moscow to Foreign Office.

49 *Savannakhet radio*, 8 December 1960, SWB/FE/510/B/2.

50 For details of the battle for Vientiane, see Hugh Toye, *Laos: Buffer State or Battleground* (London: Oxford University Press, 1971), pp. 157–164.

51 FO 371/159811, DF 1011/1, 23 June 1961, from Vientiane to Foreign Office.

52 FO 371/159813, DF 1015/21, 3 January 1961, from Washington to Foreign Office.

53 *Documents relating to British Involvement in the IndoChina Conflict 1945–1965*, (Cmnd. 2834), p. 154–155.

54 *Documents relating to Brtish Involvement in the IndoChina Conflict 1945–1965* (Cmnd. 2834), pp. 156–158; President Eisenhower, was however certain that the Soviet Union did not want the ISCC to go into Laos. See 'Memorandum of Conference on 19 January 1961 between President Eisenhower and President-elect Kennedy on the subject of Laos' in US Department of Defence, *United States-Vietnam Relations 1956–1960*, pp. 1360–1364.

55 VNA, 14 August 1960, SWB/FE/412/B/1–2. The decision to convene the 3rd Party Congress from 5 September 1960 was made at the 18th Plenary Session of the Lao Dong Party Central Committee (end-July 1960)

56 For the full text of Le Duan's political report, see SWB/FE/431/C/2–6.

57 VNA, 9 September 1960, SWB/FE/435/C/5.

58 *LSQDNDVN*, p. 128.

59 VNA, 9 September 1960, SWB/FE/435/C/3–4; for full text of Pham Van Dong' speech, see SWB/FE/439/C/1–3.

60 *LSQDNDVN*, p. 115.

61 Thanh Tin, *Hoa Xuyen Tuyet (Hoi Ky)* (California: Saigon Press, 1991), p. 130. Also, according to Hoang Van Hoan, Le Duan during the early 50s and 60s was inclined to the Chinese view regarding the strategy for unifying Vietnam and only much later was he persuaded to drift with the anti-China tide. See Hoang Van Hoan, *A Drop in the Ocean* (Beijing: Foreign Languages Press, 1988), p. 325.

62 US Department of Defence, *United States-Vietnam Relations: US Perceptions of the Insurgency 1954–1960* (Washington, 1971), pp. 48–52.

63 *LSQDNDVN*, p. 115; 23 September 1940 was when the Bac Son uprising broke out. The first guerrilla unit under the Lao Dong party leadership was also formed on that day.
64 *LSQDNDVN*, pp. 116–117.
65 Cao Van Luong, *Lich Su Cach Mang Mien Nam Vietnam: Giai Doan 1954–1960* (Hanoi: Nha Xuat Ban Khoa Hoc Xa Hoi, 1991), p. 156; *LSQDNDVN*, p. 120; Truong Nhu Tang, *Journal of a Vietcong*, (London: Jonathan Cape, 1986), pp. 79–80. According to Tang, on the morning of 21 December 1960, a special broadcast from Hanoi announcing the formation of the NLF and the good wishes of the Lao Dong Party and North Vietnamese government reached every part of South Vietnam. See also, *VNA* and *NCNA*, 29 January 1961, *SWB/FE/553/A3/2* which cited a Reuter report, and various papers published in Phnom Penh, as the sources for the 'recent' formation of the NLF.
66 Truong Nhu Tang, *Journal of a VietCong* (London: Jonathan Cape, 1986), pp. 70–74; Carlyle A. Thayer, *War by Other Means: National Liberation and Revolution in Vietnam 1954–60* (Sydney: Allen and Unwin, 1989), pp. 187–188, and 227 ftn.28; Robert K. Brigham, Guerrilla Diplomacy: The NLF's Foreign Relations and the Vietnam (Ithaca: Cornell University Press), pp. 10–11.
67 Truong Nhu the Tang, *Journal of a VietCong* (London: Jonathan Cape, 1986), pp. 81–84.
68 *LSQDNDVN*, pp. 116–122. According to the *LSQDNDVN*, on 15 February 1961, the revolutionary armed forces in the South were united under the new name 'Armed Forces for the Liberation of South Vietnam'. On 15 February 1971, the Vietnamese communists celebrated the 10th anniversary of the unification of the South Vietnamese People's Liberation Armed Forces. See *Liberation Press Agency*, 15 February 1971, *SWB/FE/3612/A3/5–9*.
69 *LSQDNDVN*, pp. 120–121.
70 At the behest of the US Department of Defence, Brigadier-General Lansdale visited South Vietnam from 2–14 January 1961. He reported that the Vietnamese communists were much further along towards accomplishing their objective of controlling South Vietnam than he had realised from the reports received in Washington. See United States Department of Defence: *United States-Vietnam Relations 1945–1967* (Book II/IV/A5/Table IV) (Washington, 1971), p. 66–77.
71 *Vietnam: The Anti-US Resistance War for National Salvation 1954–1975: Military Events*, (JPRS 80968, 3 June 1982), pp. 45–46.
72 Le Duan, *Thu Vao Nam* (Hanoi: Nha Xuat Ban Su That, 1985), pp. 31–38.
73 *LSQDNDVN*, pp. 130–135.
74 *LSQDNDVN*, pp. 136–138.

75 Hoang Van Thai is believed to be a close ally of Vo Nguyen Giap. See *Vietnam Documents and Research Notes* (Document Number 114, Part 1, July 1973): VWP-DRV Leadership, 1960–1973, pp. 60–61.
76 *LSQDNDVN*, p. 161.
77 FO 371/160123, DV 1016/22, 2 August 1961, FO minutes.
78 FO 371/166697, DV 1011/2, 15 February 1962, from Saigon to Foreign Office (1961 Annual Report for North Vietnam). According to P.J. Honey, from early March 1961, the North Vietnamese press ceased to refer to Thanh by his military title but as the 'Rural Affairs Chairman of the Party Central Committee. See P.J. Honey, *Communism in North Vietnam: Its Role in the Sino-Soviet Conflict* (Connecticut: Greenwood Press, 1973), p. 97.
79 Marek Thee, *Notes of a Witness: Laos and the Second Indochina War* (New York: Random House, 1973), Chapter 9.
80 Brigadier-General Vo Bam, ' Opening the Trail' in *Vietnam Courier*, Number 5, 1984, pp. 9–15.
81 Hoang Van Hoan, *A Drop in the Ocean* (Beijing: Foreign Languages Press, 1988), p. 382.
82 *VNA*, 27 January 1961, SWB/FE/551/B/4.
83 Brigadier-General Vo Bam, 'Opening the Trail' in *Vietnam Courier*, Number 5, 1984, pp. 9–15.
84 See Roger Hilsman, *To Move A Nation: The Politics of Foreign Policy in the Adminstration of John F. Kennedy* (New York: Doubleday, 1967), p. 133.
85 FO 371/159824, DF 1015/241, 10 February 1961, from Office of the High Commissioner for Australia (London) to Foreign Office.
86 Le Duan, *Thu Vao Nam* (Hanoi: Nha Xuat Ban Su That, 1985), pp. 39–49.
87 *LSQDNDVN*, p. 154.
88 NIE 14.3/53–61, 'Prospects for North and South Vietnam', 16 August 1961 in *US-Vietnam Relations 1945–1967, Book 11*, pp. 245–246 reproduced in Gareth Porter, *Vietnam: The Definitive Documentation of Human Decisions*,Volume II (London: Heyden and Son, 1979).
89 Denis Warner, *Reporting South-East Asia* (London: Angus and Robertson Limited, 1966), p. 171.
90 Gareth Porter, *Vietnam: The Definitive Documentation of Human Decisions*, Volume II (London: Heyden and Son, 1979), pp. 119–123. Porter's source is 'Nghi Quyet Hoi Nhgi R (mo rong). Thang 10/61', Captured Party Document, Combined Documents Exploitation Centre Log Number 1706/KTTL/69.
91 FO 371/166697, DV 1011/1, 2 January 1962, from Saigon to Foreign Office: Annual Report for 1961.
92 *LSQDNDVN*, p. 196; *Vietnam: The Anti-US Resistance War for National Salvation 1954–1975: Military Events*, (JPRS 80968, 3 June 1982), pp. 48–49.

93 *Phnom Penh Radio*, 6 April 1962, *SWB/FE/919/A3/1*.
94 *FO 371/170153*, DV 2231/1, 20 September 1963, Foreign Office Minutes.
95 Marek Thee, *Notes of a Witness: Laos and the Second IndoChinese War* (New York: Random House, 1973), pp. 245–250.
96 Tran Van Tra, *Nhung Chang Duong Lich Su Cua B2 Thanh Dong, Tap I – Hoa Binh Hay Chien Tranh* (Nha Xuat Ban Quan Doi Nhan Dan, 1992), pp. 241–242; *Vietnam: The Anti-US Resistance War for National Salvation 1954–1975: Military Events*, (JPRS 80968, 3 June 1982), pp. 50–51; See *VNA*, 13 April 1962 and *NCNA*, 14 April 1962, *SWB/FE/923/B/3–4*.
97 *Journal de Geneve*, 24 July 1962, cited by Gareth Porter in Jayne Werner and David Hunt (ed.), *The American War in Vietnam* (Southeast Asia Program) (New York: Cornell University Press, 1993), p. 11, ftn.13; Robert K. Brigham, *op. cit.*, pp. 25–27.
98 Arthur Lall, *How Communist China Negotiates* (New York: Columbia University Press, 1968), p. 180.
99 Bernard B. Fall (ed.), *Ho Chi Minh: On Revolution (Selected Writings, 1920–66)* (London: Pall Mall, 1967), pp. 352–358.
100 *NCNA*, 1 August 1962, *SWB/FE/1012/C1/1*.
101 Bernard B. Fall, *op. cit.*, pp. 352–358.
102 Le Duan, *Thu Vao Nam* (Hanoi: Nha Xuat Ban Su That, 1985), pp. 50–67.
103 Bo Quoc Phong Vien Lich Su Quan Su Viet Nam *50 Nam Quan Doi Nhan Dan Viet Nam*, (Hanoi: Nha Xuat Ban Quan Doi Nhan Dan, 1995), pp. 182–183. 1973), pp. 46–53.
104 *Lich Su Quan Doi Nhan Dan Viet Nam, Tap II – Quyen Mot* (Hanoi: Nha Xuat Ban Quan Doi Nhan Dan, 1988), pp. 200–201; Bo Quoc Phong Vien Lich Su Quan Su Viet Nam, *50 Nam Quan Doi Nhan Dan Viet Nam* (Hanoi: Nha Xuat Ban Quan Doi Nhan Dan, 1995), pp. 184–185; *Vietnam: The Anti-US Resistance War for National Salvation, 1954–1975: Military Events*, (JPRS 80968, 3 June 1982), p. 53.
105 Current Intelligence memorandum prepared in the Office of Current Intelligence, Central Intelligence Agency, 11 January 1963, *FRUS*, Vietnam 1961–1963, Volume III, pp. 19–22.
106 See Neil Sheehan, *A Bright and Shining Lie: John Paul Vann and America in Vietnam* (London: Pan Books, 1990), Book 3. This account was constructed using John Vann's after-action report and the captured communist report/document.
107 See Neil Sheehan, 'Vietnamese Ignored U.S. Battle Order', *The Washington Post*, 7 January 1963, reproduced in *Reporting Vietnam, Part One: American Journalism 1959–1969* (New York: The Library of America, 1998), pp. 68–70.
108 *Vietnam: The Anti-US Resistance War for National Salvation, 1954–1975: Military Events*, (JPRS 80968, 3 June 1982), p. 54; Van

Tien Dung, *Ve Cuoc Khang Chien Chong My Cuu Nuoc* (Hanoi: Nha Xuat Ban Chinh Tri Quoc Gia, 1996), p. 26.

109 *Ibid.*, p. 54.; Bo Tong Tham Muu Cuc Nha Truong, *Giao Trinh Lich Su Quan Su, Tap IV- Chien Tranh Va Nghe Thuat Quan Su Viet Nam Thoi Ky Khang Chien Ching My Cuu Nuoc (1954–1975)* (Hanoi: Nha Xuat Ban Quan Doi Nhan Dan, 1997), p. 56.

110 *LSQDNDVN*, pp. 212–213; Ban Chi Dao Tong Ket Chien Tranh Truc Thuoc Bo Chinh Tri, *Tong Ket Cuoc Khang Chien Chong My Cuu Nuoc: Thang Loi Va Bai Hoc* (Luu Hanh Noi Bo) (Hanoi: Nha Xuat Ban Chinh Tri Quoc Gia, 1996), p. 54–55.

111 National Intelligence Estimate–53–63, 17 April 1963, *FRUS*, Vietnam 1961–1963, Volume III, pp. 232–235.

112 *LSQDNDVN*, pp. 161, 164, 170 and 172.

113 *Ibid.*, pp. 189–190; Bo Quoc Phong Vien Lich Su Quan Su Viet Nam, *50 Nam Quan Doi Nhan Dan Viet Nam* (Hanoi: Nha Xuat Ban Quan Doi Nhan Dan, 1995), p. 186.

114 Robert S. McNamara, et.al., *Arguments Without End: In Search of Answers to the Vietnam Tragedy* (New York: Public Affairs, 1999), p. 205.

115 *Ibid.*, p. 225. The *LSQDNDVN* stated that Tra and Do were deputy commander and deputy political commissar respectively whereas in *50 Nam Quan Doi Nhan Dan Viet Nam*, Tra was described as the commander. Tran Do was not mentioned. See pp. 188–189.

116 Mieczyslaw Maneli, 'Vietnam, '63 and now' in *The New York Times*, 27 January 1975 cited in King C. Chen, 'Hanoi's Three Decisions and the Escalation of the Vietnam War' in *Political Science Quarterly*, Volume 90, Number 2, Summer 1975, pp. 239–259.

117 *LSQDNDVN*, pp. 190, 215–216.

118 Central Intelligence Agency Information Report, 2 December 1963, *FRUS*, Vietnam 1961–1963, Volume IV, pp. 647–649.

119 Memorandum from the Chairman of the Central Intelligence Agency's Working Group on Vietnam (Cooper) to the Director of Central Intelligence (McCone), 6 December 1963, *FRUS*, Vietnam 1961–1963, Volume IV, pp. 680–685.

3 The Armed Struggle Intensifies

1 See 'Landmarks in the Party's History' (*Vietnam Courier*, Number 254, 2 February 1970) reprinted in *Vietnam Documents and Research Notes*, Document 76 (Joint United States Public Affairs Office, Saigon), pp. 118–127 and 'The Communist Party of Vietnam: Historic Landmarks' in *Vietnam Courier*, Number 56, January 1977, pp. 15–16.

2 Bo Tong Tham Muu Cuc Nha Truong, *Giao Trinh Lich Su Quan Su* (Hanoi: Nha Xuat Ban Quan Doi Nhan Dan, 1999), p. 252.

3 *LSQDNDVN*, p. 221.

4 'The Communist Party of Vietnam: Historic Landmarks' in *Vietnam Courier*, Number 56, Janaury 1977, pp. 15–16.

5 See 'Forty Years of Party Activity' (Vietnam Courier, Number 254, 2 February 1970) reprinted in *Vietnam Documents and Research Notes*, Document 76 (Joint United States Public Affair Office, Saigon), pp. 64–65; 'The Vietnam Workers' Party's 1963 Decision to Escalate the War in the South' reprinted in *Vietnam Documents and Research Notes*, Number 96.

6 *Vietnam: The Anti-US Resistance War for National Salvation, 1954–1975: Military Events*, (JPRS 80968, 3 June 1982), p. 55–56; *50 Years of Activities of the Communist Party of Vietnam* (Hanoi: Foreign Languages Publishing House, 1980), pp. 156–157.

7 This may be one reason why Giap was not mentioned in the *LSQDNDVN* for this period.

8 Bui Tin, *Following Ho Chi Minh: Memoirs of a North Vietnamese Colonel* (London: Hurst and Company, 1995), pp. 44–46.

9 *LSQDNDVN*, pp. 220–234. Also, see Bo Quoc Phong Vien Lich Su Quan Su Viet Nam, *50 Nam Quan Doi Nhan Dan Viet Nam* (Hanoi: Nha Xuat Ban Quan Doi Nhan Dan, 1995), p. 190.

10 Ban Chi Dao Tong Ket Chien Tranh Truc Thuoc Bo Chin Tri, *Tong Ket Cuoc Khang Chien Chong My Cuu Nuoc Thang Loi Va Bai Hoc* (Luu Han Noi Bo)(Hanoi: Nha Xuat Ban Chinh Tri Quoc Gia, 1996), pp. 56–58.

11 Robert S. McNamara et. al., *Arguments Without End: In Search of Answers to the Vietnam Tragedy* (New York: Public Affairs, 1999), pp. 200–201.

12 *Ibid.*, p. 92.

13 Bui Tin, *op.cit.*, p. 46.

14 *Ibid.*, pp. 49–53.

15 *LSQDNDVN*, p. 164.

16 Memorandum from the Under Secretary of State for Political Affairs' Special Assistant (Jorden) to the Assistant Secretary of State for Far Eastern Affairs (Harriman), 20 March 1963, *FRUS*, Vietnam 1961–1963, Volume III, pp. 165–168.

17 *LSQDNDVN*, pp. 222–234; Bo Tong Tham Muu Cuc Nha Truong, *Giao Trinh Lich Su Quan Su* (Hanoi: Nha Xuat Ban Quan Doi Nhan Dan, 1999), p. 252.

18 Memorandum from the Joint Chiefs of Staff to the Secretary of Defence (McNamara), 2 March 1964, *FRUS*, Vietnam, 1964–1968, Volume I (1964), pp. 110–111.

19 *LSQDNDVN*, pp. 229–230; Bo Quoc Phong Vien Lich Su Quan Su Viet Nam, *50 Nam Quan Doi Nahn Dan Viet Nam*, (Hanoi: Nha Xuat Ban Quan Doi Nhan Dan, 1995), pp. 195–196 and *Hau Phong Chien Tranh Nhan Dan Viet Nam (1945–1975)* (Hanoi: Nha Xuat Ban Quan

Doi Nhan Dan, 1997), p. 151; Bo Tong Tham Muu Cuc Nha Truong, *Gia Trinh Lich Su Quan Su* (Hanoi: Nha Xuat Ban Quan Doi Nhan Dan, 1999), p. 253.

20 Memorandum from the Director of the Bureau of Intelligence and Research (Hilsman) to the Assistant Secretary of State for Far Eastern Affairs (Harriman), 24 September 1962, *FRUS*, Laos Crisis 1961–1963, Volume XXIV, pp. 897–901.

21 Special Report Prepared in the Central Intelligence Agency, 1 November 1963, *FRUS*, Laos Crisis, 1961–1963, Volume XXIV, pp. 1054–1057.

22 *Vietnam: The Anti-US Resistance War for National Salvation, 1954–1975: Military Events*, (JPRS 80968, 3 June 1982), pp. 58–59.

23 Memorandum from the Deputy Assistant Secretary of State for Far Eastern Affairs (Rice) to the Deputy Under Secretary of State for Political Affairs (Johnson), 10 April 1963, *FRUS*, Southeast Asia, 1961–1963, Volume XXIII, pp. 231–233.

24 Lt Gen. Harold G. Moore (Ret.) and Joseph L. Galloway, *We Were Soldiers Once . . . and Young* (Shrewsbury: Airlife Publishing Ltd., 1992), pp. 14–15.

25 Ilya Gaiduk, *The Soviet Union and the Vietnam War* (Chicago: Ivan R. Dee, 1996), pp. 6–11, 256 ftn. 6. Gaiduk's source on the January 1964 meeting is a top-secret memorandum of the Southeast Asia Department of the Soviet Foreign Ministry, 'Soviet Moral and Political Support of and Material Aid to the South Vietnam Patriots' (24 March 1966).

26 Memorandum from the Joint Chiefs of Staff to the Secretary of Defence (McNamara), 2 March 1964, *FRUS*, Vietnam 1964–1968, Vietnam (1964), pp. 110–111.

27 Chen Jian, 'China's Involvement in the Vietnam War, 1964–69' in *China Quarterly*, Number 142, June 1995, pp. 356–386.

28 This comes across very clearly in many of the correspondences and memorandums in *FRUS*, Laos Crisis, 1961–1963, Volume XXIV, and Laos, 1964 –1968, Volume XXVIII.

29 Nguyen Khac Vien, *Vietnam: A Long History* (Hanoi: The Gioi Publishers, 1993), p. 310.

30 Guo Ming (ed.), *Zhongyue Guanxi Yanbian Shishi Nian* (Guangxi: Guangxi Renmin Chubanshe, 1992), p. 101.

31 For details of the in-fighting within the Hanoi leadership, see Bui Tin, *op.cit.*, pp. 44–46, 54–56.

32 Bui Tin, *op.cit.*, p. 65. Ho began writing his will in May 1965.

33 'Broadcast Reportage and Ho Chi Minh Report to DRV Special Conference' in *Vietnam Documents and Research Notes* (Joint United States Public Affairs Office, Saigon), Number 98, September 1971; *50 Years of Activities of the Communist Party of Vietnam* (Hanoi: Foreign

Languages Publishing House, 1980), pp. 157–158; *Vietnam:The Anti-US Resistance War for National Salvation, 1954–1975* (JPRS 80968, 3 June 1982), pp. 57–58; *LSQDNDVN*, pp. 227–229; Bo Quoc Phong Vien Lich Su Quan Su Viet Nam, *50 Nam Quan Doi Nhan Dan Viet Nam* (Hanoi: Nha Xuat Ban Quan Doi Nhan Dan, 1995), p. 194 and *Hau Phong Chien Tranh Nhan Dan Viet Nam (1945–1975)* (Hanoi: Nha Xuat Ban Quan Doi Nhan Dan , 1997), pp. 150–151.

34 George C. Herring (ed.), *The Secret Diplomacy of the Vietnam War: The Negotiating Volumes of the Pentagon Paper* (Austin: University of Texas Press, 1985), p. 8.

35 Robert S. McNamara, et.al., *Arguments Without End: In Search of Answers to the Vietnam Tragedy* (New York: Public Affairs, 1999), pp. 202–205; Mao Zedong's conversation with Le Duan (13 August 1964, Beijing) in *New Evidence on the Vietnam/IndoChina Wars* (CWIHP).

36 *LSQDNDVN*, p. 236.

37 Gareth Porter, 'Coercive Diplomacy in Vietnam: The Tonkin Gulf Crisis Reconsidered' in Jayner Werner and David Hunt (ed.), *The American War in Vietnam* (Ithaca: Cornell Southeast Asia Program, 1993), pp. 18–20. Porter's information was based on his interviews with Bui Tin, Tran Cong Man and Nguyen Co Thach. None of them could remember the exact date of the meeting. Thach believed that it took place about a week after the Tonkin Gulf incident. See p. 19, ftn. 52.

38 Zhang Xiaoming, 'Communist Powers Divided: China, the Soviet Union, and the Vietnam War' in Lloyd C. Gardner and Ted Gittinger (ed.), *International Perspectives on Vietnam* (College Station:Texas A&M University Press, 2000), p. 84.

39 Ilya Gaiduk, *The Soviet Union and the Vietnam War* (Chicago: Ivan R. Dee, 1996), p. xv

40 Ilya Gaiduk, *op. cit.*, pp. 12–21, 258, ftn. 35–38. Gaiduk cites a combination of American and Soviet documents.

41 *LSQDNDVN*, pp. 243–244; Bo Quoc Phong Vien Lich Su Quan Su Viet Nam, *50 Nam Quan Doi Nhan Dan Viet Nam*, (Hanoi: Nha Xuat Ban Quan Doi Nhan Dan, 1995), pp. 198–199; Bui Tin, *op.cit.*, p. 61.

42 Conversation between Mao Zedong and Pham Van Dong, Hoang Van Hoan in Beijing, 5 October 1964 in Odd Arne Westad et.al. (ed.), *77 Conversations Between Chinese and Foreign Leaders on the Wars in IndoChina, 1964–1977*, Working Paper Number 22, May 1998 (CWIHP), p. 74–77.

43 *LSQDNDVN*, p. 244; US Department of State, *Working Paper on the North Vietnamese Role in the War in South Vietnam* (May 1968).

44 The letter is cited in Ilya Gaiduk, 'Turnabout? The Soviet Policy Dilemma in the Vietnamese Conflict' in Lloyd C. Gardner and Ted

Gittinger (ed.), *Vietnam: The Early Decisions* (Austin: University of Texas Press, 1997), pp. 217–218, 219, ftn. 18.

45 *LSQDNDVN*, p. 245.

46 Also known as the Eastern Nam Bo region. Forces and supplies destined for the Saigon area go through the Ho Chi Minh Trail into this region.

47 The southern part of Central Vietnam.

48 *LSQDNDVN*, p. 247–252.

49 Binh Gia is located in Duc Thanh Military Zone, forty miles southeast of Saigon.

50 *LSQDNDVN*, pp. 245–252.

51 Le Duan, *Thu Vao Nam* (Hanoi: Nha Xuat Ban Su That, 1985), pp. 68–93.

52 See *77 Conversations Between Chinese and Foreign Leaders on the Wars in IndoChina, 1964–1977*, Working Paper 22, May 1998 (CWIHP), p. 75, ftn.118.

53 Anatoly Dobrynin, *In Confidence* (New York: Times Books, 1995), p. 140.

54 Robert S.McNamara, *op.cit.*, pp. 205–212.

55 Qiang Zhai, *China and the Vietnam Wars, 1950–1975* (Chapel Hill: University of North Carolina Press, 2000), p. 167.

56 Ilya Gaiduk, *op.cit.*, p. 38.

57 Robert S. McNamara, *op. cit.*, pp. 231–232.

58 The 11th Plenary Session was listed as one of the landmarks in the Lao Dong Party's history cited in *Vietnam Courier*, Number 254, 2 February 1970. It was replaced by the 12th Plenary Session, which was held at the end of 1965, in a new list of landmarks published in *Vietnam Courier*, Number 56, January 1977.

59 Covering the northern half of South Vietnam, Military Region V coordinated the activities in Tay Nguyen and the lowland region from Danang to Nha Trang.

60 *LSQDNDVN*, p. 253.

61 For details especially of the thinking of the Vietnamese communist leadership on the Four-Points and negotiations, see Robert S. McNamara, *Arguments Without End: In Search of Answers to the Vietnam Tragedy* (New York: Public Affairs), Chapter 6.

62 Le Duan, *Letters to the South* (Hanoi: Foreign Languages Publishing House, 1986), pp. 19–45.

63 *LSQDNDVN*, pp. 259–261.

64 *LSQDNDVN*, pp. 261–262.

65 See David Chanoff and Doan Van Toai, *Portrait of the Enemy* (London: I.B.Tauris, 1986), pp. 158–161.

66 *LSQDNDVN*, p. 263.

67 Memorandum from the President's Special Assistant for National Security Affairs (Bundy) to President Johnson, Washington, 30 June

1965 in *FRUS*, Volume III (Vietnam June–December 1965), pp. 79–85.

68 Memorandum prepared in the Central Intelligence Agency, Washington, 30 June 1965 in *FRUS*, Volume III (Vietnam June–December 1965), pp. 86–89.

69 Message from Westmoreland to Sharp, 7 June 1965 and 14 June 1965 reproduced in Gareth Porter (ed.), *Vietnam: The Definitive Documentation of Human Decisions, Volume 2* (New York: Earl M. Coleman, 1979), pp. 372–375, 378–382.

70 North Vietnam's panhandle region.

71 The *LSQDNDVN* did not name the country but it was most likely the Soviet Union.

72 *LSQDNDVN*, p. 327.

73 Ilya Gaidauk, *op.cit.*, p. 60.

74 US Intelligence Memorandum, 26 July 1965 cited by Ilya Gaiduk, *ibid.*, p. 264, ftn. 12.

75 *LSQDNDVN*, pp. 297–298.

76 *LSQDNDVN*, p. 301.

77 Mao Zedong and Ho Chi Minh, Changsha (Hunan), 16 May 1965 in *77 Conversations Between Chinese and Foreign Leaders on the Wars in IndoChina, 1964–1977*, Working Paper 22, May 1998 (CWIHP), pp. 86–87.

78 Zhang Xiaoming, 'Communist Powers Divided: China, the Soviet Union, and the Vietnam War' in Lloyd C. Gardner and Ted Gittinger (ed.), *International Perspectives on Vietnam* (College Station: Texas A&M University Press, 2000), p. 87.

79 *LSQDNDVN*, p. 299.

80 Encompassing the southern tip of South Vietnam.

81 The region encompassed the southwest of Saigon, from the Cambodian border to the South China Sea.

82 *LSQDNDVN*, pp. 276–279.

83 *LSQDNDVN*, p. 276.

84 Le Duan, *Letters to the South* (Hanoi: Foreign Languages Publishing House, 1986), pp. 46–92.

85 *LSQDNDVN*, pp. 304–306.

86 *LSQDNDVN*, pp. 306–307, 312–313.

87 *LSQDNDVN*, pp. 310–311.

88 *LSQDNDVN*, pp. 311–312.

89 See George C. Herring, *The Secret Diplomacy of the Vietnam War: The Negotiating Volumes of the Pentagon Papers* (Austin: University of Texas Press, 1983); James G. Hershberg (with the assistance of L.W. Gluchowski), 'Who Murdered 'Marigold'? – New Evidence on the Mysterious Failure of Poland's Secret Initiative to Start US-North Vietnamese Peace Talks, 1966' (Woodrow Wilson International Center

for Scholars: Cold War International History Project, Working Paper Number 27).

90 For the Vietnamese communist position, see Robert S. McNamara, *op.cit.*, Chapter 6; For the Chinese position, see Zhou Enlai, Chen Yi and Nguyen Duy Trinh, Beijing, 18 December 1965 in *77 Conversations Between Chinese and Foreign Leaders on the Wars in IndoChina, 1964–1977*, pp. 91–92; Qiang Zhai, 'Beijing's Position on the Vietnam Peace Talks, 1965–1968: New Evidence from Chinese Sources', Working Paper Number 18, May 1997 (CWIHP).

91 Anatoly Dobrynin, *op.cit.*, p. 148.

92 Letter from Le Duan to Commander-in-Chief of the People's Liberation Armed Forces Nguyen Chi Thanh, March 1966 (extract) reproduced in Gareth Porter (ed.), *Vietnam: The Definitive Documentation of Human Decisions, Volume 2* (New York: Earl M. Coleman, 1979), p. 416.

93 Summary of a speech by Chairman of the Lao Dong Party Reunification Department, General Nguyen Can Vinh at a COSVN Congress, April 1966 in Gareth Porter (ed.), *Vietnam: The Definitive Documentation of Human Decisions, Volume 2* (New York: Earl M. Coleman, 1979), pp. 418–420.

94 *LSQDNDVN*, pp. 339–341, 346–347.

95 Huang Zheng, *Ho Zhiming Yu Zhongguo* (Beijing, 1987), pp. 172–173.

96 Jean Sainteny, *Ho Chi Minh and His Vietnam: A Personal Memoir* (Chicago: Cowles Book Company, 1972), pp. 161–166.

97 *LSQDNDVN*, p. 327.

98 *LSQDNDVN*, pp. 330–331.

99 *LSQDNDVN*, pp. 320–321.

100 *LSQDNDVN*, p. 348.

101 *The Diary of Ten High-Ranking V.C. Cadres* (date of publication unknown), pp. 20–21.

4 Breaking the Stalemate

1 *Vietnam: The Anti- US Resistance War for National Salvation, 1954–1975: Military Events*, (JPRS 80968, 3 June 1982), pp. 93–94; Ban Chi Dao Tong Ket Chien Tranh Truc Thuoc Bo Chinh Tri, *Tong Ket Cuoc Khang Chien Chong My Cuu Nuoc Thang Loi Va Bai Hoc* (Hanoi: Bo Nha Xuat Ban Chinh Tri Quoc Gia, 1996), p. 76.

2 Luu Van Loi, *50 Years of Vietnamese Diplomacy 1945–1995, Volume 1: 1945–1975* (Hanoi: The Gioi Publishers, 2000), pp. 177, 179.

3 Nguyen Khac Vien, *Vietnam: A Long History* (Hanoi 1993), pp. 317–318.

4 Lester A. Sobel (ed.), *South Vietnam: US-Communist Confrontation in Southeast Asia, Volume 2, 1996–67* (New York, 1973), pp. 322–323.
5 Political Letter of the Soviet Embassy in the DRV, 'The Soviet-Vietnamese Talks of April 1967 and the Following Policy of the WPV Toward Settlement of the Vietnamese Problem', August 1967, cited in Ilya V. Gaiduk, *The Soviet Union and the Vietnam War* (Chicago, 1996), pp. 110–111, 272.
6 *LSQDNDVN*, p. 128.
7 Ban Ngien Cuu Lich Su Dang Thanh Pho Ho Chi Minh, 50 *Nam Dau Tanh Kien Cuong Cua Dang Bo Va Nhan Dan Tbanh Pho* (Nha Xuat Ban Thanh Pho Ho Chi Minh 1981), pp. 172–173.
8 *LSQDNDVN*, p. 370; Pham Van Son et al., *The Viet Cong 'Tet' Offensive* (1968) (translated from the Vietnamese original by JS/JGS Translation Board, Saigon, no date, but probably 1969), pp. 44–51; translated excerpts from 1988 article by Senior General Van Tien Dung in Ronnie Ford, *Tet 1968: Understanding the Surprise* (London: Frank Cass, 1995), Annex 3, p. 206
9 Bui Tin, *Following Ho Chi Minh: Memoirs of a North Vietnamese Colonel* (London, 1995), p. 61.
10 *LSQDNDVN, op. cit.*, p. 371.
11 *Ibid.*, p. 380; Bui Tin, *op. cit.*, p. 62.
12 *LSQDNDVN, op. cit.*, p. 380.
13 *Ibid.*, p. 380.
14 See, for example, George Boudarel's introduction in Vo Nguyen Giap, *Banner of People's War, the Party's Military Line* (New York 1970), where he argued that the divergent points of view of Thanh and Giap were reconciled in practice.
15 Huang Zheng, *Ho Zhiming Yu Zbongguo* (Beijing 1987), p. 172.
16 *Vietnam: The Anti-US Resistance War for National Salvation, 1954–1975: Military Events* (JPRS 80968, 3 June 1982), p. 94.
17 NCNA, 2 September 1979. Based on interview with medical workers who had treated Ho Chi Minh between 1967 and 1968, cited by Ralph Smith, 'Ho Chi Minh's Last Decade, 1960–69: Between Moscow and Beijing', *IndoChina Report*, 27 (April/June 1991).
18 Translated excerpt from 1988 article by Senior General Van Tien Dung in Ronnie Ford, *op. cit.*, Annex 3, p. 206.
19 George C Herring (ed.), *The Secret Diplomacy of the Vietnam War: The Negotiating Volumes of the Pentagon Papers* (Austin, TX 1985), pp. 721–722.
20 David Schoenbrun in Vo Nguyen Giap, *Big Victory, Great Task* (London, 1968), p. xii.
21 Judy Stowe, '"Revisionism" in Vietnam' in *Communisme*, Number 65–66, 2001 (Paris: L'Age D'Homme). I thank the author for providing me a translated version in English.

22 Huang Zheng, *op. cit.*, p. 174.
23 There were many communist documents captured by the South Vietnamese army (ARVN) in the second half of 1967, revealing that preparation was going on for some major military offensive. See Thomas L. Cubbage III, 'Intelligence and the Tet Offensive: The South Vietnamese View of the Threat' in Elizabeth Jane Errington and B.J.C. McKercher (eds), *The Vietnam War as History* (New York, 1990).
24 *Ibid.*, p. 371.
25 *LSQDNDVN*, *op. cit.*, p. 371.
26 *Ibid.*, pp. 374–380, 381–384 are the source of the next three paragraphs.
27 *50 Nam Dau Tranh Kien Cuong*, *op. cit.*, p. 173.
28 Vo Nguyen Giap, *op. cit.*
29 Zhong Huaiwen (compiled), *Years of Trial , Turmoil and Triumph – and China from 1949 to 1988* (Beijing 1989), p. 144. For a brief account of what was happening in China during this time, see pp. 138–145.
30 See particularly, Chen Jian, 'China's involvement in the Vietnam War, 1964–1969' in *The China Quarterly*, p. 142 (June 1995).
31 Jon M. Van Dyke, *North Vietnam's Strategy for Survival* (Palo Alto, 1972), pp. 218, 221.
32 Huang Zheng, *op. cit.*, p. 176; Hoang Van Hoan in *Beijing Review*, 30 November 1979, p. 15. Hoan, however, placed this episode in 1968.
33 Guo Ming et al., *Xiandai Zhongyue Guanxi Ziliao Xuanbian, Volume 2* (Beijing 1986), pp. 446–449, 695. No details are available on this meeting with Mao.
34 *Pravda*, 24 September 1967, cited in Ilya V. Gaiduk, *op. cit.*, p. 139.
35 SNIE 14.3.–67, 'Capabilities of the Vietnamese Communists for Fighting in South Vietnam', 13 November 1967, in Gareth Porter (ed.), *Vietnam: The Definitive Documentation of Human Decisions, Volume 2* (New York: Earl M. Coleman, 1979) p. 481–482.
36 *LSQDNDVN*, p. 385.
37 Gareth Porter, *op. cit.*, pp. 477–478.
38 *Vietnam: The Anti- US Resistance War for National Salvation, 1954–1975: Military Events*, (JPRS 80968, 3 June 1982), p. 100.
39 *Tong Ket Cuoc Khang Chien Chong My Cuu Nuoc: Thang Loi Va Bai Hoc* (Hanoi: Nha Xuat Ban Chinh Tri Quoc Gia, 1996), pp. 73–74. This report is supposedly for internal circulation only.
40 Van Tien Dung, *Ve Cuoc Khang Chien Chong My Cuu Nuoc* (Hanoi: Nha Xuat Ban Chinh Tri Quoc Gia, 1996), p. 207.
41 *LSQDNDVN*, p. 389.
42 *Lich Su Nghe Thuat Chien Dich Viet Nam Trong 30 Nam Chong Phap, Chong My, 1945–1975* (Hanoi: Nha Xuat Ban Quan Doi Nhan Dan, 1991), p. 339.
43 *LSQDNDVN*, p. 388.

44 Besides the *LSQDNDVN*, also see Van Tien Dung, *op. cit.*, p. 204.

45 He was then Chief of Staff of the VPA.

46 Van Tien Dung, *Buoc Ngoat Lon cua Cuoc Khang Chien Chong My* (Hanoi: Nha Xuat Ban Su That, 1989), p. 196.

47 *Hanoi Home Service*, 1 January 1968, SWB/FE/2658/A3/6–7.

48 VNA, 1 January 1968, SWB/FE/2673/i.

49 VNA, 18 January 1968, SWB/FE/2674/A3/1.

50 Memorandum of Conversation between S.I Divilkovskii, First Secretary of the Soviet Embassy and Truong Cong Dong on 8 January 1968 cited in Ilya Gaiduk, *The Soviet Union and the Vietnam War* (Chicago: Ivan R. Dee, 1996), pp. 141–142, 276, ftn. 20.

51 *Vietnam: The Anti-US Resistance War for National Salvation 1954–1975: Military Events*, (JPRS 80968, 3 June 1982), pp. 100–1; *LSQDNDVN*, pp. 385–386; *Tong Ket Cuoc Khang*, *op. cit*, pp. 72–74.

52 Le Duan, *Letters to the South* (Hanoi, 1986), pp. 93–100.

53 VNA, 18 January 1968, SWB/FE/2674/A3/.

54 Ralph Smith, 'The Vietnam War 'from both sides': The Crisis of 1967–68 in Perspective' (unpublished paper, March 1998). Smith cites Tran Bach Dang who commanded part of the forces that attacked Saigon on Tet, and Pham Chanh Truc, then Secretary of the Saigon (communist) Youth League. I am grateful to Professor Smith for giving me a copy of his yet unpublished paper.

55 Jack Shulimson et. al, *U.S. Marines in Vietnam: The Defining Year 1968* (Washington DC: US Government Printing Office, 1997), p. 18.

56 *LSQDNDVN*, p. 388.

57 William C. Westmoreland, *op. cit.*, p. 336. Also see, Robert Pisor, *The End of the Line: The Siege of Khe Sanh* (New York: Ballantine Books, 1982), p. 3; Jack Shulimson et. al., *U.S. Marines in Vietnam: The Defining Year 1968* (Washington D.C.: History and Museums Division Headquarters, U.S. Marine Corps, 1997), Chapter 1.

58 *LSQDNDVN*, p. 388.

59 Bernard C. Nalty, *Air Power and the Fight for Khe Sanh* (Washington D.C.: United States Air Force, Office of Air Force History, 1973), p. 14.

60 General Tran Van Quang at the 1986 Vietnamese Defence Ministry Conference on Tet 1968, cited in Ngo Vinh Long, 'The Tet Offensive and Its Aftermath' in Jayne Werner and David Hunt (ed.), *The American War in Vietnam* (Ithaca: Cornell University, 1993), p. 32.

61 Tran Van Tra, 'Tet: The 1968 General Offensive and General Uprising' in Jayne S. Werner and Luu Doan Huynh (ed.), *The Vietnam War: Vietnamese and American Perspectives* (Armonk: M.E. Sharpe, 1993), p. 42.

62 *Ibid.*, p. 42.

63 David Chanoff and Doan Van Tai, *Portrait of the Enemy* (London: I.B. Tauris, 1987), pp. 156–157.

64 *LSQDNDVN*, pp. 384–385.
65 General Tran Van Quang at the 1986 Vietnamese Defence Ministry Conference on Tet 1968 cited in Ngo Vinh Long, 'The Tet Offensive and Its Aftermath' in Jayne Werner and David Hunt (ed.), *The American War in Vietnam* (Ithaca: Cornell University, 1993), p. 32.
66 Van Tien Dung, *op. cit.*, pp. 202–203.
67 *LSQDNDVN*, p. 402.
68 Van Tien Dung, *Ve Cuoc Khang Chien Chong My Cuu Nuoc* (Hanoi: Nha Xuat Ban Chinh Tri Quoc Gia, 1996), pp. 207–208.
69 *LSQDNDVN*, pp. 414–416.
70 *Paris Radio*, 22 March 1968, SWB/FE/2739/A3/1.
71 Hoang Van Hoan, *A Drop in the Ocean* (Beijing Foreign Languages Press, 1988), pp. 332–334.
72 Luu Van Loi, *50 Years of Vietnamese Diplomacy 1945–1995 Volume 1: 1945–1975*, (Hanoi: The Gioi Publishers, 2000), pp. 185–188.
73 *VNA*, 4 April 1968, SWB/FE/2739/A3/2–4.
74 *Tokyo Television Service*, 6 April 1968, SWB/FE/2741/A3/6.
75 *VNA*, 8 April 1968, SWB/FE/2743/A3/2.
76 *VNA*, 8 April 1968, SWB/FE/1743/A3/3.
77 Luu Van Loi, *op.cit.*, p. 190.
78 *New Delhi*, 12 May 1968, SWB/FE/2769/A3/9.
79 Luu Van Loi, *op.cit.*, p. 190.
80 *Vietnam: The Anti-US Resistance War for National Salvation, 1954–1975: Military Events*, (JPRS 80968, 3 June 1982), p. 110.
81 Lewis Sorley, *A Better War: The Unexamined Victories and Final Tragedy of America's Last Years in Vietnam* (New York: Harcourt Brace and Company, 1999), pp. 94, 97.
82 Bui Tin, *Following Ho Chi Minh: Memoirs of a North Vietnamese Colonel* (London: Hurst and Company, 1995), p. 62.
83 Interview with Bui Tin in Stephen Young, 'How North Vietnam Won the War in Wall Street Journal, 3 August 1995, cited in Lewis, *A Better War: The Unexamined Victories and Final Tragedy of America's Last Years in Vietnam* (New York: Harcourt Brace and Company, 1999), p. 94.
84 Tran Van Tra cited in Ngo Vinh Long, 'The Tet Offensive and its Aftermath' in Jayne Werner and David Hunt (ed.), *The American War in Vietnam* (Ithaca: Cornell University Southeast Asia Program, 1993), p. 26.
85 Ngo Vinh Long, *op. cit.*, pp. 23–45.
86 Van Tien Dung, *Ve Cuoc Khang Chien Chong My Cuu Nuoc* (Hanoi: Nha Xuat Ban Chinh Tri Quoc Gia, 1996), pp. 278–279.
87 Luu Van Loi, *50 Years of Vietnamese Diplomacy 1945–1995, Volume I: 1945–1975* (Hanoi: The Gioi Publishers, 2000), p. 199.

88 Pham Hong Son, *Nghe Thuat Danh Giac Giu Nuoc Cua Dan Toc Viet Nam* (Hanoi: Nha Xuat Ban Quan Doi Nhan Dan, 1997), pp. 299–301; Bo Quoc Phong Vien Lich Su Quan Su Viet Nam, *Hau Phuong Chien Tranh Nhan Dan Viet Nam (1945–1975)* (Hanoi: Nha Xuat Ban Quan Doi Nhan Dan, 1997), pp. 256–257; Van Tien Dung, *Ve Cuoc Khiang Chien Ching My Cuu Nuoc* (Hanoi: Nha Xuat Ban Chinh Tri Quoc Gia,.1996), pp. 275–278.

89 *LSQDNDVN*, pp. 329–338.

90 COSVN Resolution No.9, July 1969 (Extract) in Gareth Porter (ed.), *Vietnam: The Definitive Documentation of Human Decisions, Volume 2* (New York: Earl M. Coleman, 1979) pp. 532–536.

91 David Chanoff and Toan Van Tai, *Portrait of the Enemy* (London: I.B. Tauris, 1987), pp. 109, 171.

92 *Ibid.*, p. 109.

93 See, Robert K. Brigham, *Guerrilla Diplomacy: The NLF's Foreign Relations and the Vietnam War* (Ithaca: Cornell University Press, 1999), p. 41.

94 *Hanoi Home Service*, 23 August 1968, SWB/FE/2857/B/1–4; SWB/FE/2899/A3/4. The speech was subsequently broadcast in five instalments by Hanoi radio: See *Hanoi Home Service*, 16 September 1968, SWB/FE/2901/C/1–9, 17 September 1968, SWB/FE/2902/C/1–8, 18 September 1968, SWB/FE/2903/C/1–8, 19 September 1968, SWB/FE/2904/C/1–9 and 20 September 1968, SWB/FE/2905/C/1–13.

95 See Le Duan's 6 July 1969 missive to the Party Committee and Military Commission of Tri-Thien in Le Duan, *Letters to the South* (Hanoi: Foreign Languages Publishing House, 1986), pp. 101–115.

96 COSVN Resolution No.9, July 1969 (Extract) in Gareth Porter (ed.), *Vietnam: The Definitive Dcoumentation of Human Decisions, Volume 2* (New York: Earl M. Coleman, 1979), pp. 532–536. Also see, Col Hoang Ngoc Lung, The General Offensive of 1968–69 cited in Lewis Sorley, *A Better War: The Unexamined Victories and Final Tragedy of America's Last Years in Vietnam* (New York: Harcourt Brace and Company, 1999), pp. 155–157 and 427, ftn. 2.

97 Socialist Republic of Vietnam Foreign Ministry White Book on Relations with China, *Hanoi Home Service*, 4–6 October 1979, SWB/FE/6242/A3/1; NCNA, 19 October 1968, SWB/FE/2905/A3/1–2.

98 See Qiang Zhai, *China and the Vietnam Wars, 1950–1975* (Chapel Hill: The University of North Carolina Press, 2000), pp. 169–175, 179.

99 Stanley Karnow, *Vietnam: A History* (New York: Penguin Books, 1984), p. 597.

100 *Xinhua News Agency*, 2 September 1979.

101 *Hanoi Home Service*, 28 April 1969, SWB/FE/3016/A3/1.

102 For the text of Ho's will as read by Le Duan on 9 September 1969, see SWB/FE/3173/C/12–13.

103 Bo Quoc Phong Vien Lich Su Quan Su Viet Nam, *50 Nam Quan Doi Nhan Dan Viet Nam* (Hanoi: Nha Xuat Ban Quan Doi Nhan Dan, 1995), pp. 255–256.
104 *Hanoi Home Service and NCNA*, 23 May 1969, SWB/FE/3087/A3/1.
105 *Beijing Home Service and NCNA*, 29 May 1969, SWB/FE/3087/A3/1.
106 *VNA*, 6 June 1969, SWB/FE/3094/i.
107 *VNA*, 13 June 1969, SWB/FE/3100/i.
108 Tran Van Don, *Our Endless War: Inside South Vietnam* (California: Presido Press, 1978), pp. 193–196; Henry Kissinger, *White House Years*, (Boston: Little, Brown and Co., 1979), p. 277–82.
109 Stanley Karnow, *op. cit.*, p. 597.
110 *Ibid*, p. 597.
111 *Xinhua News Agency*, 2 September 1969.
112 Yang Kuisong, 'The Sino-Soviet Border Clash of 1969: From Zhenbao Island to Sino-American Rapprochement' in *Cold War History*, Volume 1 Number 1, (August 2000), pp. 21–52.
113 David Chanoff and Doan Van Tai, *Portrait of the Enemy* (London: I.B. Tauris, 1986), p. 121.
114 Truong Nhu Tang, *A VietCong Memoir* (New York: Harcourt Brace Jovanovich, 1985), p. 248.
115 Bui Tin, *op.cit.*, p. 65. Ho began writing his will in May 1965.

Selected Bibliography

I. Vietnamese Language Sources

Ban Ngien Cuu Lich Su Dang Thanh Pho Ho Chi Minh, 50 Nam Dau Tranh Kien Cuong Cua Dang Bo Va Nhan Dan Thanh Pho (Nha Xuat Ban Thanh Pho Ho Chi Minh, 1981).

Lich Su Dang Cong San Viet Nam, Tap II, De Cuong Bai Giang (Hanoi: Nha Xuat Ban Dai Hoc Trung Hoc Chuyen Nghiep, 1981).

Lich Su Dang Cong San Viet Nam, Tap III, Chuong Trinh Cao Cap (Hanoi: Nha Xuat Ban Sach Gio Khoa Mac-Lenin, 1985).

Le Duan, *Thu Vao Nam* (Hanoi: Nha Xuat Ban Su That, 1985).

Ho Chi Minh: Toan Tap, Tap VII (7/1954–12/1957) (Hanoi: Nha Xuat Ban Su That, 1987).

Lich Su Bo Doi Dac Cong, Tap I (Hanoi: Nha Xuat Ban Quan Doi Nhan Dan, 1987).

Lich Su Quan Doi Nhan Dan Viet Nam, Tap II (Hanoi: Nha Xuat Ban Quan Doi Nhan Dan, 1988 and updated in 1999).

Cao Van Luong, *Lich Su Cach Mang Mien Nam Viet Nam: Gioi Doan 1954–1960* (Hanoi: Nha Xuat Ban Khoa Hoc Xa Hoi, 1991).

Vo Tran Nha (chu bien), *Lich Su Dong Thap Muoi* (Hanoi: Nha Xuat Ban Thanh Pho Ho Chi Minh, 1993).

Bo Quoc Phong Vien Lich Su Quan Su Viet Nam, *50 Nam Quan Doi Nhan Dan Viet Nam* (Hanoi: Nha Xuat Ban Quan Doi Nhan Dan, 1995).

Bo Quoc Phong Vien Lich Su Quan Su Viet Nam, *Lich Su Nghe Thuat Chien Dich Viet Nam 1945–1975* (Hanoi: Nha Xuat Ban Quan Doi Nhan Dan, 1995).

Bo Quoc Phong Vien Lich Su Quan Su Viet Nam, *Lich Su Khang Chien Chong My Cuu Nuoc 1954–1975 Tap I–IV* (Hanoi: Nha Xuat Ban Chinh Tri Quoc Gia, 1996–1999).

Ban Chi Dao Tong Ket Chien Tranh Truc Thuoc Bo Chinh Tri, *Tong Ket Cuoc Khang Chien Chong My Cuu Nuoc Thang Loi Va Bai Hoc* (Hanoi: Nha Xuat Ban Chinh Tri Quoc Gia, 1996).

Pham Hong Son, *Nghe Thuat Danh Giac Gu Nuoc Cua Dan Toc Viet Nam* (Hanoi: Nha Xuat Ban Quan Doi Nhan Dan, 1997).

Bo Quoc Phong Vien Lich Su Quan Su Viet Nam, *Hau Phong Chien Tranh Nhan Dan Viet Nam 1945–1975* (Hanoi: Nha Xuat Ban Quan Doi Nhan Dan, 1997).

Bo Tong Tham Muu Cuc Nha Truong, *Giao Trinh Lich Su Quan Su, Tap IV and Tap V* (Hanoi: Nha Xuat Ban Quan Doi Nhan Dan, 1997 and 1998).

Ho Khang, *Tet Mau Than 1968 Tai Mien Nam Viet Nam* (Hanoi: Nha Xuat Ban Quan Doi Nhan Dan, 1998).

Luu Van Loi, *Nam Muoi Nam Ngoai Giao Viet Nam 1945–1995* (Hanoi: Nha Xuat Ban Cong An Nhan Dan, 1998).

Bo Tong Tham Muu Cuc Nha Truong, *Giao Trinh Lich Su Quan Su* (Hanoi: Nha Xuat Ban Quan Doi Nhan Dan, 1999).

Bo Quoc Phong Vien Lich Su Quan Su Viet Nam, *May Van De Chi Dao Chien Luoc Trong 30 Nam Chien Tranh Giai Phong 1945–1975* (Hanoi: Nha Xuat Ban Quan Doi Nhan Dan, 1999).

Le Mau Han, *Cac Dai Hoi Dang Cong San Viet Nam* (Hanoi: Nha Xuat Ban Chinh Tri Quoc Gia, 2000).

Ban Chi Dao Tong Ket Chien Tranh Truc Thuoc Bo Chinh Tri, *Chien Tranh Cach Mang Viet Nam 1945–1975: Thang Loi Va Bai Hoc* (Hanoi: Nha Xuat Ban Chinh Tri Quoc Gia, 2000).

II. Memoirs/First-Person Accounts

Duong Ho Chi Minh: Hoi Ky Truong Son (Nha Xuat Ban Tac Pham Moi/ Hoi Nha Van Viet Nam, 1982).

Chen Geng, *Chen Geng Riji,Volume II* (Beijing: Jiefang Jun Chubanshe, 1984).

Thanh Tin, *Hoa Xuyen Tuyet (Hoi Ky)* (California: Saigon Press, 1991).

Mat That: Hoi Ky Chinh Tri cua Bui Tin (California: Saigon Press, 1993).

Tran Van Tra, *Nhung Chang Duong Lich Su Cua B2 Thanh Dong, Tap I: Hoa Binh Hay Chien Tranh* (Hanoi: Nha Xuat Ban Quan Doi Nhan Dan, 1992).

Zhongguo Wai Jiao Guan Huiyi Lu: Xin Zhongguo Waijiao Fengyun (3 volumes) (Beijing: Shijie Zhishi Chubanshe, 1994).

Van Tien Dung, *Ve Cuoc Khang Chien Chong My Cuu Nuoc* (Hanoi: Nha Xuat Ban Chinh Tri Quoc Gia, 1996).

Dang Vu Hiep, *Ky Uc Tay Nguyen* (Hanoi: Nha Xuat Ban Quan Doi Nhan Dan, 2000).

III. Memoirs/First-Person Accounts (in English)

Bui Tin, *Following Ho Chi Minh: Memoirs of a North Vietnamese Colonel* (London: Christopher Hurst, 1995).

Chanoff, David and Doan Van Toai, *Portrait of the Enemy: The Other Side of the War in Vietnam* (London: I.B. Tauris and Co. Limited, 1987).

Dobrynin, Anatoly, *In Confidence* (New York: Random House, 1995).

Gromyko, Andrei, *Memories* (London: Hutchinson Limited, 1989).

Hoang Van Hoan, *A Drop in the Ocean* (Beijing: Foreign Languages Press, 1988).

Karnow, Stanley, 'An Interview with General Giap' in Capps, Walter (ed.), *The Vietnam Reader* (London: Routledge, 1991).

Kaznacheev, Aleksandr, *Inside a Soviet Embassy: Experiences of a Russian Diplomat in Burma*, (Philadelphia: J.B. Lippincott, 1962).

Lall, Arthur, *How Communist China Negotiates* (New York: Columbia University Press, 1968).

Langer, Paul F. and Zasloff, Joseph J., *The North Vietnamese Military Adviser in Laos: A First Hand Account* (California: Rand Corporation, 1968).

Mai V. Elliot (transl.), *No Other Road to Take (Khong Con Duong Nao Khac): Memoir of Mrs. Nguyen Thi Dinh* (Ithaca: Cornell University, Department of Southeast Asian Studies, Southeast Asia Programme, Data Paper Number 102, June 1976).

Maneli, Mieczyslaw, *War of the Vanquished* (New York: Harper and Row, 1971).

Macmillan, Harold, *Riding the Storm, 1956–1959* (London: Macmillan, 1971).

——. *Pointing the Way, 1959–1961* (London: Macmillan, 1972).

Radvanyi, Janos, *Delusion and Reality* (Indiana: Gateway Limited, 1978).

——. 'Vietnam War Diplomacy: Reflections of a Former Iron Curtain Official' in Lloyd, Matthews and Brown, Dale E. (ed.), *Assessing the Vietnam War: A Collection from the Journal of the US Army War College* (Washington, DC: Pergamon-Brassey's International Defence Publishers, 1987).

Schecter, Jerrod L and Luchkov Vyacheslav V., *Khrushchev Remembers: The Glasnost Tapes* (Boston: Little, Brown and Company, 1990).

Sihanouk, Norodom and Burchett, Wilfred, *My War with the CIA: Cambodia's Fight for Survival* (Harmondsworth: Penguin Books Limited, 1973).

Sisouk Na Champassak, *Storm Over Laos: A Contemporary History* (New York: Frederick A. Praeger, 1961).

Strong, Tracy B. and Keyssar, Helene, 'Anna Lousie Strong: Three Interviews with Chairman Mao Zedong' in *China Quarterly*, Number 103, September 1985.

Talbot, Strobe, *Khrushchev Remembers* (London: Sphere Books Limited, 1971).

——. *Khrushchev Remembers: The Last Testament* (London: Andre Deutch Limited, 1974).

Thee, Marek, *Notes of a Witness: Laos and the Second IndoChina War* (New York: Random House, 1973).

Tran Van Tra, *Vietnam: History of the Bulwark B2 Theatre: Concluding the 30 Years War* (Ho Chi Minh City, 1982).

Truong Nhu Tang, *Journal of a VietCong* (London: Jonathan Cape Limited, 1986).

Wang Bingnan, *Nine Years of Sino-US Talks in Retrospect* (JPRS-CPS–85-079, 7 August 1985).

'We Lied to You' (interview with Generals Vo Nguyen Giap and Vo Bam) in *The Economist*, 26 February 1983.

Wu Xiuquan, *Eight Years in the Ministry of Foreign Affairs (January 1950–October 1958): Memoirs of a Diplomat* (Beijing: New World Press, 1985).

IV. Chinese Language Sources

Meiguo Dui Yuenan Nanfang De Ganshe He Qinlue Zheng Ce (Beijing: Shijie Zhishi Chubanshe, 1963).

Huang Guoan, et al., *Zhongyue Guanxi Jian Bian* (Guangxi Renmin Chubanshe, 1986).

Guo Ming, et al., *Xiandai Zhongyue Guanxi Ziliao Xuanbian, Volume I and II* (Beijing: Shishi Chubanshe, 1986).

Huang Zheng, *Ho Zhiming Yu Zhongguo* (Beijing: Jiefang Jun Chubanshe, 1987).

——. *Zhongyue Guanxi Shi Yanjiu Ji Gao* (Guangxi Renmin Chubanshe, 1992).

Wang Qi, *Zhonghua Renmin Gongheguo Dui Wai Guanxi Gaishu* (Shanghai Waiyu Jiaoyu Chunbanshe, 1989).

Xie Yixian, *Zhechong Yi Gongchu – Xin Zhongguo Dui Wai Guanxi Sishinian* (Henan Renmin Chubanshe, 1990).

Zhongguo Junshi Guwentuan Yuanyue Kangfa Douzheng Shishi (Beijing: Jiefang Jun Chubanshe, 1990).

Dang De Junshi Shilue Zhuanbian Yu Renmin Jundui Jianshe (Beijing: Guofang Daxue Chubanshe, 1990).

Guo Ming, *Zhongyue Guanxi Yanbian Sishinian* (Guangxi Renmin Chubanshe, 1992).

Wang Xiangen, *Yuanyue Kangmei Shilu* (Jinan Chubanshe, 1992).

Han Suyin, *Zhou Enlai Yu Ta De Shiji 1898–1998* (Beijing: Zhongyang Wenxian Chubanshe, 1992).

Li Deng, et al., *Jianguo Yilai Junshi Bai Zhuang Da Shi* (Beijing: Zhishi Chubanshe, 1992).

'Huan Nan Zhi Zhong Jian Zhen Qing: Mao Zedong Yu Ho Zhiming' in *Congren Ribao*, 28 November 1993.

Shi Yinghong, *Meiguo Zai Yuenan De Ganshe He Zhanzheng*, 1954–1968 (Beijing: Shijie Zhishi Chubanshe, 1993).

Jie (Xie) Lifu, *Yuenan Zhanzheng Shilu (2 volumes)* (Beijing: Shijie Zhishi Chubanshe, 1993).

Zhou Enlai Waijiao Huodong Da Shiji (Beijing: Shijie Zhishi Chubanshe, 1993).

Xie Yixian, *Zhongguo Waijiao Shi – 1949–1979* (Henan Renmin Chubanshe, 1994).

V. Communist Documentation/Publications in English

Concerning the Situation in Laos (Beijing: Foreign Languages Press, 1959).

Fascist Terror in South Vietnam: Law 10/59 (Hanoi: Foreign Languages Publishing House, 1961).

The South Vietnam National Liberation Front (Hanoi: Foreign Languages Publishing House, 1962).

Ho Chi Minh: Selected Works, Volume IV: Period from the Re-establishment of Peace in July 1954 to the 3rd National Congress of the Vietnam Workers' Party in September 1960 (Hanoi: Foreign Languages Publishing House, 1962).

Third National Congress of the Vietnam Workers' Party: Documents, Volume I–III (Hanoi: Foreign Languages Publishing House, 1960).

Le Duan, *On the Socialist Revolution in Vietnam, Volume I-III* (Hanoi: Foreign Languages Publishing House, 1967).

Fall, Bernard B. (ed.), *Ho Chi Minh: On Revolution (Selected Writings, 1920–66)* (London: Pall Mall Press, 1967).

John Woddis (ed.), *Ho Chi Minh: Selected Articles and Speeches, 1920–1967* (London: Lawrence and Wishart Limited, 1969).

McGarvey, Patrick J., *Visions of Victory: Selected Vietnamese Communist Military Writings, 1964–1968* (Stanford: Hoover Institute on War, Revolution and Peace, 1969).

Le Duan, *The Vietnamese Revolution: Fundamental Problems and Essential Tasks* (New York: International Publishers, 1971).

——. *Selected Writings* (Hanoi: Foreign Languages Publishing House, 1977).

Ho Chi Minh: Selected Writings, 1920–1969 (Hanoi: Foreign Languages Publishing House, 1977).

Truong Chinh: *Selected Writings* (Hanoi: Foreign Languages Publishing House, 1977).

An Outline History of the Vietnam Workers' Party, 1930–1975 (Hanoi: Foreign Languages Publishing House, 1978).

Black Paper: Facts and Evidences of the Acts of Aggression and Annexation of Vietnam against Kampuchea (Phnom Penh, September 1978, reprinted in New York).

Socialist Republic of Vietnam Foreign Ministry White Book on Relations with China (Hanoi Home Service, 4–6 October 1979, SWB/FE/6238 and 6242).

'Chinese Government and Hoang Van Hoan's replies to Vietnam Foreign Ministry White Book' in *Beijing Review*, 23 November, 30 November and 7 December 1979; 12 October, 19 October and 2 November 1981.

'Facts about Sino-Vietnamese Relations' in *China and the World* (Beijing Review, Foreign Affairs Series I, 1982).

The Anti-US Resistance War for National Salvation, 1954–1975 (translated by FBIS/US Joint Publications Service, Washington, DC, June 1982).

The Ho Chi Minh Trail (Hanoi: Foreign Languages Publishing House, 1982).

The Chinese Rulers' Crimes against Kampuchea (Ministry of Foreign Affairs, People's Republic of Kampuchea, April 1984).

Le Duan, *Letters to the South* (Hanoi: Foreign Languages Publishing House, 1986).

China's Foreign Relations: A Chronology of Events, 1949–1988 (Beijing: Foreign Languages Press, 1989).

Zhong Huaiwen (compiled), *Years of Trial, Turmoil and Triumph – China from 1949 to 1988*, (Beijing: Foreign Languages Press, 1989).

Nguyen Khac Vien, *Vietnam: A Long History* (Hanoi: Foreign Language Publishing House, 1993).

Luu Van Loi and Nguyen Anh Vu, *Le Duc Tho-Kissinger Negotiations in Paris* (Hanoi: The Gioi Publishers, 1996).

McNamara, Robert S, et. al., *Argument Without End: In Search of Answers to the Vietnam Tragedy* (New York, Public Affairs, 1999).

Luu Van Loi, *Fifty Years of Vietnamese Diplomacy 1945–1995 (Volume I: 1945–1975)* (Hanoi: The Gioi Publishers, 2000).

Vietnam Documents and Research Notes (Joint United States Public Affairs Office, Saigon).

VI. Non-Communist Documentation

British Foreign Office General Political Correspondence (FO 371), 1956–1963 (Public Record Office).

Documents Relating to British Involvement in the IndoChina Conflict, 1945–1965 (Cmnd. 2834).

Reports of the International Commission for Supervision and Control in Laos (Cmnd.314).

The Quynh Luu Uprisings (Saigon, 1958).

Confidential United States State Department Central Files, 1956–1959.

United States: Congress, Senate, Committee on Foreign Relations – Top-Secret Hearings, 1959–1966.

United States: Office of Strategic Services (OSS)/State Department Intelligence and Research Reports.

United States Department of State, A Threat to the Peace: North Vietnam's Effort to Conquer South Vietnam (Washington: US Government Printing Office, December 1961).

United State Department of State, Aggression from the North: The Record of North Vietnam's Campaign to Conquer South Vietnam (Washington: US Government Printing House, February 1965).

United States Department of State, Working Paper on North Vietnam's Role in the South (including Appendices) (Washington: US Government Printing House, 27 May 1968).

The Viet Cong Tet Offensive 1968 (History Section, J5/Joint General Staff, RVN Armed Forces, Saigon, August 1968).

Background Information Relating to Southeast Asia and Vietnam (Committee on Foreign Relations, US Senate) (Washington: US Government Printing Office, 1969).

United States Department of Defence, United States-Vietnam Relations, 1945–1967 (Washington: US Government Printing Office, 1971).

The Pentagon Papers: The Defence Department History of US Decision Making on Vietnam (The Senator Gravel Edition) (Boston: Beacon Press, 1971).

Who's Who in North Vietnam (no publisher given but believed to be CIA, November 1972).

Nalty, Bernard C., Air Power and the Fight for Khe Sanh (Office of Air Force History, US Fair Force, Washington, 1973).

Porter, Gareth (ed.), Vietnam: The Definitive Documentation of Human Decisions, Volume II (London: Heyden and Son, 1979).

Herring, George (ed.), The Secret Diplomacy of the Vietnam War: The Negotiating Volumes of the Pentagon Papers (Austin: University of Texas, 1983).

United States Marine Corps, U.S. Marines in Vietnam: The Defining Year 1968 (Washington: US Government Printing Office, 1997).

United States Department of State, Foreign Relations of the United States (FRUS) (Washington: US Government Printing House), Volume I (Vietnam, 1955–1957), Volume I (Vietnam 1958–1960), Volume I (Vietnam, 1961), Volume II (Vietnam, 1962); Volume III (Vietnam, January–August 1963), Volume IV (Vietnam, August-December 1963), Volume I (Vietnam, 1964), Volume II (Vietnam, January–June 1965), Volume III (July-December 1965), Volume IV (Vietnam 1966); Volume XXI (Cambodia and Laos, 1955–1957), Volume XVI (Cambodia and Laos, 1958–1960), Volume XXIV (Laos Crisis, 1961–1963), Volume XXVII (Mainland Southeast Asia, 1964–1968), Volume XXVIII (Laos, 1964–1968).

VII. Monitored Broadcasts/Reports

Keesing's Research Report: The Sino-Soviet Dispute (Keesing's Publications Limited, 1970).
Keesing's Research Report 5: South Vietnam – A Political History, 1954–1970 (New York: Charles Scribner, 1970).
Sagar, D.J., *Major Political Events in Indo-China* (Oxford: Facts on File, Inc., 1991).
Summary of World Broadcasts (Far East Series) (Caversham: BBC Monitoring Service).
Summers, Harry G., Jr., *Vietnam War Almanac* (New York: Facts on File, Inc., 1985).
Vietnam, Laos and Cambodia: Chronology of Events, 1945–68 (London: Central Office of Information, 1968).

VIII. Books and Compilations

Adams, Nina and McCoy, Alfred W., *Laos: War and Revolution* (New York: Harper and Row Publishers, 1970).
Ang, Cheng Guan, *Vietnamese Communists' Relations with China and the Second Indochina Conflict, 1956–1962* (Jefferson, North Carolina: McFarland & Company, Inc., 1997).
Brigham, Robert K., *Guerrilla Diplomacy: The NLF's Foreign Relations and the Vietnam War* (Ithaca: Cornell University Press, 1999).
Boudarel, George, *Cent Fleurs Ecloses dan la Nuit du Vietnam: Communisme et Dissidence, 1954–1956* (Jacques Bertoin, 1991).
Burchett, Wilfred, *North of the 17th Parallel* (Hanoi: Red River Publishing House, 1957).
———. *Mekong Upstream* (Hanoi: Red River Publishing House, 1957).
———. *The Furtive War: The US in Vietnam and Laos* (New York: International Publishers, 1963).
———. *My Visit to the Liberated Zones of South Vietnam* (Hanoi: Foreign Languages Publishing House, 1966).
———. *The China Cambodian Vietnam Triangle* (London: Zed Press, 1981).
Cable, James, *The Geneva Conference of 1954 on IndoChina* (New York: St. Martin's Press, 1986).
Caldwell, Malcom and Lek Hor Tan, *Cambodia in the Southeast Asian War* (New York: Monthly Review Press, 1973).
Cameron, Allan W. (ed.), *Vietnam Crisis: A Documentary History, Volume I: 1940–1956* (Ithaca: Cornell University Press, 1971).
Castle, Timothy Neil, *At War in the Shadow of Vietnam: US Military Aid to the Royal Lao Government, 1955–1975* (New York: Columbia University Press, 1993).

Chandler, David P., *The Tragedy of Cambodian History: Politics, War, and Revolution since 1945* (New Haven: Yale University Press, 1991).
——. *A History of Cambodia* (Boulder: Westview Press, 1992).
——. *Brother Number One: A Political Biography of Pol Pot* (Boulder: Westview Press, 1992).
Charlton, Michael and Moncrieff, Anthony, *Many Reasons Why: The American Involvement in Vietnam* (London: Scolar Press, 1978).
Currey, Cecil B., *Victory at any Cost: The Genius of Vietnam's Gen. Vo Nguyen Giap* (Washington: Brassey's Inc., 1997).
Davidson, Philip B., *Vietnam at War: The History, 1946–1975* (California: Presido Press, 1988).
Dommen, Arthur J., *Conflict in Laos: The Politics of Neutralisation* (New York: Frederick A. Praeger Publishers, 1967).
——. *Laos: Keystone of IndoChina* (Boulder: Westview Press, 1985).
Donnell, John and Gurtov, Melvin, *North Vietnam: Left of Moscow, Right of Peking* (California: Rand Corporation, 1968).
Dudley, Williams and Bender, David (ed.), *The Vietnam War: Opposing Viewpoints* (San Diego: Greenhaven Press, 1990).
Duiker, William J., *The Communist Road to Power in Vietnam* (Colorado: Westview Press, 1981).
——. *China and Vietnam: The Roots of Conflict* (Institute of East Asian Studies, University of California at Berkeley, IndoChina Research Monograph I, 1986).
——. *Sacred War: Nationalism and Revolution in a Divided Vietnam* (New York: McGraw-Hill, Inc., 1995).
——. *Ho Chi Minh: A Life* (New York: Hyperion, 2000).
Dyke, Jon M. Van, *North Vietnam's Strategy for Survival* (Palo Alto: Pacific Books Publishers, 1972).
Errington, Elizabeth Jane and McKercher B.J.C., *The Vietnam War as History* (New York: Praeger Publishers, 1990).
Fall, Bernard, *Vietnam Witness, 1953–66* (London: Pall Mall Press, 1966).
——. *The Two Vietnams: A Political and Military Analysis* (London: Pall Mall Press, 1967).
——. *Last Reflections On a War* (New York: Doubleday and Company, 1967).
——. *Anatomy of a Crisis: The Laotian Crisis of 1960–1961* (New York: Doubleday and Company, 1969).
Fishel, Wesley R. (ed.), *Vietnam: Anatomy of a Conflict* (Illinois: F.E. Peacock Publishers, 1968).
Ford, Ronnie, *Tet 1968: Understanding the Surprise* (London: Frank Cass, 1995).
Gaiduk, Ilya V., *The Soviet Union and the Vietnam War* (Chicago: Ivan R Dee, 1996).
Gardner, Lloyd C. and Gittinger Ted (ed.), *Vietnam: The Early Decisions* (Austin: University of Texas, 1997).

——. *International Perspectives on Vietnam* (College Station: A&M University Press, 2000).

Gettleman, Marvin E. (ed.), *Vietnam: History, Documents and Opinion on a Major World Crisis* (Middlesex: Penguin Books, 1966).

Gettleman, Marvin and Susan, and Kaplan, Lawrence and Carol (ed.), *Conflict in IndoChina: A Reader to the Widening War in Laos and Cambodia* (New York: Random House, 1970).

Gilbert, Marc Jason and Head, William (ed.), *The Tet Offensive* (Westport: CT, 1996).

Gurtov, Melvin, *Hanoi on War and Peace* (California: Rand Corporation, 1967).

Gurtov, Melvin and Byong-Moo Hwang, *China Under Threat: The Politics of Strategy and Diplomacy* (Baltimore: Johns Hopkins University Press, 1980).

Han Suyin, *Eldest Son: Zhou Enlai and the Making of Modern China, 1898–1976* (London: Jonathan Cape, 1994).

Hannah, Norman B., *The Key to Failure: Laos and the Vietnam War* (London: Madison Books, 1987).

Hearden, Patrick J. (ed.), *Vietnam: Four American Perspectives* (Indiana: Purdue University Press, 1990).

Honey, P.J. (ed.), *North Vietnam Today: Profile of a Communist Satellite* (New York: Frederick A. Praeger Publishers, 1962).

——. *Communism in North Vietnam: Its Role in the Sino-Soviet Dispute* (Connecticut: Greenwood Press, 1973).

Hudson, G.F., Lowenthal, Richard and MacFarquhar, Roderick, *The Sino-Soviet Dispute* (London: China Quarterly Publication, 1961).

Kahin, George McT., *Intervention: How America Became Involved in Vietnam* (New York: Alfred A. Knopf, 1986).

Karnow, Stanley, *Vietnam: A History* (London: Penguin Books, 1988).

Kirk, Donald, *Wider War: The Struggle for Cambodia, Thailand and Laos* (New York: Praeger Publishers, 1971).

Kolko, Gabriel, *Vietnam: Anatomy of War, 1940–1975* (London: Unwin Hymnan Limited, 1987).

Lacoutre, Jean, *Vietnam: Between Two Truces* (London: Secker and Warburg Limited, 1966).

——. *Ho Chi Minh* (Middlesex: Penguin Books, 1968).

Langer, Paul F. and Zasloff J. Joseph, *North Vietnam and the Pathet Lao* (Cambridge, Mass. Harvard University Press, 1970).

Langer, Paul F., *The Soviet Union, China and the Pathet Lao: Analysis and Chronology* (California: Rand Corporation, no date indicated).

Lanning, Michael Lee and Cragg, Dan, *Inside the VC and the NVA: The Real Story of North Vietnam's Armed Forces* (New York: Ballantine Books, 1992).

Lee Chae Jin, *Chinese Communist Policy in Laos, 1954–1965* (PhD dissertation, University of California in Los Angeles, 1966).

Lowe, Peter (ed.), *The Vietnam War* (London: Macmillan Press, 1998).

MacAlister, Brown and Zasloff, Joseph J., *Apprentice Revolutionaries: The Communist Movement in Laos, 1930–1985* (Stanford: Hoover Institution Press, 1986).

MacDonald, Peter, *The Victor in Vietnam: Giap* (London: Fourth Estate, 1993).

MacFarquhar, Roderick, *The Origins of the Cultural Revolution, Volume I: Contradictions among the People, 1956–57; Volume II: The Great Leap Forward, 1958–1960; Volume III: The Coming of the Cataclysm, 1961–1966* (London: Oxford University Press, 1974, 1983 and 1997 respectively).

McMahon, Robert J. (ed.) *Major Problems in the History of the Vietnam War* (Lexington: D.C. Heath and Company, 1990).

Modelski, George, *International Conference on the Settlement of the Laotian Question, 1961–62* (Department of International Relations, Research School of Pacific Studies, ANU, 1962).

Moise, Edwin Evaviste, *Land Reform in China and North Vietnam: Revolution at the Village level, Volumes I and II* (PhD dissertation, University of Michigan, 1977).

Moore, John Norton, *The Vietnam Debate: A Fresh Look at the Arguments* (Lanham: University Press of America, 1990).

Morris, Stephen J., *Why Vietnam Invaded Cambodia* (Stanford: Stanford University Press, 1999).

O'Ballance, Edgar, *The Wars in Vietnam, 1954–1973* (London: Ian Allan Limited, 1975).

Osborne, Milton, *Sihanouk: Prince of Light, Prince of Darkness* (Sydney: Allen and Unwin, 1994).

Papp, Daniel S., *Vietnam: The View from Moscow, Peking and Washington* (North Carolina: McFarland and Company, 1981).

Pike, Douglas, *Viet Cong: The Organisation and Techniques of the National Liberation Front of South Vietnam,* (Cambridge, Mass.: MIT Press, 1968).

——. *History of Vietnamese Communism, 1925–76* (Stanford: Hoover Institution Press, 1978).

——. *PAVN: People's Army of Vietnam* (California: Presido Press, 1986).

——. *Vietnam and the Soviet Union: Anatomy of an Alliance* (Colorado: Westview Press, 1987).

Qiang Zhai, *China & the Vietnam Wars, 1950–1975* (Chapel Hill: University of North Carolina Press, 2000).

Race, Jeffrey, *War Comes to Long An: Revolutionary Conflict in a Vietnamese Province* (Berkeley: University of California Press, 1972).

Randle, Robert F., *Geneva 1954: The Settlement of the IndoChina War* (New Jersey: Princeton University Press, 1969).

Raskin, Marcus G. and Fall, Bernard B. (ed.), *The Vietnam Reader: Articles and Documents on American Foreign Policy and the Vietnam Crisis* (New York: Random House, 1965).

Rupen, Robert A. and Farrell, Robert, *Vietnam and the Sino-Soviet Dispute* (New York: Praeger Publishers, 1967).

Salisbury, Harrison E., *Behind the Lines – Hanoi* (London: Secker and Warburg, 1967).

Shaplen, Robert, *The Lost Revolution: Vietnam, 1945–1965* (London: Andre Deutsch, 1966).

Short, Anthony, *The Origins of the Vietnam War* (London: Longman, 1989).

Smith, Ralph B., *An International History of the Vietnam War, Volume I: Revolution versus Containment, 1955–61* (London: Macmillan Press, 1983); *Volume II: The Struggle for Southeast Asia, 1961–65* (London: Macmillan Press, 1985); *Volume III: The Making of a Limited War, 1965–66* (London: Macmillan, 1991).

Smith, Roger M., *Cambodia's Foreign Policy* (PhD dissertation, Cornell University, 1964).

Smyser, W.R., *The Independent Vietnamese: Vietnamese Commmunism Between Russia and China, 1956–1969* (Ohio: Ohio University Centre for International Studies, 1980).

Sorley, Lewis, *A Better War* (New York: Harcourt Brace and Company, 1999).

Stevens, Richard L., *The Trail: A History of the Ho Chi Minh Trail and the Role of Nature in the War in Vietnam* (New York: Garland Publishing, Inc., 1993).

Tai Sung An, *The Vietnam War* (Madison: Fairleigh Dickinson University Press, 1998).

Thai Quang Trung, *Collective Leadership and Factionalism: An Essay on Ho Chi Minh's Legacy* (Singapore: Institute of Southeast Asian Studies, 1985).

Thayer, Carlyle Alan, *The Origins of the National Liberation Front for the Liberation of South Vietnam* (PhD dissertation, ANU, 1977).

——. *War By Other Means: National Liberation and Revolution in Vietnam, 1954–60* (Sydney: Allen and Unwin, 1989).

Toye, Hugh, *Laos: Buffer States or Battleground* (London: Oxford University Press, 1971).

Turley, William S., *Army, Party and Society in the Democratic Republic of Vietnam: Civil-Military Relations in a Mass-Mobilisation System* (PhD dissertation, University of Washington, 1972).

——. *The Second IndoChina War: A Short Political and Military History, 1954–1975* (Colorado: Westview Press, 1986).

Turner, Robert F., *Vietnamese Communism: Its Origins and Development* (Stanford: Hoover Institution Press, 1975).

Warner, Denis, *Reporting Southeast Asia* (Sydney: Angus and Robertson Limited, 1966).

Werner, S. Jayne and Luu Doan Huynh (ed.), *The Vietnam War: Vietnamese and American Perspectives* (New York: M.E. Sharpe, 1993).

Werner, Jayne and Hunt, David (ed.), *The American War in Vietnam*, (Ithaca: Cornell University Press, 1993).

White, Christine Katherine Pelzer, *Agrarian Reform and National Liberation in the Vietnamese Revolution, 1920–1957* (PhD dissertation, Cornell University, 1981).

Wirtz, James, *The Tet Offensive: Intelligence Failure in War* (Ithaca: Cornell University Press, 1991).

Zasloff, Joseph J. and Goodman, Alan E., *IndoChina in Conflict: A Political Assessment* (Lexington: Lexington Books, 1972).

Zasloff, Joseph J., *The Pathet Lao: Leadership and Organisation* (Toronto: Lexington Books, 1973).

Zasloff, Joseph J. and MacAlister, Brown, *Communism In IndoChina: New Perspectives* (London: D.C. Heath and Company, 1975).

IX. Articles

Boudarel, Georges, 'Intellectual dissidence in the 1950s: The Nhan-Van and Giai-Pham Affair' in *The Vietnam Forum*, Number 13 (Yale University Southeast Asia Studies, 1990).

Cameron, Allan W., 'The Soviet Union and Vietnam: The Origins of Involvement' in Duncan, W.Raymond (ed.), *Soviet Poliicy in Developing Countries* (Toronto: Ginn-Blaisdell, 1970).

Carver, George A. Jr., 'The Faceless VietCong' in *Foreign Affairs*, Volume 44, Number 3, April 1966.

Chen Jian, 'China and the First Indo-China War, 1950–54' in *China Quarterly*, Number 133, March 1993.

——. 'China's Involvement in the Vietnam War, 1964–1969' in *China Quarterly*, Number 142, June 1995.

Chen, King C., 'North Vietnam in the Sino-Soviet Dispute, 1962–64' in *Asian Survey*, Volume IV, Number 9, September 1964.

——. 'Hanoi's Three Decisions and the Escalation of the Vietnam War' in *Political Science Quarterly*, Volume 90, Number 2, Summer 1975.

Crozier, Brian, 'Peking and the Laotian Crisis: An Interim Appraisal' in *China Quarterly*, Number 7, July–September 1961.

——. 'Peking and the Laotian Crisis: A Further Appraisal' in *China Quarterly*, Number 11, July–September 1962.

Fall, Bernard B., 'Crisis in North Vietnam' in *Far Eastern Survey*, January 1957.

——. 'The International Relations of Laos' in *Pacific Affairs*, Volume XXX, Number 1, March 1957.

Garver, John W., 'New Light on Sino-Soviet Relations: The Memoirs of China's Ambassador to Moscow, 1955–62' in *China Quarterly*, Number 122, June 1990.

——. 'The Chinese Threat in the Vietnam War' in *Parameters*, Spring 1992.

Heder, Stephen, 'Kampuchea's Armed Struggle: The Origins of an Independent Revolution' in *Bulletin of Cocerned Asian Scholars*, Volume 11, Number 1, 1979.

Hirohide Kurihara, 'Changes in the Literary Policy of the Vietnamese Workers' Party, 1956–1958' in Takeshi Shiraishi and Motoo Furuta (ed.), *IndoChina In the 1940s and 1950s* (Ithaca: Cornell University Southeast Asia Programme, 1992).

Hoang Giang, 'La Revolte des Intellectuels au Viet-nam en 1956' in *The Vietnam Forum*, Number 13 (Yale University Southeast Asia Studies, 1990).

Honey, P.J., 'Pham Van Dong's Tour' in *China Quarterly*, Number 8, October–December 1961.

Hunt, David, 'Images of the Viet Cong' in Robert M. Slabey (ed.), *The United States and Vietnam from War to Peace* (Jefferson: McFarland, 1996).

Lee Chae Jin, 'Communist China and the Geneva Conference on Laos: A Reappraisal' in *Asian Survey*, Volume IX, Number 7, July 1969.

Leifer, Michael, 'Cambodia and her Neighbours' in *Pacific Affairs*, Volume XXXIV, Number 4, Winter 1961–62.

McLane, Charles B., 'The Russians and Vietnam: Strategies of Indirection' in *International Journal*, Number 24, Winter 1968.

Phan Thien Chau, 'Leadership in the Vietnam Workers Party: The Process of Transition' in *Asian Survey*, Volume XII, Number 9, September 1972.

Pike, Douglas, 'Origins of Leadership Change in the Socialist Republic of Vietnam' in Taras, Raymond C. (ed.), *Leadership Change in the Communist States* (London: Unwin Hyman Limited, 1989).

Porter, Gareth D., 'The Myth of the Bloodbath: North Vietnam's Land Reform Reconsidered' in *Bulletin of Concerned Asian Scholars*, Volume 5, Number 2, September 1973.

Pringsheim, Klaus H., 'China and the Soviet Satellites: New Dimensions in China's Foreign Policy' in *China Quarterly*, Number 4, October–December 1960.

Qiang Zhai, 'China and the Geneva Conference of 1954' in *China Quarterly*, Number 129, March 1992.

——. 'Opposing Negotiations: China and the Vietnam Peace Talks, 1965–1968' in *Pacific Historical Review*, February 1999.

Race, Jeffrey, 'The Origins of the Second IndoChina War' in *Asian Survey*, Volume X, Number 5, May 1970.

Shabad, Theodore, 'Economic Developments in North Vietnam' in *Pacific Affairs*, Volume XXXI, Number 1, March 1958.

Shao Kuo-kang, 'Zhou Enlai's Diplomacy and the Neutralisation of IndoChina, 1954–55' in *China Quarterly*, Number 107, September 1986.

——. 'Chou En-lai's Diplomatic Approach to Non-aligned States in Asia: 1953–60' in *China Quarterly*, Number 78, June 1979.

Shaw, Brian, 'China and North Vietnam: Two Revolutionary Paths, Part I and II' in *Current Scene*, Volume IX, Number 11 and 12, 1971.

Smith, R.B., 'Cambodia in the Context of Sino-Vietnamese Relations' in *Asian Affairs*, Volume XVI, Part III, October 1985.

Thayer, Carlyle A., *Revisionism in Communist Vietnamese Historiography: The Issue of Central Party Control over the Southern Party Organisation, 1954–1961* (Canberra: ANU, Research School of Pacific Studies, Department of Pacific and Southeast Asian History Seminar Series, 8 August 1989).

Trager, Frank N., 'Never Negotiate Freedom: The Case of Laos and Vietnam' in *Asian Survey*, Volume I, Number 11, January 1962.

Turley, William, 'The Vietnamese Army' in Adelman, Jonathan R., *Communist Armies in Politics* (Colorado: Westview Press, 1982).

Woodside, Alexander, 'Peking and Hanoi: Anatomy of a Revolutionary Partnership' in *International Journal*, Number 24, Winter 1968.

Yang Kuisong, 'The Sino-Soviet Border Clash of 1969: From Zhenbao Island to Sino-American Rapprochment' in *Cold War History*, Volume 1, Number 1, August 2000.

X. Journals/Periodicals

Beijing Review.
China News Analysis.
Cold War International History Project Bulletin.
Far Eastern Economic Review.
Nhan Dan.
News from Xinhua News Agency.
Su Kien Va Nhan Chung.
Tap Chi Nghien Cuu Lich Su.
The World Today.
Vietnam Courier.
Vietnamese Studies.

Index

Ap Bac battle 67–68, 70, 81–82, 85

Ba Gia campaign 92–93
Bau Bang-Dan Tieng campaign 101
Ben Tre uprisings 42–43
Binh Gia Campaign 84–85
Brigham, Robert K. 3, 4
Bucharest Conference (1960) 46
Bui Tin, 21, 54, 74, 75, 134
Burchett, Wilfred 7

Cambodia 14, 16, 36, 49, 54, 77, 106
Central Highlands (Tay Nguyen) 25,
    32, 57, 62, 67, 76–77, 83,
    87–88, 91, 93, 100–102, 106,
    117, 122
Chen Jian 3
Chen Yi 39, 63–64
Chu Huy Man 77, 92, 101, 118, 121
Cold War International History
    Project 4
CP 38 Committee 60

Deng Xiaoping 27, 45, 79
Doan Khue 5, 76
Dobrynin, Anatoly 86, 108
Dong Duong campaign 101
Dong Xoai campaign 90–91
Duiker, William J. 3, 4

Eastern Nam Bo Command 27, 28

Fall, Bernard 63–64

Five-Year Military Plan 8, 59, 68–69,
    75
Ford, Ronnie 3

Gaiduk, Illya 3, 4, 115, 123
Geneva Conference (1954) 6, 14, 18
    (1962) 62, 77
Group 959 36

Han Suyin 39
Harriman, Averell 131
Ho Chi Minh 5, 10–11, 15, 86, 94,
    119–120, 126, 131, 140–142
    closing speech at 9th Plenary
    session 16–17, address at re-
    education class (Ministry of
    Defence) and at 12th
    anniversary of independence of
    North Vietnam 22–23, speech
    at 13th plenary session 25, in
    China 27, at 15th Plenary
    session 29–30, meeting with
    Janos Radvanyi 32, in the
    Soviet Union and China
    37–39, 44, 46–47, meeting with
    Bernard Fall 64, at 9th Plenary
    session 80, meeting with Mao
    98, at 12th Plenary session
    103–104, meeting with Jean
    Sainteny 109–110, meeting
    with Mao 123
Ho Chi Minh Trail 35–36, 48, 60, 76,
    113

Hoang Cam 83, 90, 101
Hoang Minh Chinh 10, 79, 120
Hoang Minh Thao 118
Hoang Tung 35
Hoang Van Hoan 8, 21, 40, 46, 60, 78, 82, 123, 138
Hoang Van Thai 59, 111, 118
Hunt, David 4

International Supervisory and Control Commission (ISCC) 18, 31, 52
Interzone IV 26
Interzone V 25, 26, 28, 32, 35, 42, 54, 57

Khe Sanh 4, 35, 48, 125, 127–130
Khrushchev 14, 15, 38, 47, 78, 79
Kissinger, Henry 141
Kong Lae 50–52
Kontum campaign 135
Kosygin, Alexi 86, 142

Laos 7, 26, 30, 31, 35, 36, 48–52, 54, 58, 59–62, 77, 79, 99, 129
Law 10/59 7, 8, 33, 40
Le Duan 9–10, 24–25, 28–34, 42–44, 68–69, 74, 78, 80, 85–86, 120, 123, 138–139
    and 14–point plan 15–16, and 'The Road to the South' 18–21, letter of 7 February 1961 57, letter of 20 April 1961 61, letter of July 1962 64–65, letter of May 1965 89, letter of November 1965 102–103, letter of 18 January 1968 126–127, and Paris negotiations 131
Le Duc Tho 21, 74, 78, 120
Le Ngoc Hien 124
Le Quang Dao 125
Le Thanh Nghi 29, 123
Le Trong Tan 83, 90, 101, 124
Liu Shaoqi 79
Long Khanh campaign 135
Luo Ruiqing 78
Ly Ban 123

Mai Van Bo 126, 131

Mao Zedong 8, 9, 39, 82–83, 98, 123, 133
Marek Thee 63
Mieczslaw Maneli 69
Military Transportation Group 559 34–35, 60, 66, 88, 98, 128
Moscow Conference (1957) 24 (1960) 47–48

Nam Bo Regional Committee 16, 20, 27, 54, 61, 62, 69
National Liberation Front for South Vietnam (NLFSV) 4, 55, 63, 135
Ngo Dinh Diem 7, 8, 15, 26, 27, 33–34, 69–70
Ngo Vinh Long 4, 135
Nguyen Chanh 76
Nguyen Chi Thanh 23, 59, 74, 89, 105, 108, 114, 116–118
    in Beijing 46, appointed commander of military operations in the South 83
Nguyen Duy Trinh 28, 123, 126, 132
Nguyen Huu Tho 33
Nguyen Huu Xuyen 20
Nguyen Kien Giang 10, 79
Nguyen Minh Duong 20
Nguyen Van Linh 20, 69, 121
Nguyen Van Tien 141
Nguyen Van Vinh 37, 108
Nixon, Richard 11, 38, 135, 142

Operation An Lac 66
Operation Attleboro 112
Operation Cedar Falls 113
Operation Crimp 104
Operation Deckhouse V 113
Operation Flaming Dart 86
Operation Junction City 114–115
Operation Morning Star 66
Operation Niagara 128
Operation Rolling Thunder 87, 96
Operations Thayer I & II 112

Paris talks/negotiations 11, 131, 132, 133, 135, 139, 141, 142, 143
Pathet Lao (see Laos)
Pham Hung 24, 60, 99, 118

Pham Van Dong 8, 9, 47, 53, 132
  meeting with Janos Radvanyi 33,
    with Zhou Enlai 45, with
    Bernard Fall 63–64, with Mao
    Zedong 82, and Four-point plan
    86, 88, in Beijing and Moscow
    115, meeting with M. Aubrac
    and David Schoenbrun
    119–120
Phoumi Nosavan 49–52, 60
Phu Loi incident 38
Plenary sessions (of Lao Dong Party)
  6th 13, 14, 19
  9th (enlarged) 16
  11th 19, 20
  12th 21, 22, 44
  13th 24, 25
  14th 28
  15th 7, 8, 29–30
  (after 3rd Congress)
  9th 8, 73–75
  11th 87, 94
  12th 103–104, 106, 107
  13th 113–114
Pleiku campaign 101
Pol Pot (Saloth Sar) 90

Qiang Zhai 3
Quinim Pholsena 77

Radvanyi, Janos 32–33, 38–39
Rung Sat Special Military Region
  108

Sainteny, Jean 109–110, 142
Sau Duong 19
Sihanouk 62–63, 77, 90
Smith, R.B. 2, 3, 4, 6
Strong, Anna Louise 39

Tay Nguyen (see Central Highlands)
Tay Ninh-Bing Long campaign 133

Tet Offensive 4, 9, 116–119, 120,
  124, 125, 126–131, 132,
  133–134, 135, 136
Thayer, Carlyle A. 2, 4
Third Party Congress (of Lao Dong
  Party) 43, 52–54
To Huu 74, 78
Tonkin Gulf incident 8, 10, 80–81,
  95
Tra Bong uprisings 41
Tran Do 69, 83, 90, 114
Tran Quang Huy 35
Tran Quoc Hoan 74
Tran Quy Hai 125
Tran Van Huu 63
Tran Van Quang 128–129
Tran Van Tra 30, 37, 69, 113,
  128–129, 134–135
Truong Cong Dong 126
Truong Chinh 26, 28, 54, 138
Truong Nhu Tang 142
Turley, William S. 3, 4
Tuu Ky 40, 142

Van Tien Dung 74, 76, 126, 130, 135
Vietnamisation policy 11, 136
Vo Bam 34, 48
Vo Chi Cong 28, 75, 118
Vo Nguyen Giap 10, 21, 35, 44, 53,
  74, 79,
  report at 3rd Party Congress 53, in
    Moscow 86, in Beijing and
    Moscow 115, and Tet Offensive
    118–119, 122, 123
Vo Van Kiet 121

Warner, Denis 61

Xuan Thuy 133, 141, 142

Zhou Enlai 9, 15, 27, 39, 44, 45–46,
  79, 85, 133, 142